The Psychology of Women
under Patriarchy

School for Advanced Research
Advanced Seminar Series
Michael F. Brown
General Editor

Since 1970 the School for Advanced Research (formerly the School of American Research) and SAR Press have published over one hundred volumes in the Advanced Seminar Series. These volumes arise from seminars held on SAR's Santa Fe campus that bring together small groups of experts to explore a single issue. Participants assess recent innovations in theory and methods, appraise ongoing research, and share data relevant to problems of significance in anthropology and related disciplines. The resulting volumes reflect SAR's commitment to the development of new ideas and to scholarship of the highest caliber. The complete Advanced Seminar Series can be found at www.sarweb.org.

Also available in the School for Advanced Research Advanced Seminar Series:

How Nature Works: Rethinking Labor on a Troubled Planet edited by Sarah Besky
    and Alex Blanchette
Negotiating Structural Vulnerability in Cancer Control edited by Julie Armin, Nancy J. Burke,
    and Laura Eichelberger
Governing Gifts: Faith, Charity, and the Security State edited by Erica Caple James
Puebloan Societies: Homology and Heterogeneity in Time and Space edited by Peter M. Whiteley
New Geospatial Approaches to the Anthropological Sciences edited by Robert L. Anemone
    and Glenn C. Conroy
Seduced and Betrayed: Exposing the Contemporary Microfinance Phenomenon edited by
    Milford Bateman and Kate Maclean
Fat Planet: Obesity, Culture, and Symbolic Body Capital edited by Eileen P. Anderson-Fye
    and Alexandra Brewis
Costly and Cute: Helpless Infants and Human Evolution edited by Wenda R. Trevathan and
    Karen R. Rosenberg
Why Forage? Hunters and Gatherers in the Twenty-First Century edited by Brian F. Codding
    and Karen L. Kramer
Muslim Youth and the 9/11 Generation edited by Adeline Masquelier and Benjamin F. Soares

For additional titles in the School for Advanced Research Advanced Seminar Series,
please visit unmpress.com.

The Psychology of Women under Patriarchy

Edited by Holly F. Mathews and Adriana M. Manago

SCHOOL FOR ADVANCED RESEARCH PRESS • SANTA FE
UNIVERSITY OF NEW MEXICO PRESS • ALBUQUERQUE

© 2019 by the School for Advanced Research
All rights reserved. Published 2019
Printed in the United States of America

ISBN 978-0-8263-6083-0 (paper)
ISBN 978-0-8263-6084-7 (electronic)

Library of Congress Control Number:
2019945841

Cover illustration: *Women of the World Unite*,
2011. Original Painting by Cheryl Braganza.
Courtesy of Miguel Da Costa Frias.

Composed in Minion Pro and Gill Sans

Acknowledgments   vii
Foreword. Women of the World Unite   ix
    Miguel Da Costa Frias

CHAPTER ONE. Introduction: Understanding Women's Psychological Responses to Various Forms of Patriarchy   1
    Holly F. Mathews and Adriana M. Manago

CHAPTER TWO. Historical Circumstances and Biological Proclivities Surrounding Patriarchy   31
    Naomi Quinn

CHAPTER THREE. Growing Up Female in North India   51
    Susan C. Seymour

CHAPTER FOUR. To Make Her Understand with Love: Expectations for Emotion Work in North Indian Families   71
    Jocelyn Marrow

CHAPTER FIVE. Perspectives on Gender Roles and Relations across Three Generations of Maya Women in Southern Mexico   91
    Adriana M. Manago

CHAPTER SIX. Contested Terrains of Female Education in Rural Muslim Pakistan   111
    Ayesha Khurshid

CHAPTER SEVEN. Moving beyond Notions of Resistance and Accommodation: Understanding How Women Navigate Conflicting Models of Marriage in Rural Mexico   133
    Holly F. Mathews

CHAPTER EIGHT. What Women's Experiences in Disadvantaged Families in Ankara, Turkey, Have to Tell about Patriarchy   157
    Gülden Güvenç

CHAPTER NINE. Theorizing Female Consent: Familism, Motherhood, and Middle-Class Feminine Subjectivity in Contemporary South Korea   175
  Kelly H. Chong

CHAPTER TEN. Property, Patriarchy, and the Chinese State   195
  Leta Hong Fincher

CHAPTER ELEVEN. Reflections on Kidnap and Rape Culture: A Cross-Cultural Comparison of Patriarchy   211
  Cynthia Werner

CHAPTER TWELVE. Conclusion: Charting a Way Forward   235
  Holly F. Mathews and Adriana M. Manago

References   245
Contributors   271
Index   273

ACKNOWLEDGMENTS

This volume grew out of an organized session called "The Psychology of Patriarchy" held in March 2013 at the annual meeting of the Society for Psychological Anthropology in Los Angeles, California. We especially thank participants Jeanette Mageo, Carol Mukhopadhyay, and Karen Sirota for their valuable contributions to the discussions that helped to inspire this follow-up volume. The book's contributors participated in a week-long Advanced Seminar in April 2015 at the School for Advanced Research in Santa Fe, New Mexico, organized by Holly F. Mathews and Adriana M. Manago. Advanced planning for the seminar and preliminary travel to Santa Fe were made possible by funding from the Veronica Campbell Brown Foundation, and efforts to bring the seminar to fruition were strongly facilitated by James Brooks, the former president of SAR, to whom we are deeply indebted. We appreciate the staff members at SAR who made the conference a success, and we are grateful to our contributors for their collegiality, insight, and commitment to critical scholarship and feminist engagement. Suad Joseph served as a discussant in the seminar and generously shared her recent work on families and youth in the Middle East. We especially thank Sarah Soliz, the acquisitions editor for SAR Press, for her critical reading, editing, and guidance in the development of the manuscript. Finally, we thank Michell Gilman, who assisted in the initial preparation and editing of the chapters, and Merryl Sloane, whose careful copyediting improved greatly the readability and accuracy of this book.

FOREWORD

Women of the World Unite

MIGUEL DA COSTA FRIAS

My mother, Cheryl Braganza, was a Montreal artist and human rights activist. Her painting on the cover of this book, *Women of the World Unite* (2014), sends a message of empowerment to girls and women. It envisions a future where women of all cultures join hands to collectively enact positive change. In speaking about the painting, she said, "Power, especially the power to effect real and meaningful change, is rarely a solitary achievement. More often, power is born out of a deep connection with others and a sense of ourselves in the world." The authors in this book bring to light the issues that confront women who live within patriarchal systems that often oppress and divide them. Yet as Ayesha Khurshid points out in her chapter on rural Pakistan, women are active participants in these patriarchal systems as they attempt strategically to claim their rights and navigate hierarchy through their connections to others. In so doing, these women often transcend boundaries, reshaping the opportunities open to them and the systems in which they live. My mother did just that in her lifetime, and her personal story as well as her artwork continue to inspire the hope that other women can as well.

Born in Bombay, India, and raised in Lahore, Pakistan, my mother grew up within the strictures of patriarchy. She was raised Catholic in a Muslim country and attended a convent school run by Belgian nuns. She reported that in school she was never asked to give her opinion about anything and that home was not that different. "No one asked for my opinion. I just obeyed.... Respect and family values were so important that even if I had different ideas on anything, I kept them to myself." A gifted musician, my mother auditioned on piano at age 14 for a professor from the Julliard School of Music. She didn't hear anything more until six months later when her piano teacher mentioned in passing that she had been accepted and offered a scholarship but that her parents had refused to let her go and had chosen not to tell her. They had decided for her. My mother later wrote about this experience: "I thought back to the traditional way South Asian society regarded daughters. In a very general sense, we were considered burdens to families. . . . I couldn't help but feel the burden of an oppressive tradition. I was allowed to excel but just in the confines of a certain frame, within certain boundaries." She would later say that as a young woman she felt she had no voice.

In the 1960s, her family finally allowed her to go to college in London, where she discovered her talent for painting. In 1966, she made her way on her own to Montreal, Canada. The young girl from Pakistan who could never speak up began to communicate through her music, her writing, and especially through her art. Married with three young sons, she encountered racism in the suburbs of Montreal that caused her to doubt herself. Eventually, however, she found the courage to leave an unhappy marriage to a controlling man, and without any support, she went on to build a life and career for herself as an artist.

Her activism began when she was approached in the streets by a woman promoting a benefit for the women of Afghanistan. When she asked the woman why she should get involved, the woman answered, "Why not?" This simple answer struck a chord with my mother and motivated her to paint their suffering and their hopes. In 2008, she was named Montreal Woman of the Year by the Montreal Council of Women for using her art to fight for women's rights all over the world. In her acceptance speech, she noted that people are not, for the most part, moved to action by written information. Rather, they are moved by images that touch the common center, inspire, and provoke thought and understanding.

On her sixtieth birthday, my mother was diagnosed with a bone-related cancer. For the last decade of her life, she developed her painting talent with exponential speed noting, "I am in a race against time. I have so much to say and so much more to bring into the world." Confronting the reality of death enabled her to blossom with unlimited creativity, courage, and joy. She died peacefully in December of 2016, after seeing her three children. She once said, "When people look for hope, as in times like now, they turn to the arts, to the symbols and images that hold and heal." Her painting *Women of the World Unite* is one such symbol of hope and healing. It offers the promise that together women can overcome the restrictions of patriarchy and forge the relational connections needed to shape a more humane, caring, and enlightened society. She would wholeheartedly support the efforts of these authors to examine the psychological underpinnings of patriarchy in order to improve the lives of women and men around the world.

The Psychology of Women
under Patriarchy

CHAPTER ONE

Introduction
Understanding Women's Psychological Responses to Various Forms of Patriarchy

HOLLY F. MATHEWS AND ADRIANA M. MANAGO

In her chapter in this volume, Adriana M. Manago analyzes interviews with first-generation Maya college students in Chiapas, Mexico. Susana commutes daily from her village to the city and tells how her world view and aspirations have changed due to education. When asked why she did not want to get married right away, Susana answered: "Because I want to study, I want other experiences, I don't know exactly. I'm free to go out at any time, to wake up at any time, late, early, I don't have a schedule, that is, I get phone calls, let's go, and well, there's nobody to ask permission to go out, just my parents, [I say] 'I'm going out.' . . . I have this freedom to do what I want." She seems to have embraced the individualistic goals that many feminist scholars argue accompany economic development and the spread of Western discourses. In contrast, contributor Ayesha Khurshid reports that many of her rural female Pakistani respondents, who were among the first to be educated and find jobs, still agree to traditional arranged marriages. In explaining why, one young teacher, Salma, said: "How could I refuse my father's wishes? He has educated us [the sisters] against the wishes of the family. He did everything for us. So I knew that I had to do this [accept the marriage proposal] for him. I proved [to the community] that my father was right in educating us." While Salma values education and the rights of women to work outside the home, her duty to uphold her family's honor by obeying her father's wishes remains central to her sense of self. How are we to understand these seemingly contradictory beliefs and behaviors? Are they simply the result of incomplete or uneven forces of modernization and the survival of archaic patriarchal value systems in isolated regions?

No country has modernized more rapidly than South Korea, which arguably has one of the world's most highly educated populations. Yet when contributor

Kelly Chong interviewed well-educated, middle-class Korean housewives, many of their views about marriage and gender roles appeared to echo traditional Confucian values. As one woman explained, "I really believe sincerely that for any woman, obedience is something she has to deal with and accept.... A wife obeying, raising her husband continuously and making him the leader, that is the most essential aspect of marriage." Contributor Leta Hong Fincher questions why a new generation of highly educated, urban Chinese women continue an old custom of registering joint property solely in the husband's name, compromising their marital power in the process. One of her respondents explained her agreement with the traditional custom by saying, "His family thinks I'm more capable than him. Even though I'm younger, the companies I worked for are better than his. So his mother thinks her son needs some kind of guarantee.... His mother started crying on the phone and I thought, forget it.... After all, she's my elder [*zhangbei*]. Since she started crying, I knew that this issue was also really hurting her. So I thought, forget about it, whatever works is fine."

Clearly, patriarchal beliefs and practices flourish even in modernized societies and among well-educated women. Deniz Kandiyoti (1987, 324) highlights the central paradox confronting feminist theorists seeking to understand and change gender oppression cross-culturally: what is the relationship, if any, between emancipation and liberation? She reports that while the formal emancipation of Turkish women was achieved through a series of legal reforms and the establishment of a secular republic, corporate kin control of female sexuality continued to reproduce a culturally specific experience of gender for many. Kandiyoti (1987, 324) concludes, "Insofar as subjective experiences of femininity and/or oppression have a direct bearing on the shaping of what we might imprecisely label a 'feminist consciousness,' they have to be taken seriously and analyzed in far greater detail than they have been."

Contributors to this volume met for a week-long seminar at the School for Advanced Research in Santa Fe, New Mexico, in April 2015 to examine how women's subjective experiences shape and are shaped by changing sociocultural and political conditions. Noting the need to move beyond a dichotomy of accommodation and resistance, the organizers brought together a group of feminist scholars with field research experience and in-depth qualitative data from different parts of the world in order to probe how patriarchy works psychologically and what constitutes agency in patriarchal systems. Embracing the feminist goals of intersectional and interdisciplinary analysis (Bolles 2016), participants sought to bridge preexisting divides between biopsychological, sociological, and cultural perspectives and to begin explicating the ways that women's desires, goals, and identities interact with culturally situated systems of patriarchy (see Chong 2008). These scholars explored why and how patriarchy persists as a cultural model even as the material and social conditions supporting it are eroding worldwide. In other words, participants attempted to delineate the "sticky" parts of patriarchy in different cultural contexts and determine why these remain persuasive to women.

This work raises the issue of motivation, and the authors included here explore the innate human proclivities that are shaped in the course of child and adolescent socialization and show how these are affected by state policies, religion, local cultural beliefs and practices, and larger historical moments. The goals of this volume, therefore, are to stimulate the development of more complex theories about the psychological underpinnings of patriarchy and to potentially inform more socially progressive policies to improve the lives of women and men globally.

Reclaiming the Concept of Patriarchy

The concept of patriarchy, once of central importance in women's studies, fell out of favor with many feminists in the 1980s and 1990s. They argued that it was based on an essentialized view of society; was used uncritically to advance universalist claims; reflected a white, middle-class agenda; and was politically counterproductive (Acker 1989; Gottfried 1998; Hunnicutt 2009; Pollert 1996). Moreover, because it was applied to virtually any situation in which men dominated women, some scholars maintained that the concept's specificity and theoretical utility were compromised (Kandiyoti 1988, 275). More recently, Vrushali Patil (2013) has critiqued the concept's unidimensional characterization of gender and the binary division of gendered individuals into women and men.

With the demise of patriarchy as a concept, some scholars substituted capitalism as the explanation for persistent gender inequalities, while others maintained that such inequalities could not be explained by any commonality of structures across social systems. Sylvia Walby (1990, 155) pointed out, however, that patriarchy both pre- and postdates capitalist systems. And although patriarchy takes historically specific forms, it remains in tension with capitalism. Walby (1990, 169) concluded by arguing for the importance of a more flexible concept of patriarchy to explain both the continuities and the historical and cross-cultural variability in forms of gender inequality.

Around the same time, Heidi Tinsman (1998, 183) reported that historians were reinvigorating the concept, treating it not as an overarching system, but as a central dynamic that mediates race, class, culture, and politics. Nonetheless, Patil (2013) finds that the concept of intersectionality has largely replaced patriarchy in twenty-first-century feminist scholarship. First formulated by Kimberlé Crenshaw in 1991, intersectionality foregrounds the differences between categories of race, sexuality, ethnicity, and nationality and explores the relationships among them as a way of describing how people experience simultaneous forms of domination. Crenshaw has documented how women of color in the United States experience not only patriarchy, but also racial inequality, arguing that the feminist focus on patriarchy is insufficient. She argues that the term *intersectionality* "articulate[s] the interaction of racism and patriarchy" (1991, 1265).

Yet while intersectionality has untangled various aspects of oppression in the Global North, Patil (2013, 857) argues that "we do not have an intersectional analysis of gender relations in the modern world that is sufficiently historical and transnational." The work of Valentine Moghadam (2004) emphasizes the urgent need for analyses of the ways in which forms of social organization interact with political factors, state policies, and existing patriarchal beliefs to create neopatriarchal gender relations. Newer analyses of patriarchy are helping to fill these gaps (see Szoltysek et al. 2017).

In November 2017, United Nations secretary-general António Guterres (2017) reported that around the world, more than one in three women face violence during their lifetimes, 750 million women are married before age 18, and more than 250 million have undergone female genital mutilation. There is increasing recognition, he said, that violence against women is a major barrier to the fulfillment of human rights and a direct challenge to women's participation in sustainable development and peace. This violence is the most visible sign of patriarchy, which continues to affect women's well-being. Moreover, the increase in reports detailing sexual harassment in organizations worldwide indicates that patriarchal practices are still entrenched, even in the Global North. Indeed, Kashtan (2017) argues that patriarchy may be harder to pinpoint in the United States and Europe because people have internalized the neoliberal logic that says social problems are individual issues requiring individual solutions. She calls for us to refocus our attention on the structural dimensions of patriarchy and our responses to it.

For these reasons, the contributors to this volume agree that this is the moment to reinvigorate the concept of patriarchy in the social sciences. We cannot hope to understand the nature of the changes we are witnessing, moreover, without the development of new theories about the psychological processes of appropriating patriarchal ideas and the effects that these have on the experiences and subjectivities of both women and men. As the historian Pavla Miller (2017) writes, patriarchy is a powerful tool to think with.

Defining and Situating Patriarchy Historically

Because of its adaptability to changing contexts, patriarchy has been a powerful organizing concept through which social orders have been understood, maintained, enforced, and contested around the world (Miller 2017). Patriarchy was never the same in all places, and it has now come to look very different in different places. Thus, it becomes important, first, to define the concept and, second, to trace the geographic and historical variations in patriarchal systems as prerequisites to understanding the enduring influence of patriarchy's practices and beliefs.

In her famous book *The Creation of Patriarchy*, Gerda Lerner (1986, 239) wrote, "Patriarchy in its wider definition means the manifestation and institutionalization of male dominance over women and children in the family and the extension of male dominance over women in society in general." Only two years later, however, social scientists like Deniz Kandiyoti (1988, 275) found definitions like this too general because they applied patriarchy to any situation in which men dominated women. She and other researchers in the Middle East and elsewhere tried throughout the 1980s and 1990s to define patriarchy more specifically and to delineate its key features (Inhorn 1996; Joseph 1994, 1999; Kandiyoti 1988, 1998; Mernissi [1975] 1987; Mukhopadhyay and Seymour 1994).

Contributors to this volume take as their point of departure the definition of classic patriarchy first articulated by Kandiyoti (1988): it was a precapitalist social formation that stretched from northern Africa across the Middle East to South and East Asia, in what has been termed the *patriarchal belt* or *arc* (see also Caldwell 1982, 209). For Kandiyoti (1988, 278), the defining feature of classic patriarchy is women's accommodation to it (which she counterposes to the active resistance of women in sub-Saharan Africa to male domination). Chief among the reasons for women's collusion is what she terms the "patrilineal-patrilocal complex," originally rooted in the operation of the patrilocally extended household, which, she says, has had remarkably uniform implications for women living in agrarian peasant societies, regardless of religion (278). New brides join their husband's household as low-ranking members subordinate to all men and to senior women. They are separated from claims on their father's estate and are encouraged to produce children, particularly sons, to provide for their own security (278; see also Wolf 1960). Importantly, both Kandiyoti (1988) and Joseph (1999) argue that the cyclical nature of women's power in the household and their anticipation of inheriting authority as senior women encourage "a thorough internalization of this form of patriarchy by the women themselves" (Kandiyoti 1988, 279). This pioneering body of research demonstrates the advantages of viewing patriarchy as a historical formation. Such a perspective enables analysts to recognize similarities among the varieties of beliefs and practices that support patriarchy cross-culturally and to explain some women's motivations in response. As Kandiyoti (1987, 325) points out, in many societies the corporate control of female sexuality, the psychological effects of sex segregation, and the characteristics of the female life cycle combine to produce a specific, subjective experience of gender that, in turn, shapes consciousness.

THE DEVELOPMENT OF FAMILISM AS A PRECURSOR TO PATRIARCHY

Quinn (this volume) calls our attention back to biology in order to set the stage for the historical evolution of patriarchal systems. She summarizes the work of anthropologists who equate the transition from ape to human with the acquisition of the skills needed for cooperation, and she suggests that two cultural strategies to foster cooperation—deference and familism—built on these human proclivities and survived into the rise of agrarian societies, thereby providing the structural framework for the later emergence of patriarchy. Quinn proposes that deference is originally learned within the extended household (Seymour, this volume) and that kinship comes to operate as a tool for keeping track of hierarchical relationships (Marrow, this volume), enforcing deference, inculcating deference patterns in children, and extending deference into other spheres, such as politics. *Familism* is a social structure in which the needs of the family take precedence over those of the individual members (Chong, this volume). More importantly, Quinn argues, family reputations rise or fall based on individual propriety or misbehavior, and thus preserving the reputation of one's family becomes highly motivating.

Around the world, family reputation is equated with honor, which James Bowman (2007, 4) defines as the good opinion of people who matter to us because we regard them as a society of equals who have the power to judge our behavior. Familism and notions of honor thus set the stage for the emergence of some of the features of patriarchy. Patrilocal families emphasize the authority of senior male members. As stratification emerged, daughters became a resource for contracting alliances with other families, and honor became bound up with men's efforts to protect their daughters' purity and control their decisions. Goody (1973) writes that Eurasian familism also correlated with notions of female virginity and the existence of concubinage, but he does not explore the implications of this pattern for women, stating only that the parental right to arrange marriages was threatened if young people could elope or form other romantic bonds. To reduce such possibilities, families began to limit contact between the sexes and to place a high value on a girl's premarital virginity (Goody 1973, 17), which then became a chief indicator of her family's honor.

While familism partially explains the emergence of patriarchy's distinctive features, processes of state formation enabled the consolidation of patriarchal systems over time, further circumscribing the roles of women.

PRECAPITALIST STATE FORMATION AND THE EMERGENCE OF THE CLASSIC PATRIARCHAL BARGAIN

Karen Sacks (1982) proposes that precapitalist state formation was crucial in transforming the status of women within families. As long as corporate kin groups controlled the rights to land and production, upon which the power of elites depended, they limited state expansion. Sacks (1982, 242) maintains that states deliberately attempted to break down the autonomy of corporate kin groups by making families the key units of power in the relationship between the individual and the state. The emerging civil sphere, according to Christine Gailey (1987, 56), became an arena wherein people could, for the first time, be considered solely on the basis of abstract features, like sex and race, rather than as categories of kin. Because women's access to resources was rooted in kin group membership, the erosion of these ties reduced women to dependents of men, who were persuaded to accept state authority in return for legal recognition as heads of households with the right to exercise exclusive authority over women and junior male members within that sphere (Sacks 1982, 7).

Motherhood also underwent a profound transformation. With male household heads in positions of authority, they—not the kin group—assumed responsibility for controlling the labor of subordinates and for protecting their patrimonies against outsiders. Women's roles in these family units became increasingly circumscribed. Irene Silverblatt (1988, 443) contends that state ideologies often reinforced these processes by depicting women as valuable only for the reproduction of heirs and laborers.

Other factors, such as militarism and religion, have also been important in the consolidation of patriarchal practices in state systems (Rapp 1977). As threats to women increase, restrictions on their behavior intensify to protect them and the honor of the group. Thus, patriarchy becomes "a system of domination enforced through violence and the threat of violence" (Christ 2016, 218). Abeda Sultana (2012) further contends that male violence is systematically condoned by the state's refusal to intervene against it except in rare cases (Werner, this volume; Kwiatkowski 2016).

While Kandiyoti (1988) correctly observes that patriarchy predates the rise of monotheistic religions, religious beliefs and practices have shaped distinctive forms of patriarchy in many parts of the world. Goody (1976, 119), for example, finds that patrilineal clans that took up Islam in parts of South Asia and the Middle East emphasized patrilateral, parallel cousin marriage in order to preserve the status, resources, and religious purity of the lineage (see also Barth 1954). This practice necessitated a more rigid separation of male and female cousins, which led eventually to residential segregation for all of the women in the extended family, a pooling of unmarried elite women at the top of the hierarchy, and the emergence of the harem and life in purdah (see also Mernissi 1994).

As historian Judith Bennett (2006) points out, the origins of patriarchal systems were complex, and women's accommodations to them were rooted in the particular constraints they faced (Kandiyoti 1988, 275). Nonetheless, Kandiyoti finds a blueprint for the bargain that underlay classic patriarchy. Generally, she says, women traded submissiveness, virtuous behavior, and deference for male protection. This patriarchal bargain acted as an implicit script to define and inflect women's options, and it shaped the gendered subjectivities that permeated early socialization and became part of the adult cultural milieu across the patriarchal arc (Kandiyoti 1988, 283, 285).

THE RELATIONSHIP BETWEEN PATRIARCHY AND CAPITALISM

Feminists have long studied the problematic relationship between the emergence of capitalism in Europe and the patriarchal practices and ideologies that accompanied it. The influential historian Carole Pateman (1988, 18) argues that capitalism was built on the original subordination of women to men in the marriage contract: men, the workers, have conjugal rights over women, the reproducers, to whose labor men are entitled. Because of the preexisting patriarchal contract, "the attributes and activities of the 'worker' are constructed together with, and as the other side of, those of his feminine counterpart, the 'housewife'" (Pateman 1988, 135).

In contrast, Walby (1990, 185) describes "the tension between capitalism and patriarchy ... over the exploitation of women's labour," which was resolved, she contends, when patriarchy moved from a private to a public form: "On the one hand, capitalists have interests in the recruitment and exploitation of female labour, which is cheaper than that of men because of patriarchal structures. On the other, there is resistance to this by that patriarchal strategy which seeks to maintain the exploitation of women in the household. . . . An alternative patriarchal strategy developed of allowing women into paid employment, but segregating them from men and paying them less" (see also Johnson 1996).

The result in contemporary times, according to Nancy Folbre and Heidi Hartmann (1989, 93), is sex segregation, lower wages for women, and the devaluing of nonmarket work, which are "expressions of a basic complementarity between patriarchy and capitalism that has made patriarchy quite resistant to change." Thus, women are now exploited both within and outside the home, a development well suited to the need of modern capitalism for a flexible, inexpensive labor force (Walby 1990, 199).

COLONIALISM AND PATRIARCHY

As European colonial empires expanded, capitalism penetrated other parts of the world. April Gordon (1996, 5–6) argues that European capitalism did not create patriarchy in these different world regions. Rather, the collision of colonial capitalism with existing social systems modified gender relations and furthered colonial economic objectives. Most often, these modifications gave men more authority and opportunity and sometimes also entailed importing European forms of patriarchy into new contexts. Historian Elizabeth Schmidt (1991, 734) documents how British colonial policies undercut peasant agricultural production in southern Rhodesia, leading to the further subordination of women by men, freeing up the best agricultural lands for British use, and strengthening the control of indigenous men over bridewealth and the products of women's labor.

This mutual reinforcement of capitalism and patriarchy took different forms in different parts of the world, influenced by relationships between competing ethnic groups and emerging social classes. For example, the capitalist transition in highland Peru between 1900 and 1950 involved men from different social classes and ethnicities using their control over women as a resource in changing forms of class struggle (Mallon 1987, 393). Florencia Mallon (1987, 380) concludes that the transition to capitalism cannot be understood solely by studying class formation; rather, "pre-existing forms of patriarchy have as great an effect on processes of capitalist class formation as class formation has on the forms taken by patriarchy." Research like that of Schmidt and Mallon clearly demonstrates the complexity of the relations between capitalism and patriarchy and the ways that these, in turn, shaped postcolonial preoccupations and identities in local contexts (see also Loomba 2015).

EVOLVING FORMS OF CONTEMPORARY PATRIARCHY

In the 1980s, Kandiyoti (1984, 1988, 281–82) found that the bases of classic patriarchy were crumbling under the impact of new market forces and capitalism's penetration of rural areas. While she maintains that there was no single trajectory of this breakdown, she does enumerate some common effects, including the earlier emancipation of young men from their fathers and their earlier separation from paternal households. For women, the establishment of neolocal households meant liberation from the control of mothers-in-law but also that they could no longer look forward to a future position of power in the extended family. Paradoxically, Kandiyoti finds that women in many areas resisted the transition from patriarchy, especially when they lacked other empowering alternatives.

Moghadam (2004) builds on Kandiyoti's observations to suggest that worldwide socioeconomic changes beginning in the 1980s led to the collapse of extended family households in many areas and to the emergence of new forms of stratification based on gendered classes, personhood, and nation. To describe this situation, she adopts the term *neopatriarchy*: "the product of the encounter between modernity and tradition in the context of dependent capitalism; it is modernized patriarchy" (Moghadam 2004, 148). While the outward forms of neopatriarchal families and states vary, Moghadam finds that their internal structures remain rooted in patriarchal values and social relations characterized by the dominance of the father in the household and at the level of the state (see Güvenç, this volume; White [1994] 2004). Yet Moghadam (2004, 144) reports that the infiltration of neopatriarchal forms has been uneven, noting the strong pockets of traditional patriarchy that remain in regions of the Middle East and South Asia (see Khurshid, this volume).

The nature and objectives of the state, political systems, and ruling elites also strengthen or weaken patriarchy. Moghadam (1992, 38) writes, "States that base and legitimize their power on patriarchal structures[,] such as the extended family or rural groups, foster and encourage its perpetuation through legislation subordinating women to the control of men." Stacey (1983) documents one such example in the establishment of the Chinese socialist state after the 1949 revolution. She points out that the state's initial goal was to reform the patriarchal structure of the prerevolutionary society. However, the new state lacked the resources to reward male peasants who supported the revolution, so instead they ceded to them control over the women in their families by recognizing these men as legitimate heads of household.

Michael Mann (1986, 50) proposes that the growth of formal education gave women the skills they needed to enter the workforce and attain more autonomy in their daily lives, further contributing to the breakdown of classic patriarchy. Moghadam (1992, 49) highlights the importance of parallel ideological and cultural changes in the West that emphasized women's equality, autonomy, and liberation. She concludes that the mass education of girls and women, the entry of women into the workforce, and the expanded activities of women's organizations, along with Western influence, pose the strongest challenges to patriarchy and the neopatriarchal state. Yet the chapters in this volume by Fincher and Chong demonstrate that these transitions are far from guaranteed.

WHAT COMES AFTER PATRIARCHY?
FATHER RIGHT VERSUS FRATERNAL RIGHT

In June 1996, a panel entitled "What Comes after Patriarchy? Reflections on Gender and Power in a Post-Patriarchal Age" was convened at the Berkshire Conference on the History of Women, and the papers were subsequently published in *Radical History Review* (1998). One contributor, Stacey (1998, 66), argues that contemporary Euro-American societies are postpatriarchal in part because the system of gender domination rooted in the prerogatives of fatherhood is over. Fatherhood, she contends, is no longer the foundation of the most significant features of gender subordination in the United States, and she suggests that the contemporary scene might be conceptualized as a diversity of "post-patriarchal gender bargains." Although Stacey does not elaborate, Arlie Hochschild and Anne Machury (1989) have proposed that middle-class American women during the late 1970s gave up their roles as full-time housewives in return for paid employment but in the process agreed to assume the burden of a second shift at home after the workday ended. Sharon Hays (1996) finds that middle-class US women solve the conflict between full-time work and the needs of children by committing themselves to an ideology of intensive mothering (see Manago and Khurshid, both this volume).

Teresa Meade and Pamela Haag (1998, 92) draw on the work of Pateman (1988) to argue that patriarchy in the West was transformed as father right was replaced by a broader fraternal right, or the domination of society by "the brotherhood of men." At the end of the Enlightenment era, in other words, patriarchy expanded from its original basis in the family to become a bond among men, who exercised control over society and its institutions. While men may no longer head patriarchal families, they still maintain patriarchal-fraternal bonds of power through control of administrative hierarchies in corporations, government, the military, and "a thousand other institutions that hold dear to the principles of the 'old boy network'" (Meade and Haag 1998, 93). These scholars also raise concern about Stacey's use of the term *postpatriarchy* because it suggests "that patriarchy and all its evils are now past and we have entered a world, like postimperialism, that is somehow an improvement" (Meade and Haag 1998, 94). Instead, write Linda Gordon and Allen Hunter (1998), patriarchy is a system that endlessly redesigns itself and assumes new forms.

NEOLIBERALISM AND NEW FORMS OF PATRIARCHAL CONTRACTS

Neoliberalism refers to a set of economic policies that emphasize the removal of barriers to competition, the deregulation of labor markets, the dismantling of the welfare state, and the opening of global borders to the free flow of capital and goods. Often, these policies are accompanied by the privatizing of government assets and services (Kingfisher 2016; Mies 2007). Aihwa Ong (2006, 3) clarifies, however, that neoliberalism is more than an economic doctrine; it is also a new mode of political organization that reconfigures the relationship between the government and the governed, power and knowledge, sovereignty and territoriality. Government actions are recast, she says, as nonpolitical and nonideological solutions to technical problems, and notions of citizenship and entitlement are rearticulated within forces set into motion by the market. Thus, "mobile individuals who possess human capital or expertise are highly valued and can exercise citizenship-like claims in diverse locations. Those judged not to have tradable competence or potential become devalued and vulnerable to exclusionary practices" (Ong 2006, 7).

Sarah Mies (2007, 2014) writes that capitalism is the latest avatar of patriarchy. Noting the recruitment of young women as preferred laborers in border zones, the rapid rise and spread of prostitution and human trafficking, and the enormous increases in rates of male violence against women, she argues that new forms of neoliberal patriarchy are emerging. Paradoxically, she says, feminists call for equality but do not demand an end to patriarchy or capitalism, in part because neoliberal logic portrays inequality as an individual and not a systemic problem. Yet it remains true "that capitalism needs patriarchy to maintain different layers of inequality and exploitability" (Mies 2014, 272–73). She concludes that under neoliberalism, the new equality is most likely seen between women and men at the bottom, who enjoy equal status as the cheapest labor worldwide (but see Kingfisher 2016, 258).

In many places, various groups, including multinational corporations, religious organizations, UN agencies, and NGOs, are intervening to deal with the specific issues of the poor and neglected in neoliberal systems (Ong 2006, 24). Often, they reinforce neoliberal notions of individual responsibility and autonomy while importing pieces of patriarchal ideology from the Global North. Zeynep Atalay (2017, 14), for example, finds that Western faith-based groups in Turkey are providing needed services while also promulgating religious familism, gender complementarity, and a traditional mode of social reproduction based on pronatalism. He concludes that faith-based organizations co-constitute neoliberalism by providing theological and political legitimacy to neoliberal social welfare systems and, in the process, reinforce the patriarchal gender contract in the public and private spheres (see Khurshid, this volume).

Ortner (2014) has urged scholars to renew their attention to patriarchy under neoliberal capitalism, and it is a key contention of the authors in this volume that patriarchy remains a remarkably resilient ideological system even though the material conditions that originally supported it have eroded. Although Keith Hart (2014) argues that humanity's emancipation from unequal societies has suffered reverses as a result of the synthesis between industrial capitalism and the nation-state, he fails to mention what seems obvious: the enduring power of patriarchy and the ongoing struggle of women for equality throughout the world. This omission provides telling evidence for patriarchy's persistence as a taken-for-granted ideological framework.

The case studies in this volume suggest that it is the ability of patriarchal beliefs and practices to adapt to changing contexts that accounts for their persistent power. Patriarchy, which never was identical in all places, has now come to seem almost unique in different places. Therefore, women's psychological responses to it are also likely to vary and must be the subject of careful empirical investigation in each case.

A Psychological Approach to Women's Responses to Patriarchy

While many explanations for the evolution of patriarchal systems mention the psychological mechanisms involved in women's responses to patriarchy, these remain overgeneralized and undertheorized. Just as blanket definitions of patriarchy are inadequate to the analytical task before us, so too are vague assertions that women are socialized to patriarchy, that they internalize beliefs that oppress them, or that they are motivated to contract strategic marriages. Without psychological theories, feminists cannot adequately address how women come to regulate their own public and private behaviors, why they want to obey family dictates, what appeals to them about conservative religious ideologies that run counter to values learned in the context of Western schooling, or why they sometimes assist men who kidnap brides or blame rape victims for the violent acts committed against them.

In 2004, volume contributor Susan Seymour edited a special issue of the journal *Ethos* titled "Contributions to a Feminist Psychological Anthropology." In the introduction she noted that feminism and psychological anthropology have moved on largely separate and sometimes antagonistic trajectories but that scholars in both fields could have much to say to one another (Seymour 2004a, 416). Unfortunately, this situation has not improved in the interim. Katherine Frank (2006, 282) suggests several reasons that scholars in today's academic climate are reluctant to do more than nod toward the interior domain of human life: an intellectual backlash against ahistorical and culturally imperialist uses of psychology; the tendency of psychologists to explain actions as the result of individual pathologies alone, rather than as responses to systems of power; and the deconstruction of the unitary subject or coherent self, which is currently fashionable in the academy.

Feminist researchers who rejected psychological approaches tended initially to embrace neo-Marxist frameworks relying, for example, on Gramsci's (1971) views of hegemonic ideology and consciousness derived from analyses of class-based systems. This led them to explain women's collusions with patriarchy as instances of "mystification" or false consciousness, which would presumably be corrected with consciousness raising and education (Dworkin 1974; MacKinnon 1989). Poststructural feminist scholars, influenced by the work of Foucault, called attention to the ways that knowledge is produced within a structure of power relations. Chris Weedon (1987, 19), for example, proposed that the concept of subjectivity could connect the power relations structuring public discourse and social institutions with individual consciousness.

Practice theorists critiqued poststructuralism for its lack of a theory of human agency, and they began, as Seymour (2006, 304) writes, to define agency as "the capacity for action, resistance, and accommodation in the face of cultural hegemony." Many studies have focused on the subaltern, asking how relations of power and inequality are both reproduced and changed through practice (Ortner 1997, 3). Such ideas made their way into feminist analyses through investigations of the ways that women, even while dominated, attempt to resist oppression. However, as Abu-Lughod (1990) points out, these studies often romanticize resistance and ignore the particularly thorny issue of women's own assent to patriarchal structures.

Saba Mahmood (2005) draws on Butler's (1997) ideas in analyzing the reasons that urban Egyptian women actively support a conservative Muslim mosque movement that seems inimical to their interests. Critical of feminists who assume the universality of the autonomous liberal subject, Mahmood (2005, 15) argues that agentival capacity is also affected by the ways in which people inhabit norms. In other words, repeated, embodied practice leaves a permanent mark on the character of the person. She writes, "The moral virtues (such as modesty, honesty and fortitude) are acquired through a coordination of outward behaviors (e.g., bodily acts, social demeanor) with inward dispositions (e.g., emotional states, thoughts, intentions) through the repeated performance of acts that entail those particular virtues" (139). Exactly how this process works psychologically, however, is left unexplained by Mahmood, which leaves her unable to clarify why women who practice the same rituals vary in their commitments to norms. Moreover, as Frank (2006, 285) points out, Mahmood's (2005, 188) removal of agency from the individual to the level of culture and discourse allows her to sidestep troubling questions about universal psychological processes and the nature of individual consciousness and leads her to conclude that it is best not to propose a theory of agency at all.

While poststructural and practice theories have provided powerful frameworks for understanding relations between actors in different positions in the social hierarchy, they do little, as Kandiyoti (1998, 143) notes, to help us understand how social actors internalize ideological precepts or become motivated to act against them (see also Strauss and Quinn 1997, 36–47). Moreover, these frameworks may be particularly ill suited for analyses of the power dimensions of gender relationships because, as Joseph (1994) has documented, gendered power tends to fluctuate throughout women's and men's life cycles. Additionally, gender relations (which have some basis in biology, giving them a sense of "naturalness") may themselves serve as templates for the reproduction of patriarchal relations in other realms of social life (see Inhorn 1996; Kandiyoti 1998; Scott 1988).

We agree that an analysis of the structural conditions giving rise to various forms of patriarchy is crucial, but we also maintain that the studies we have reviewed do not sufficiently explain internalization, a complex interpersonal and intrapsychic process negotiated by individuals. Lamenting the dearth of scholarship on the tensions between women's resistance to and accommodation of oppressive ideologies, Chong (2008) stresses the need for new approaches that can explicate how culturally situated systems of patriarchy and power are both shaped by and constitutive of the identities of women. Inevitably, the approaches that she is calling for are psychological.

THE PSYCHOLOGICAL APPROACH

Psychology as a discipline is primarily concerned with mental processes and the subjective worlds of individuals. Psychological states are assumed to derive from physical activities in the brain but cannot be reduced to them because of emergent properties at higher levels of complexity, which introduce distinct operating principles. Agency is one such property. Albert Bandura (2001, 2) proposes that human agency is characterized by a number of core features that operate through phenomenal and functional consciousness. These include the temporal extension of agency through intentionality and forethought; self-regulation by self-reactive influence; and self-reflectiveness about one's capabilities, quality of functioning, and the meaning and purpose of one's life pursuits. The self, conceptualized as a "coherence creator" by Susan Harter (2015), is central to human agency. Bandura's theory of agency illuminates how the human mind is not just reactive, but also generative, deliberative, and purposeful in constructing courses of action. Importantly, human agency enables individuals to affect their own biological functioning, potentially changing the self and also contributing to cultural change.

Nevertheless, decades of psychological research have discovered that human behavior arises from unconscious biases, attitudes, networks of associations, and contextual priming. In fact, John Bargh (2008) argues that the vast majority of psychological functioning, from the way humans parse visual stimuli in the environment to the way they produce language in everyday conversation, is unconscious. Over the course of development, brain maturation results in the formation of automatic patterns of sensing, perceiving, thinking, and feeling. Brain maturation unfolds in a sequence programmed by genetics, yet it is an open-ended process that requires social and sensory input. Although the brain remains plastic throughout the lifespan, it is particularly sensitive to sculpting during critical periods of development in infancy, childhood, and adolescence (Dehaene et al. 2010; Galván 2014; Strauss and Quinn 1997; Vygotsky 1978).

While not all of the contributors to this volume are psychologists or psychological anthropologists, we agree on the importance of exploring the psychological dimensions of women's experiences. We also agree that this is best accomplished by immersing ourselves in the everyday lives of women through long-term, ethnographic fieldwork and by attending closely to what women have to say as clues to their thoughts and feelings. To analyze these materials and to address the broader questions orienting this volume, we draw on several key psychological theories that illuminate the varied reasons for women's participation in their own subjugation. We hope that these findings provide the basis for further scholarship and for improving women's lives in different cultural contexts.

ATTACHMENT, SOCIALIZATION PRACTICES, AND CHILD DEVELOPMENT

Socialization practices are rooted in the biological universality of attachment between human infants and their caregivers. Erik Erikson (1950, 220) posited an initial stage of ego formation in which infants learn, through the co-regulation of arousal in the form of physical contact with caregivers, to trust others as sources of comfort and security and, by extension, to trust themselves as worthy of love. Since the 1960s, attachment researchers have produced extensive evidence that the infant-caregiver relationship serves as the initiating conditions for personality development (Sroufe 2005).

Although most attachment research has been done in Western countries, developmentalists working in different settings have begun to shed light on cultural variations in the attachment bond and how caregiving styles support culturally configured pathways of self-development (see Otto and Keller 2014; Quinn and Mageo 2013). Heidi Keller (2007), for example, has documented how proximal caregiving (characterized by constant close body contact, anticipation of rather than reaction to babies' emotional cues, and emphasis on bodily rather than cognitive stimulation) is more common among mothers in rural environments with less wealth and formal schooling, whereas distal parenting (characterized by greater face-to-face cognitive stimulation and object play) is more common in Western, educated, middle-class families with higher levels of schooling. Keller (2007, 258–59) contends that proximal parenting socializes an interdependent self, a more communal agent who is role oriented and compliant, while distal parenting socializes an independent self, a more autonomous agent who is bounded, self-contained, and unique (see also Keller et al. 2004). Along these lines, Seymour's chapter in this volume describes in great detail the proximal and distributed caregiving practices among North Indian families in Bhubaneswar, which socialize children, regardless of gender, into interdependent meaning systems (see also Seymour 2013). The lessons in valuing interdependence are reinforced in a variety of contexts, resulting in experiential constancy, one of the universal features of child-rearing posited by Quinn (2005b, 478).

Establishment of the attachment bond also motivates the universal human need for social approval, according to Quinn (2005b). Physical comfort and attention communicate safety to the preverbal infant, and any disruption of this attachment system is experienced as an existential threat. With maturation into toddlerhood, all children acquire increased capacities for agency, including physical mobility, language, self-regulation, and self-awareness, and thus the ability to experience self-conscious emotions, such as embarrassment, shame, and pride. In Erikson's (1950, 223) theory, children in this second stage of development are faced with the task of coordinating their newfound capacities for self-determination with their need for social acceptance. Quinn (2005b) suggests that child-rearing at this point in development focuses on predisposing children to experience emotions appropriate for the further internalization of cultural lessons, and she references a host of neurobiological research showing that lessons are most memorable when they are emotionally arousing (see also Quinn and Mathews 2016).

The kinds of emotion used in socialization provide insights into the emotional architecture of women's identities that may generate compliance with patriarchal roles. Developmentalists Ying Wong and Jeanne Tsai (2007, 210) have observed contrasting cultural models of shame and guilt in child-rearing practices. Shame arises when transgressions of moral standards are attributed to a global and stable self and thus leads to self-effacement; guilt arises when transgressions are attributed to transitory states or actions and thus preserves an expansive, positive view of the self. Wong and Tsai (2007, 212) argue that in more familistic cultural contexts, shame is a valued feeling that contributes a sense of self-worth and purpose in tight-knit interdependent relationships in which others' feelings and thoughts are just as important as one's own. Describing the North Indian family, Seymour points out that a girl's first menstruation is the moment when she comes of age and must, for the first time, begin following the rules of adult female decorum with their attendant sense of shame (*lajya*). They come to learn what is required of them as wives and daughters-in-law, lessons that are effective because they have been predisposed to experience shame early in development.

THE DEVELOPMENT OF SELF AND THE SATISFACTION OF AFFILIATIVE NEEDS

The origins of self-understanding, as Seymour's observations demonstrate, are first and foremost relational, beginning in the very first experiences of infants with caregivers. Yet Seymour stops short of explicitly theorizing about the construction of the self as the way in which girls create meaning out of cultural circumstances, experience and internalize specific emotions related to this cultural meaning, and thus become motivated to assume adult roles.

British psychologists Melanie Klein (1949) and W. R. D. Fairbairn independently formulated the principles of what is now called object relations theory. Fairbairn ([1952] 1981) departed from Freud ([1894] 2013) by proposing that people do not attempt to satisfy basic biological drives, but rather need the satisfaction that comes from being in relation to real others. The theory holds that an infant's relationship with the primary caregiver is the key determinant of personality formation and that the infant's need for attachment motivates the development of the infantile self. The infant forms internal objects through repeated experiences with caregivers, and *object relations* refers to the dynamic, internalized relationships between the self and objects (i.e., significant others). The images of these relationships are subjectively constructed by the infant and have enduring qualities that serve as templates for future relationships. From this perspective, the *self* refers to the combination of ego and internal objects in a unique, dynamic relation that creates a sense of personal identity that remains relatively constant over the life course.

Contributor Jocelyn Marrow explores how such self-construction takes place in the context of elder-junior relationships in North Indian families. She draws on the work of the psychoanalyst Heinz Kohut (1971), who focuses on the processes whereby an infant moves from conceiving of objects as external to internalizing certain qualities that objects are perceived to possess, thereby making these qualities the infant's own. Kohut (1984) proposes that the external becomes internalized through three basic psychological processes: people must be admired for who they are (mirroring); they must be allowed to form an idealized image of a significant other (idealization); and they must feel similar to others and be included in relationships with them (twinship).

In the North Indian family communication model that Marrow describes, elders and juniors inhabit complementary roles with respect to the types of interrelational work they perform. Elders shape juniors (and demonstrate love for them) by making them understand, while juniors listen to their seniors and take advantage of the opportunity to become more like them. By taking in the perspectives of their elders and transforming their own thoughts and behaviors, newly married women can strengthen their claim to full membership in their conjugal families. In this context, idealization and twinship are paramount, and mirroring is largely absent, which suggests that these processes may be universal features of patrilocal extended families.

Socialization to interdependence is also psychological, and Joseph (1999) labels the tendency to define oneself in relationship with others as "intimate selving." Joseph warns that the forging of relational selves does not cause patriarchy, nor does patriarchy always lead to relational selves. The combination, however, may result in patriarchal connectivity, which she defines as relationally oriented feminine and masculine selves organized for a gendered and aged hierarchy (Joseph 1993b, 466). She explains, "Intertwined, connectivity and patriarchy have helped produce selves trained in the psychodynamics of domination, knowing how to control and be controlled" (Joseph 1999, 13). Moreover, we might hypothesize that because connectivity reinforces family solidarity, it may be particularly resistant to change in situations where such solidarity is necessary for social, economic, or political survival.

SELF-INTEREST, DEFERENCE, AND THE FORGING OF PARTIAL ACCOMMODATIONS TO PATRIARCHY

Before children can fully experience shame in the context of familial interactions, they must forge intersubjective understandings of themselves and others. Peter Fonagy (2001) describes this process as the development of mentalization, which is the capacity to recognize and anticipate the mental states of self and other. Katherine Ewing (1991, 132) distinguishes between the formation of interpersonal autonomy, which is often suppressed in extended families with deference hierarchies, and intrapsychic autonomy, which she defines as the "ability to maintain enduring mental representations of sources of self-esteem and comfort, permitting a more flexible adaptation to the vicissitudes of the immediate environment."

Feminist relational psychologists, like Jean Baker Miller (2012), caution that the attainment of intrapsychic autonomy may exact an emotional toll, depending on the type of family system in which people live, because individuation unfolds within family systems that vary considerably in their tolerance for separation and independence (see also Joseph 1999, 9). Where individuation is viewed as a betrayal of family or as a threat to its stability, such as might be expected in the traditional patrilocal household, individuals may be required to sacrifice agency for communion or forgo individuation for a sense of belonging, which can lead to a host of psychic conflicts requiring more mental work to resolve.

In a reanalysis of two articles by Ewing, Quinn (2006, 373–74) argues that Pakistani women's use of indirect, subtle political strategies is a cultural task solution to the otherwise unbearable demands of formal deference in a severely hierarchical system of family relations. Pakistani children observe others enacting deference while keeping their true feelings to themselves; they also practice these behaviors by advancing relatively minor desires for things, like special foods. Each time they are successful, the positive emotions they experience help to reinforce the practice. The use of this strategy by the Pakistani woman is evidence, according to Quinn (2006, 376), "of the practiced ability to suppress her desires rather than expressing them in a way that would violate powerful cultural expectations of deference; and an equally practiced strategy for pursuing these desires within the strictures of deference."

While Quinn does not suggest that this shared task solution is found elsewhere, we might hypothesize that children face similar dilemmas in other regions where the patrilocal extended family system engenders conflicts between the pursuit of individual goals and the need to pay deference to elders. We might further speculate that this shared task solution creates an early mental template for compromise and, as such, serves as a defense against the feelings of frustration, anxiety, and hostility that are evoked when individual desires and goals must be subordinated to family wishes and cultural expectations.

These insights help us to understand how young women, who are socialized to be deferent and to both express and receive love by merging with the wishes of elders, can ever come to resist patriarchal practices rooted in family hierarchy. Two anecdotes recounted earlier in this chapter further illustrate this dilemma. We contrasted Susana's appreciation of the freedom afforded by her education in Chiapas with Salma's willingness, despite being educated and employed, to comply with an arranged marriage in rural Pakistan. Susana's story is more complicated than it first appears, however, because in a subsequent interview reported in the chapter by Adriana M. Manago, Susana says that her right to an education was given to her by her father, and she is thus indebted to him. This sense of indebtedness motivates Susana to behave appropriately even in the absence of community and family supervision. Similarly, Khurshid reports in her chapter that while Salma views herself as an "educated" woman, she also believes that she represents her family and her father and must behave appropriately so as not to dishonor them. Both young women, despite living in very different cultural contexts, confront a similar contradiction between autonomy and obedience, a challenge that they attempt to resolve while struggling to forge a coherent sense of self under rapidly changing social conditions. In doing so, they appropriate some aspects of new discourses about rights and freedoms while retaining older emphases on the importance of family and the value of intergenerational relationships.

COGNITIVE SCHEMATA AND CHANGING FORMS OF PATRIARCHY

Two important criticisms can be raised about the explanations presented thus far about the psychological mechanisms that animate adherence to the dictates of the traditional patrilocal extended family. First, as the Arab Families Working Group (2008) documents, patrilocal families share certain overall characteristics, but they also vary considerably in their constitution and operation on the ground. Second, given that variability, children in patrilocal families likely observe a range of behaviors and absorb a diversity of ideas, making self-construction a less monolithic process. In the patrifocal North Indian family, for example, Seymour (2013) reports that girls learn patterns of deferent behavior but often see women wielding considerable power. They learn that women move through various roles and statuses in life, which are differentially restricting and empowering. Competing discourses, derived from male insecurities in a patriarchal society and women's diverse experiences and roles, may include critiques of the patrifocal family voiced in particular contexts (Seymour 2006, 311). Even when these critiques do not form the basis for collective resistance, Seymour maintains that they provide important mental preparation for a changing future and serve to remind us that the links between beliefs and actions are complex.

Schema theory provides a mechanism for analyzing alternative gender scripts within a cultural group. Schemata can be defined as mental representations used to organize and simplify knowledge about the world. Claudia Strauss and Naomi Quinn (1997, 48–88) argue that a schema can be understood as a generic version of (some part of) the world built up from experience and stored in memory. Moreover, Quinn (2005a, 37) explains, "to the degree that people share experiences, they will end up sharing the same schemata—having, we would say, the same culture (or subculture)." On the other hand, all people have experiences that are only partially shared with others or that are completely idiosyncratic. Thus, schema theory predicts that women's responses to patriarchal ideals and practices are often varied and complex, even when they grow up in the same cultural tradition.

Strauss (2005, 203) points out that shared schemata become powerful when they are so deeply internalized that people are hardly aware of them and do not consider alternatives to them as viable. In her chapter, Holly F. Mathews provides an example of such a schema found in her research community in southern Mexico in the 1970s. Over the course of more than forty years of fieldwork, however, Mathews observed changes in beliefs about marriage and gender roles, and a new schema began to spread into this region during the 1980s. Daughters of women who had grown up with the old schema began to articulate a desire to marry men who would stay with them, support them, and love them. Their shared emotional trauma played a key role in shaping them. Defining themselves as "modern," many rejected old ideas of patrilocal residence and strict gender segregation in favor of the nuclear family built on the basis of choice, love, and friendship.

People assemble their understandings of the world from exposure to the different sets of beliefs that circulate throughout a community (see Strauss 2012). These may include formal ideologies that come from religion and politics, folk wisdom and popular cultural precepts that represent tradition, or values transmitted through Western schooling or by the activities of NGOs and international development agencies. Assuming that people are exposed to multiple schemata in this way, we must ask, which ones motivate them and why?

Quinn (2005b, 489) posits that one of the four universal features of childrearing systems is emotional arousal; socialization techniques that arouse emotion are more effective motivators for desired behavior. More generally, we might expect that schemata tied to emotional arousal are likely to be more powerful than those that are not. Quinn and Mathews (2016, 369–70) contend that emotional arousal imbues an experience with an enhanced sense of ownership, perhaps because we feel what we are experiencing so deeply that we *become* that experience. Further, who we are has a large role in guiding our commitments and our resulting behavior (or making us feel badly if we do not live up to who we think we should be). So, they conclude, our emotionally arousing experiences play a key role in the development of the selves we become, largely because they are more memorable (Quinn and Mathews 2016, 369). For a generation of girls with absent fathers in rural Mexico, the shared experience of abandonment and loss, coupled with the perception of their parents' marriages as bearing the blame for this situation, seemed to prompt a widespread shift toward free choice and companionate marriage.

COLLAPSING PATRIARCHAL BARGAINS AND INCREASING COGNITIVE DISSONANCE

Obviously, not all mental conflicts caused by changing public discourses can be resolved. Contributors to this volume document many instances in which the traditional patriarchal bargain highlighted by Kandiyoti (1988, 281) is collapsing under the weight of social change, yet women have no other satisfying options. Social psychologists in the 1950s and 1960s argued that people strive for cognitive consistency (Abelson et al. 1968) because cognitive inconsistency or contradiction generates tension and causes dissonance, a negative drive state that people feel compelled to eliminate. Elliot Aronson (1968, 8) notes that these perceptions of cognitive inconsistency are not necessarily logical; they are psychological. He also maintains that individuals are most likely to experience distress when certain beliefs call for behaviors that are inconsistent with their self-concept (23). Dissonance also occurs when people's beliefs conflict with those held by members of their social reference group and thus compromise their identity, a key part of self-representation. Strauss (2012, 102) finds that people experience ambivalence when they are aware of and concerned about such conflicts but seem unable to resolve them to make decisions and take action. Erika Bourguignon (2004) and Jocelyn Marrow (2013) suggest that ambivalence for women (and, presumably, other less powerful groups) can also be unconscious and manifest through embodied forms of expression, like possession trance and psychosomatic illness.

Güvenç's (this volume) research in Ankara clearly illustrates this ambivalence and the psychological toll it takes on women. Under difficult circumstances, much as Kandiyoti (1988) predicted, women tried to make men live up to their obligations under the old patriarchal bargain. Men, frustrated and angry, frequently beat their wives, who in turn beat their children, suffered from extreme guilt afterward, and frequently expressed their interpersonal distress as somatic complaints, including severe headaches and other pains. While women are aware of the problems they face, they do not know of any way to solve them. As a result, they live in an ambivalent state and pay an enormous emotional price for doing so.

Similarly, by the early 2000s the women in rural Mexico studied by Mathews (this volume) were once again confronting unstable social conditions, which left them anguished and ambivalent. Much like the Turkish women studied by Güvenç (this volume), they were unable to resolve the contradictions between old ways of life and new. Some of the Mexican women clung to traditional ideas, hoping to coerce absent men into honoring the terms of the older patriarchal bargain, while others escaped by fantasizing about finding a prince, a rich man who would rescue them from a life of hardship and loneliness—paradoxically longing for the return of the good patriarch (see also Stern 1998).

Quinn (1996) argues that when people confront similar cognitive dilemmas on a recurring basis, they forge common task solutions to them, and these sometimes work as a shared psychological defense that reduces the anxiety caused by conflicting views of the self. In her chapter in this volume, Chong describes a common task solution adopted by upper- and middle-class South Korean women. These women's new aspirations conflict with their gender identities, which are still strongly rooted in their family-oriented view of themselves, causing them to experience cognitive dissonance and anxiety (see Welter 1966).

Chong hypothesizes that conversion to the Korean evangelical church is a solution to the intrapsychic conflicts these women share and that conversion serves as a psychological defense against the anxieties caused when their rising emancipatory sensibilities are frustrated by a lack of work opportunities and by an enduring patriarchal value structure that expects them to fulfill traditional family duties. Because church conversion is a well-established and culturally available option, it becomes, for many of these women, a shared task solution to a common psychic dilemma (see Christensen 1963; McGinty 2006; Wallace 1956).

External Constraints: Coercion and Conformity

Our discussion thus far has concentrated on why certain ideas are psychologically motivating to women and how women come to adjust their self-perceptions and regulate their behaviors in response to them. Yet accommodations to patriarchy are not solely the result of internal motivations. Coercion, whether in the form of community gossip or acts of violence and rape, has been widely employed to keep women in line with systems that oppress them. At one extreme are "honor" killings, defined as acts of vengeance taken by men against women who are seen as bringing shame on a family or kin group. Unni Wikan (2008, 15) argues that honor killings are not crimes of passion motivated by emotions like jealousy. Instead, they are planned and presuppose an audience that will reward and honor the assailant.

Groups that share common ideas can be real or imagined. Strauss (2012, 15–16) labels these "opinion communities." Members do not need to hold all of the same attitudes; what they share is exposure to conventional ways of thinking and talking (16). These communities usually include members of a person's social network (family, friends, neighbors, co-workers), but they can also include members of one's profession, ethnic group, religion, or the like, whose ideas are supposed from the comments of a few. Sociologists refer to these as "reference groups," which they define as the groups to which we compare ourselves in order to identify our social norms (Newcomb 1953). When individuals counter these norms, it is reference groups that are likely to impose sanctions to punish and correct the offending behaviors. Because individuals meet needs for social approval and belonging through group membership, the standards and opinions of reference groups are often emotionally compelling and can be incorporated into aspects of the self known as "social identities" (Tajfel 1982).

Several contributors in this book identify the extended family and the residential community as traditional reference groups that regulate family honor and women's behavior. Werner (this volume) calls attention to the importance of patriarchal value systems that transcend individual families and cut across existing ethnic, religious, and national lines. She compares the resurgence of bride kidnapping in Kazakhstan with the epidemic of sexual assaults on college campuses in the United States. In each case, members of the broader community say and do things that reinforce the idea that these acts of violence against women are acceptable. Both the women who feel forced to accept the grooms who kidnap them and the women who feel pressured not to report sexual assault are making choices in a context where they would be judged negatively for resisting the patriarchal system.

Werner concludes that the patriarchal value system is so powerful because its ideas, exemplified by rape and kidnap myths, are shared by a large segment of society and comprise schemata tied to fundamental assumptions about the nature of men and women. In these situations, it is the larger community or public, not the household or residential community (as Kandiyoti 1988 suggests), that serves as the social reference group, rendering commentary and judgment based on these schemata about women's sexual assault or kidnapping.

Social psychologists Peter Glick and Susan Fiske (2001, 2011) have formulated ambivalent sexism theory to explain why community members, especially women, often support beliefs that are harmful to them. They argue that sexism manifests in two complementary ways. Hostile sexism is an adversarial view of gender relations in which women are seen as seeking to control men. It leads to overt prejudice against women who embody nontraditional gender roles. In contrast, benevolent sexism characterizes women in seemingly more positive ways — as pure creatures who ought to be protected and adored and whose love is needed to make men complete (Glick and Fiske 2001, 109). Of course, this idealization of women simultaneously implies that they are best suited for conventional gender roles, confined to the pedestal. Glick and Fiske point out that benevolent sexism is a more subtle form of prejudice, a legitimizing ideology that helps to justify and maintain inequality.

Acceptance of benevolent sexism, moreover, may reduce women's resistance to patriarchy. Glick and Fiske (2001, 111) write, "Not only is it subjectively favorable in its characterization of women, but it promises that men's power will be used to women's advantage, if only they can secure a high status male protector." To the extent that women depend on men as protectors and providers, they are less likely to protest men's power or to seek their own. Perhaps more significant, benevolent sexism rewards women who embrace conventional gender roles and power relations, while hostile sexism punishes women who challenge the status quo. Radke and colleagues (2017) analyzed data from the New Zealand Values and Attitudes Survey, which polled 10,485 New Zealanders (men and women), and they conducted an online survey with 269 women recruited in the United States. The researchers found that women who endorse an ideology of benevolent sexism also believe that social hierarchy is natural and good and perceive women's lower position in the social hierarchy as legitimate. The researchers propose that women often adopt benevolent sexism because they assume that it affords them protection from more hostile forms of sexism, such as domestic violence and sexual assault.

A number of other scholars have theorized about the motivating force of ideologies, not only in terms of affiliation and social belonging, but also because these confer a sense of existential security in an unpredictable world. Thus, as Kandiyoti (1988) observes and Güvenç's chapter in this book illustrates, women often aggressively support the classic patriarchal bargain even as patriarchal systems are eroding because it provides them with a sense of security and stability in times of social change.

System justification theory, as articulated by John Jost and Mahzarin Banaji (1994), explains that certain groups of people are predisposed to defend existing systems but for very different reasons. According to Jost, Banaji, and Mosek (2004, 908–10), younger people and those with newly formed aspirations are more likely to question prevailing norms and practices. Alternatively, those who hold power and privilege are more likely to support the status quo because it benefits them directly and because it decreases their feelings of guilt about personal power by legitimizing their positions of privilege. Paradoxically, those at the bottom of the hierarchy are also likely to support the status quo because the system provides a rationale for their low position, which helps to mitigate the anxiety of feeling oppressed by others. By rationalizing their own suffering, they reduce the cognitive dissonance produced when the realities of their lives do not meet societal expectations.

One implication of system justification theory is that some groups pursue change while others actively oppose it, which may lead to conflicts between elites and lower classes, between older and younger generations, or between men and women. Chong's (this volume) description of women in Korea clearly illustrates this process. Fincher (this volume) describes another relevant example. After the Chinese population control campaigns of the 1970s and 1980s, a generation of only daughters in urban areas received the benefits of education once reserved for men and went on to attain high-paying and high-status jobs. Yet state media campaigns pushed these women to marry, while parents and in-laws pressured them to register titles to land and houses in their husbands' names. The episode recounted above illustrates how a mother-in-law's emotional appeal worked on one prospective Chinese bride, who agreed to record her property in her husband's name. System justification theory would suggest that even though she was well educated and forward thinking, this woman acquiesced to her in-laws in part to mitigate her feelings of oppression and powerlessness in this situation.

In these examples, the sticky parts of patriarchy vary and suggest different explanations of the motivating factors behind women's responses to them. The chapters in this volume sketch out some of these factors and attempt to link sociostructural parameters with psychological motivations and responses. We propose that only by continuing in these endeavors can we hope to elucidate the dynamics of what Bennett (2006, 81) refers to as the "patriarchal equilibrium," which has persisted throughout history because of the ability of patriarchal institutions "to adapt remarkably well to the conflicts, contradictions and confusions they produce."

Organization of the Volume

When Naomi Quinn first presented her paper to our seminar, she acknowledged that biological explanations were unpopular in feminist circles because of past attempts to reduce gender differences to certain innate proclivities (see Vandermassen 2005). We open the volume with her chapter. Urging us not to throw the baby out with the bathwater, Quinn argues that more sophisticated explorations of the evolution of human cooperation are beginning to shed light on how human predispositions to both submission and dominance structure the systems of deference that are so basic to the workings of patriarchy. Her contribution is followed by chapters by Susan Seymour and Jocelyn Marrow, who offer nuanced illustrations of how repetitive, affect-laden prescriptive and proscriptive lessons transmit patterns of deference and honor to children and adolescents in North Indian families.

The volume shifts focus in chapters by Adriana Manago and Ayesha Khurshid, who consider the implications of socioeconomic change in, respectively, southern Mexico and rural Pakistan, areas where the extended patrilocal family has traditionally been strong. These authors consider the ways that economic modernization, children's exposure to Western education, and the rights discourses of NGOs challenge patriarchal control rooted in the extended family by opening new arenas for women outside the household. In both sites, the strong commitment to family remains, but the nature of family roles and relations is changing as young women take on the burden of regulating their own behaviors, including their sexuality.

Traditional extended family patterns in many parts of the world are breaking apart under the onslaught of population dislocations, economic collapse, and the spread of Western values. Holly Mathews and Gülden Güvenç explore the implications of these changes for women in, respectively, southern Mexico and urban Turkey. With traditional family forms no longer functional, women and men struggle to adapt to new circumstances and changing values. In the absence of suitable cultural solutions for these new situations, they are forced to cope individually and often experience psychic distress along with increasing levels of interpersonal violence.

In the next two chapters, Kelly Chong and Leta Hong Fincher each consider the role of state policies as these interact with family dynamics to shape women's perceptions of themselves and others and to affect their behaviors. Chong examines the experience of South Korean women who adopt a culturally shared task solution—conversion to the Korean evangelical church—to ease their psychic distress. Fincher highlights the role of persistent patriarchal values in the parental generation in China and describes how these influence young professional women to acquiesce to traditional marriages.

In parts of the Global North, vestiges of patriarchy are found in more isolated places where networks of men control the institutional hierarchy and reinforce dominance by excluding women or by attempting to control them sexually. In her chapter, Cynthia Werner examines rape culture on US college campuses as one of these bubbles of patriarchy that tacitly sanctions the use of violence against women, and she compares it to state-sanctioned violence against women in Kazakhstan.

We end this volume by returning to the question that motivated our seminar: Why do women accommodate practices that are oppressive to them? We attempt to disaggregate what women do from why they do it. The conclusion by Mathews and Manago summarizes our explanations for women's varied responses to patriarchy, charts an agenda for continued research, and considers the possibilities for change.

CHAPTER TWO

Historical Circumstances and Biological Proclivities Surrounding Patriarchy

NAOMI QUINN

In this chapter, I argue that the particular historic formation we call patriarchy is built on certain universal human proclivities. These propensities are not universally realized, however, and not all human societies are patriarchal. Patriarchy came to fruition in the context of a specific set of structural circumstances that pertained across Asia and Europe, in what I think of as the patriarchal arc, from Japan to the British Isles, including all of the settler colonies and the many contexts into which colonial rule — and, with it, patriarchy — have been introduced.[1]

The two human proclivities I think are most fundamentally implicated in patriarchy are deference and familism. In order to describe how they are so implicated, I first have to say more about the extent and shape of patriarchy itself and the circumstances giving rise to this historic formation in some human societies. Together, these particular human proclivities and these particular historical circumstances set the stage for patriarchy.

My chapter, with its evolutionary and materialist tilt, may seem out of place in this volume. However, I take up the burden of laying groundwork for the ethnographic chapters to follow. The ethnographic chapters are informed by their authors' close and revealing present-day fieldwork. These contributors do not, for the most part, historicize this ethnography or put it in an evolutionary context. But to fully understand these individual stories about patriarchy, its persistence, and the turns it has taken, the larger historical and evolutionary context is necessary.

The Extent of Patriarchy

My argument for the extent of patriarchy bears a strong family resemblance to that made by Deniz Kandiyoti, a scholar of gender relations, politics, and economic development in the Middle East, in a dazzling paper. Kandiyoti (1988) contrasts what she terms "the sub-Saharan African pattern" of patriarchy—which I elect not to label patriarchy at all, in order to avoid diluting the term beyond usefulness—with "classic patriarchy," which she locates in South and East Asia and the Middle East.

At first blush, these regional limits to the extent of classic patriarchy may appear to be much more restrictive than my own designation of a patriarchal arc reaching across all of Asia and Europe and beyond. Kandiyoti (1988) considers that, historically, patriarchy has broken down in many places, even as it has fostered a female conservative reaction. That her description of it, like mine, recognizes the historic reach of patriarchy beyond Asia and the Middle East is implicit in her acknowledgment that historical parallels to patriarchal breakdown "may be found in very different contexts, such as the industrialized societies of Western Europe and the United States" (Kandiyoti 1988, 283). That its vestiges, which she views as reactive female conservatism, live on in the latter societies suggests that patriarchy was in full force at one time in their histories or those of their colonizers.

Elsewhere in her article Kandiyoti (1988, 278) provides another clue to the extent of patriarchy across Eurasia when she notes in passing that the forms of control and subordination common to classic patriarchy "cut across cultural and religious boundaries, such as those of Hinduism, Confucianism, and Islam"—to which she might have added Christianity. I hope that she would agree with me that patriarchy once cut a continuous swath across all of Asia and Europe, including but not limited to the Middle East and parts of Asia.

Women's Accommodation to Patriarchy

However widespread across human societies some type or degree of male dominance or attempted dominance may be, what is especially distinctive of patriarchy is that women accommodate to being so dominated. As Kandiyoti (1988, 278) notes, her examples of African "women's open resistance" stand in stark contrast to women's accommodations to classic patriarchy. In the southern Ghanaian case that I know best, men do attempt to assert their domination over others, including their wives and other women, and this is the case even in matrilineal societies. Nevertheless, women will have none of it, and the result appears to be a continuous war of the sexes. North of the Sahara, women's accommodation to male dominance, a defining feature of patriarchy, amounts to "their active collusion in the reproduction of their own subordination" (Kandiyoti 1988, 280). Of course, there are exceptions to this broad dichotomy between Eurasia and Africa, on both sides of the Sahara.

Kandiyoti offers insight as to why women's accommodation to or collusion with male dominance has occurred in these Eurasian societies. The most general factor that she names is "the operation of the patrilocally extended household," a "patrilineal-patrilocal complex" that she declares has had "remarkably uniform" implications for women across societies characterized by agrarian peasantry (Kandiyoti 1988, 278). In this complex, more particularly, "girls are given away in marriage at a very young age into households headed by their husband's father," where "they are subordinate not only to all the men but also to the more senior women, especially their mother-in-law" (278). She notes further about the dowry system once widespread across Asia and Europe:

> Women do not ordinarily have any claim on their father's patrimony. Their dowries do not qualify as a form of premortem inheritance since they are transferred directly to the bridegroom's kin and do not take the form of productive property, such as land. . . . In Muslim communities, for a woman to press for her inheritance rights would be tantamount to losing her brothers' favor, her only recourse in case of severe ill-treatment by her husband or divorce. The young bride enters her husband's household as an effectively dispossessed individual who can establish her place in the patriliny only by producing male offspring. (Kandiyoti 1988, 279)

Virtually the only resource that wives marrying into patrilineal-patrilocal households can convert into a modicum of influence and status is their offspring, specifically the sons that they bear. One consequence of this predicament is "a powerful incentive for higher fertility" (Kandiyoti 1988, 281). Another consequence is the waiting game that in-marrying women are forced to play (described so well in Margery Wolf's 1972 ethnography of rural Taiwanese families) in order to ultimately become relatively influential mothers-in-law. As Kandiyoti (1988, 279) concludes, "The cyclical nature of women's power in the household and their anticipation of inheriting the authority of senior women encourages a thorough internalization of this form of patriarchy by the women themselves."

In a subsequent article, Kandiyoti (1998, 146–47) expands on this insight: "Women's life cycle in the virilocally extended household may be such that the deprivation and hardships they experience as young brides is [sic] eventually superseded by the control and authority they enjoy over their sons' wives." This and other elements of the patriarchal complex that Kandiyoti describes may receive greater or lesser cultural elaboration, and they may take on slightly different appearances in particular locales, but the central features of the patriarchal complex are highly identifiable.

The Origins of Patriarchy in Intensive Agriculture

For a comprehensive explanation for Kandiyoti's (1988) "patrilineal-patrilocal complex" among Eurasian agrarian peasantry, we must go back even further in the anthropological literature to Jack Goody's important comparative works: his 1973 essay "Bridewealth and Dowry in Africa and Eurasia" and his 1976 book *Production and Reproduction*. The choice of Goody, among all his contemporaries and forebears in anthropology and related fields, may seem a curious one. After all, in today's antimaterialist climate in the discipline, Goody's anthropological contribution tends to get discounted. But it should not be. Moreover, he is particularly informative regarding one of the aforementioned tasks I address in this chapter: laying the historical groundwork for patterns of patriarchy in Asia, Europe, and by extension the European settler colonies. A useful way of thinking about this is that Goody finishes Kandiyoti's argument.

In Goody's (1976) view, the impetus for the dowry and the distinctive Eurasian complex of institutions and practices to which it belonged was the introduction of the plow, along with other features of intensive agriculture. This agricultural innovation of the plow made farmland roughly ten times as productive as it had been under the hoe, encouraging a population explosion. In sub-Saharan Africa, by contrast, hoe cultivation persisted, and plentiful land and corporate descent group landownership with individual usufruct were the rule. The resulting land shortage in Eurasia and the solution to familial perpetuation of landholding rights that it dictated were at the heart of the Eurasian dowry system.[2] Goody (1973, 25) writes: "Upon these differences status largely but not exclusively depended. Consequently it became a strategy of utmost importance to preserve those differences for one's offspring, lest the family and its fortunes decline over time. . . . Sons might inherit all the productive capacity but daughters had to be assured of a marriage that would provide them with the same (or better) standard of life to which they were accustomed. They had to be endowed with property to attract a husband of the same rank."

Goody's overall argument is not primarily focused, nor is it intended to be, on the implications of this gendered rule of inheritance for women's position. Thus he does not stress these implications. However, in addition to those named by Kandiyoti, he does note in passing several features of the Eurasian system that are absent in Africa, which have consequences for women. Along with arranged marriage, monogamy, and concubinage, the Eurasian dowry system is typically accompanied by a concern for the virginity of unmarried women. In the latter instance, "sex before marriage could diminish a girl's honour, and reduce her marriage chances.... indeed premarital sex might also lead to a forced marriage, to an inappropriate husband" (Goody 1976, 17). Arranged marriage, of course, is necessary to make a good match, that is, "a husband of the same rank" for a daughter.

Monogamy follows from the unlikelihood of even a relatively wealthy landholder being able to afford more than one wife. As Goody (1976, 51) explains, under the dowry system "it is difficult to repeat this type of funded marriage, since the spouses have to commit their property in order to get a partner of the right standing." Under this system, the wife brings a dowry to the marriage, but the husband must match the resources she brings with his own. Furthermore, multiple wives mean more heirs born, and "only the very rich can afford the luxury of many children without dropping in the economic hierarchy" (17). Concubinage, which does not require such a financial commitment on a man's part, either to the concubine herself or the children she bears, is an adaptation to monogamy. In Africa, by contrast, there is no such economic constraint on accumulating additional wives, each of whom has the full rights attendant to that role, and so polygyny is widespread.

Human Proclivities toward Patriarchy

I suggest that the constraints on women in patriarchal societies are more than circumstantial or learned; men and women are predisposed to patriarchy by their human nature as well. New levels of cooperation and the distinctive biological capacities that evolved to make such cooperation possible are thought by a growing number of evolutionists to differentiate humans from the other great apes and our common ancestor. This insight has led to a twenty-first-century explosion of books (Boehm 2012; Bowles and Gintis 2011; Hrdy 2009; Sterelny 2012; Tomasello 2014; for an earlier rendition of this argument, see Richerson and Boyd 1998), all arguing, according to various scenarios, that the critical difference between nonhuman apes' social organization and that of the earliest humans was an unprecedented pressure for the human hunter-gatherers to cooperate.³

In agreement on this fundamental point, these authors sometimes disagree sharply with regard to the primary need that led to such cooperation. This may be deemed to have been the need for cooperation in large game hunting (Tomasello 2014, who thinks that this transition occurred in two cognitive steps); in alloparenting due to the uncommonly slow development of human offspring (Hrdy 2009; Crittenden and Marlowe 2013, 69–70); or in defense against hostile groups (Richerson and Boyd 1998, 1999). Kim Sterelny (2012, xii) is skeptical of all such single "magic moment, key innovation models," arguing instead for a larger human syndrome growing out of these various ventures. More recently, Robert Paul (2015) has identified yet another possible factor—the potentially violent male competition for mates—which prompted communities to eliminate or contain that tendency by means of cultural strategies.⁴

These accounts, along with others in the literature, are interesting for their contributions to the general discussion of human evolution—even if this is a debate that for lack of more conclusive evidence from, say, genetics or experimental findings may never be settled with finality. It is not my job in this chapter to adjudicate the validity of this evolutionary argument about human cooperation and its multiple variants. Nevertheless, these evolutionary anthropologists' accounts are important in the present context because they raise the possibility of analogous human proclivities more directly related to patriarchy.

This is where culture enters the story about patriarchy. Christopher Boehm in his 2012 book, *Moral Origins: The Evolution of Virtue, Altruism, and Shame*, reasons that two innate tendencies of humans, egoism (self-interest) and nepotism (kin selection), are both stronger instincts than altruism, the willingness to help others unrelated to oneself (and, as Boehm explains, not reducible to reciprocal altruism), which fosters non-kin cooperation. Cultural practices have therefore evolved to reinforce altruism and cooperation. For example, Boehm (2012) posits, two practices that work against self-interest and kin selection and for larger group cooperation are a cultural emphasis on the value of harmonious relationships, and explicit injunctions to behave generously. Such cultural emphases, widespread among hunter-gatherers, survived the transition to groups that cultivate—as the example of the Golden Rule suggests. Here, I want to draw attention to two other cultural strategies that are relevant to patriarchy wherever it arises. These approaches not only have survived into the post-forager world but under the right conditions flourish there. Importantly, these two strategies receive distinctive elaboration and significance in patriarchal societies.[5]

The first of these strategies is deference. Systems of deference, so widespread in farming communities, may be overlooked by evolutionary scholars because deference in interpersonal relationships tends to be actively suppressed or at least deemphasized in hunter-gatherer groups in favor of their prized egalitarianism. However, the propensity for deference is present in humans, awaiting strategic use and cultural elaboration in more complex societies. I argue that these rules for deference go a long way toward accounting for the position of women in patriarchal societies.

The second of these cultural strategies revolves around reputation. In hunter-gatherer societies, Boehm (2012) notes, gossip can damage the reputations of individuals, operating not only as a first line of defense to punish bullies and cheaters, but also as a threat to keep other potential free-riders, as evolutionists call them, in line. Further, gossip can escalate into the more severe social sanctions of shunning or ostracism, outright exile, or even murder. Settled farming communities continue to be rife with gossip, but now, key to the argument of this chapter, the reputations at stake are not just those of individuals, but of the larger, stable households and the (typically extended) families who inhabit them. Those whose behavior attracts gossip are representatives of these larger entities. This concern with family reputation provides a powerful control on egoism in favor of the interests of the group. Both the requirement for deference and the concern for family reputation exert new pressures to cooperate that were unnecessary in achieving cooperation in foraging groups. And like the hierarchical system of deference, this brand of familism has an undue effect on the position of women under patriarchy.

These strategies, like cooperation, likely have roots in human and prehuman biology: deference has a basis in the inclination of individuals to submissiveness, and reputation, including family reputation, in the inclination to dominate. Indeed, as innate propensities, submissiveness in the face of domination and the tendency to domination itself can both be traced back to the primate and even more remote mammalian past of humans; chimpanzees and many other mammals exhibit these tendencies. As Peter Richerson and Robert Boyd (1998, 79) comment, "Coercion and deference to coercion are very widespread in animal societies in the form of dominance hierarchies and similar principles of social organization." Interestingly, there may be a counterimpulse to being dominated in humans, one at least incipient in chimps; this may be an effect of self-interest or perhaps a wholly independent disposition, and it may generalize more broadly to a reaction against inequality of any kind. Richerson and Boyd (1999, 254) attribute this rebellion against inequality to people's "egalitarian impulses and love of autonomy." Sterelny (2012, 181) postulates a somewhat narrower inborn disposition: to retaliate.

Of course, among humans such strategies are culturally elaborated. Without language, nonhumans can coerce others and submit to such coercion, and they can ostracize bullies, drive them out of the group, or murder them outright. But they cannot shame them with gossip, an important initial strategy for dealing with deviance in human groups. Without culture more generally and the other cognitive advances that accompanied the acquisition of culture, people could neither learn the local rules specifying to whom deference is owed and from whom it is to be expected, nor keep track of these others, nor come to agreement as to what breaches of deference or other sociocultural violations deserve gossiping about or even more extreme sanctions. In this chapter, I assume the biological basis of the culturally elaborated strategies of deference and familism, two complexes of belief and practice that are illustrated consistently in the chapters that follow.

Cooperation after Foraging

Before considering more closely the implications of family reputation and deference for patriarchy, I briefly call attention to a limitation of the evolutionary theory on which this chapter has been relying. Boehm's (2012) and the other evolutionary works on the origins of human cooperation largely stop with consideration of hunting-gathering societies. This is because these writers are intent on capturing the transition from ape to human life, which they identify with the acquisition by the earliest humans—who were hunter-gatherers—of the new cognitive, emotional, motivational, and cultural skills needed to cooperate. As Boehm (2012, 313; see also Richerson and Boyd 1999, 254) states, that evolutionary transition is viewed as having been completed with the acquisition of these new skills, modern humans evincing the same biological equipment as that of the early hunter-gatherers. Therefore, as Michael Tomasello (2014, 152) puts it, "We have given only cursory attention to humans after agriculture and all of the complexities of mixing cultural groups, from literacy and numeracy, and from institutions such as science and government. And so our attempt is less of an explicitly historical exercise than an attempt to carve nature at some of its most important joints, specifically, at some of its most important evolutionary joints."

This "cursory attention" given by evolutionary thinkers to "humans after agriculture" includes, of course, inattention to patriarchal societies. Moreover, it must be said that even with regard to hunter-gatherers, most of these writers, not being cultural anthropologists after all, tend to give only passing consideration to human culture. Having laid the evolutionary groundwork for humans living in societies of all kinds, in the remainder of this chapter I focus on the cultural beliefs and practices of certain post-foraging societies—those that came to be patriarchal.

What we know of the farming (horticultural and subsequently agricultural) societies that followed and overtook the hunting-gathering way of life comes from the ethnographic record, which I can only briefly discuss here. As I have noted, early farmers and many farming communities up to the present day appear to have continued the cooperative tradition that characterized hunter-gatherers before them. In addition to their continued emphasis on harmony and on generosity, farming societies were and still are, like hunting-gathering groups, predominantly kin-based, including fictive kin and adoptive ties, in their reckoning of relationships. As with hunter-gatherers, kinship serves as both a claim on cooperation and an idiom for reinforcing and extending it beyond actual nepotistic ties. Indeed, it could be said that kinship played an even greater role in the lives of early farmers than in those of foragers, governing the household structure and rules of inheritance, both largely absent among nomadic peoples but increasingly important among settled ones.

Extended households, which do not exist in most hunting-gathering societies, are the rule in farming societies. This is because most agriculture is more labor-intensive than hunting and gathering, but at the same time farming is productive enough to support the additional members. As Eric Wolf (1966, 65) states, "Extended families and domestic groups larger than the nuclear family occur more frequently among cultivators where the tasks of cultivation *and* the pursuit of part-time specialties both permit and require a larger labor force" (italics in original).[6] These larger family groups may be composed of three or more generations of kin. Additionally, they may include single, divorced, or never-married relatives, all living if not under the same roof, then in the same compound or in close proximity, under the authority or direction of one senior resident man or couple.

A further complexity of these communities is that separate farming households may share labor and resources with one another in the form of work cooperatives (especially at harvest time), rotating credit associations, ceremonies organized around family giving, or more informal arrangements in which families help others or make gestures expressing their readiness to do so. Such practices may have the effect of leveling, at least temporarily, emergent economic and social differences within communities. Further, farming communities often are still isolated and insulated enough from outside influences—a feature that Wolf (1957) captures in the term *closed corporate communities*—to prevent the influx of new ideas and artifacts and to discourage the out-migration of community members and the exposure to new influences that this would bring, including less cooperative beliefs and practices. Along with the many and often thorny interrelationships within extended households themselves, these extra-household arrangements put new burdens on cooperation.

Hunter-gatherers and farmers are different, then, in important ways.[7] New cultural strategies had to be invented to reinforce cooperation under the more complex circumstances of life in farming communities, which included extended household interests, the assignment of landed property to these households, and their obligations to other households. One of these new strategies, largely absent among hunter-gatherers, was a distinctive kind of hierarchical system based on relations of authority and deference to that authority.

Hierarchy in Human Societies

In one respect, post-hunter-gatherer societies differ quite radically from their forebears. That is, they become, as evolutionary theorists (e.g., Tomasello 2014, 133) recognize, markedly more inegalitarian.[8] Boehm (2012, 255) suggests the following minimal explanation: "For tribal people who are tied to agricultural land use, it's much more costly to pick up and move, and such sedentary egalitarians are more likely to invest some limited authority in their headmen so that preemptive conflict resolution can become more effective."

Sterelny (2012, 190–97) likewise recognizes that post-hunter-gatherer, or Holocene, societies are more inegalitarian than the hunter-gatherer societies that peopled the Pleistocene. He concludes that this is not only because they are sedentary, but as a result of their sedentary life, they are larger and more vertically complex, composed of many more "functionally important units intermediate between individual agents and the social world as a whole," therefore requiring "top-down mechanisms of command and control" (194). Richerson and Boyd (1999, 265) elaborate: "In complex societies, we are expected to live in social systems whose size, degree of division of labor, requirements for subordination, frequency of interaction with strangers, degree of status differences, and so on, are far outside the range of even the most complex foraging societies." At the same time, these authors remind us, this greater social complexity fosters a countertendency in humans: "People's egalitarian impulses and love of autonomy rebel at the striking inequality and coercion present in complex societies" (Richerson and Boyd 1999, 254).

I think these explanations in terms of sedentary life, size, and complexity are only part of the story. A clue to what is missing is provided in the way that some evolutionary anthropologists conflate the distinctive kind of hierarchy that characterizes these isolated farming communities with later forms of domination and powermongering, which emerged with the state and state-supported economies. Richerson and Boyd (1999, 265), for example, appear to skip right from hunter-gatherer egalitarianism to "beliefs and institutions that allow deep hierarchy, strong leadership, inegalitarian social relations, and an extensive division of labor."[9] Sterelny (2012, 195) recognizes the retention of cooperative life in post-foraging communities but cannot reconcile these cooperative impulses with the rise of other seemingly coercive ones; as he says, "the survival—indeed, the elaboration—of collective action throughout this period is puzzling." Sterelny worries about the "unsolved chicken-and-egg problem in the transition from the bottom-up organization of collective action in small, relatively egalitarian worlds to the top-down, coercion-backed organization of collective action in larger inegalitarian social worlds" (196–97). In other words, he wonders how formerly deeply egalitarian societies became so inegalitarian.

The problem is resolved if we recognize an intermediate stage between the "bottom-up organization of collective action" and its successor, the "top-down, coercion-backed organization." This middle stage is represented in the farming communities that supplanted hunter-gatherers, which indeed folded some of the egalitarian aspects of foraging life into a distinctive and carefully delimited system of hierarchy. It is true that these farming communities became too sedentary, large, and complex for communal consensus to be any longer possible. Hierarchy, I argue, was a new cultural resource that evolved to foster a continuation of cooperative ways of life. Studiously suppressed in foraging societies, hierarchy became one of the signature traits of post-foraging ones. However, while humans, with their innate inclination to dominance, are predisposed to hierarchy, this earliest type of hierarchical system is culturally distinctive. It is based not on top-down coercion, as Sterelny (2012) imagines, but on deference to authority and the cultivation of this deference in household relationships.

I argue that the new kind of extended household that characterizes farming communities was the birthplace of this system of hierarchy and deference.[10] These extended households seem to be crucibles for the enculturation and enforcement of deference behavior. They provide the small-scale context in which the innate human propensities for dominance and submissiveness can be recruited to a set of culturally learned and perpetuated practices having to do with a hierarchical system of interpersonal deference that one must observe and with the reputation not only of oneself but of the family one represents. These practices, in turn, help to preserve some degree of cooperation in human communities of a size and complexity that make hunter-gatherer forms of cooperative action no longer feasible.

Systems of Deference

The newly extended households of settled cultivators must have posed new interpersonal problems nonexistent or at least not as prominent in the nuclear families that came before them. Wolf (1966, 68–70) describes well the tensions that commonly arise between generations, between siblings, between mothers-in-law and daughters-in-law, and between core members of the household and peripheral ones, such as unmarried aunts and uncles, stepchildren, or servants (by contrast, the tensions between husband and wife that arise in nuclear households pale). As Wolf (1966, 69) concludes, "We may expect that a society containing such family units will have to provide strong reinforcements to keep the unit from flying apart," and they do so "by inculcating appropriate behavior patterns in the young." As examples of this, Wolf discusses training in dependence and in impulse control.

I propose that deference systems evolved as the vehicle for inculcating the requirement of suitably submitting to appropriate others, and those systems encompass the full complex of learned capacities needed to enact deference, including but not limited to the two that Wolf identifies. Such a system of deference, in all its local elaboration, was a general cultural device to preserve cooperation in newly extended households during the transition from hunting and gathering to farming. The system preserves cooperation in the household not only by making clear the limits of juniors' autonomous rights, but also by containing the domination of the more senior members within acceptable limits. It is true that being deferred to may serve nepotistic ends by giving seniors, both male and female, control over juniors, who may be sons, daughters, or grandchildren or who, like in-marrying wives and daughters-in-law, may be key to the reproduction of such kin. The reciprocal requirements of deference relationships do limit self-interest in the way I describe below. Nevertheless, girls and junior women are unfailingly among those who have to defer and who have to learn to do so. These deference requirements play a key role in ensuring women's willing subordination to men and other authorities in patriarchal societies.

Deference and the cultural beliefs and practices surrounding it are thus staples of farming societies. In such societies, however, egalitarian relationships are still valued and inequality deemphasized. This egalitarian value persists, albeit in abridged form, especially in relations between households and representatives of them. Within households, deference is paid in every paired relationship: juniors to seniors, women to men, children to adults, and, more generally, all young people to their elders. Deference is even observed in the fine-grained kinship distinction between younger and older siblings: the younger must defer to the older. At each of these levels, the requirement of deference ensures the compliance of juniors with instructions, orders, and advice from their seniors. However, seniors must not overstep their bounds. As Jocelyn Marrow (this volume) so vividly portrays in her ethnography of North Indian family relationships, seniors are expected to act in the best interests of those in their charge (see Chapin 2014 for another beautiful ethnographic example of this). Thus, the system of deference is reciprocal; it ensures that neither those owed deference nor those who defer to them will act out of sheer self-interest. It is worth remembering that the relationships between households in these communities are also well served by this restraint on domination.

Undoubtedly, deference requirements and the reciprocal obligations they impose on those deferred to often get extended to relationships in the community beyond the household. In many societies, chiefs and other community leaders hold their positions only as long as they do not overreach their power and influence. They tend to exercise humility, bow to public opinion, and cultivate a perception of themselves as no more than wise elders. In the wider community, as in the household, kinship operates as a rich tool for keeping track of hierarchical relationships, enforcing the deference owed to those above one in the hierarchy, softening the authority of those higher-ups, and inculcating appropriate deference in children.

Systems of Familism

The second kind of system that is critical to reinforcing cooperation in patriarchal societies is familism. In settled farming communities, individuals are representatives of the larger, stable households, which are often extended over generations and laterally. In this kind of group living among humans, the reputations at stake are not just those of individuals, but those of the households in which the individuals reside or, more broadly, the families for which these households stand. Family reputations rise or fall with individual propriety or misbehavior, and the preservation of the reputation of one's family becomes highly motivating for everyone belonging to it. Thus we have the famous renditions of household reputation known as "family honor" in the Middle East and India (and, as the chapters in this volume by Adriana M. Manago and Holly F. Mathews show, in Mexico via Spain and perhaps North Africa) or as "family duty" and "filial piety" farther to the east in Asia (as exemplified in the chapters by Kelly Chong and Leta Hong Fincher). The seminar participants who became the contributors to this volume agreed to use the more general term *familism* to refer to both variants, and I have adopted this good suggestion here.

As many of the chapters in this book illustrate, the concern with family honor or family obligation means that individual members are not only willing to accept their family's dictates with regard to important life decisions—marriage, schooling, choice of profession—but are also at pains to deport themselves in public in ways that reflect well on their families. Moreover, they do so even when they harbor different, conflicting wishes for themselves.[11] Thus, Goody (1976, 17) suggests that "sex before marriage could diminish a girl's honour," and presumably that of her family too. Nor are households at liberty to pursue their collective family goals unimpeded. The larger community exerts actual and anticipated pressure on its households to see that members of each behave according to community dictates and that households as units distribute spare resources to other households (with a leveling effect on the community-wide distribution of wealth), participate in community-wide events, and otherwise act in the perceived interest of the whole community. Both deference and familism, then, suppress individual self-interest in favor of the interests of larger groups—the household and the community—and the senior members of each.

Neither deference nor familism are ever good for women. To begin with, women are undersized in average physique in comparison to men, due to the developmental requirements of childbearing. Alesina, Giuliano, and Nunn

(2013, 470), taking up a possibility suggested by Ester Boserup's (1970) contrast between hoeing and plowing economies, attribute women's exclusion from employment outside the home (which the authors use as a proxy for gender inequality; see Alesina, Giuliano, and Nunn 2013, 471n2) to the assumption that women do not have the upper-body strength, grip strength, or capacity for bursts of power necessary to plow or to control the animals that pull the plow. In this ambitious cross-cultural study, the authors find a strong set of correlations between the use of the plow and women's historic exclusion from employment outside the home both across nations and across the finer grain of subnational districts and, within districts, ethnicities.

The scheme that these authors lay out also coincides with my inclusion of European and Asian settler colonies in the range of patriarchal societies. They note that the correlation they find and the associated cultural beliefs have outlasted plow agriculture in many places. This, they say, is either because these beliefs have found other institutional reinforcement, because in some ways they complement both plow agriculture and the subsequent industrial structure of society, or simply because they are "inherently sticky" (Alesina, Giuliano, and Nunn 2013, 476), providing people with helpful rules of thumb.

However, the authors' explanation for the correlation they find—that "societies characterized by plough agriculture, and the resulting gender-based division of labor, developed a cultural belief that the natural place for women is within the home" (Alesina, Giuliano, and Nunn 2013, 475)—does not provide a full and persuasive explanation for the origins of such a cultural belief. They merely conclude, "Boserup's hypothesis suggests that in societies that engaged in plough agriculture, cultural beliefs about gender inequality were relatively beneficial. Therefore, these norms may have evolved in plough agriculture societies but not hoe agriculture societies" (Alesina, Giuliano, and Nunn 2013, 476). *How* might cultural beliefs about gender inequality and specifically women's confinement to the home have been beneficial? These authors do not provide an explanation for women's exclusion from employment outside the household or for a whole cluster of related patriarchal institutions and practices—but Goody's (1976) account of land shortage and the resultant emergence of patrilocal extended households, patrilineal inheritance, and the dowry in Eurasia does. While the plow and the greater upper-body strength that its use required may have contributed to the division of labor leading up to patriarchy, they are only a fraction of the story.[12]

Moreover, Alesina, Giuliano, and Nunn base the assignment of plowing to men on their greater physical strength, when that aspect of the division of labor has elsewhere been attributed instead to the demands of nursing and the subsequent care for infants and small children, everywhere primarily the responsibility of adult women (e.g., Brown 1970; Hrdy 1999, 209–13). (Exceptions are found where institutions for alternative care, such as childcare centers, exist, though the providers of institutional childcare are predominantly female too; or where older children, both girls and boys, act as caregivers, though even in those cases women are called on to supervise.) Brown argues that the requirements of childcare limit women to tasks not requiring rapt concentration; tasks that can be easily interrupted and then resumed; nondangerous tasks; and tasks keeping them relatively close to home, such as hoeing or food processing. Childcare is thus incompatible with large game hunting, large animal herding, deep-sea fishing, and plowing, since one cannot care for children while doing these tasks. Brown (1970, 1074) rejects explanations like that of Alesina and his co-authors as "naïvely physiological," saying that such explanations are "contradicted by numerous ethnographic accounts of heavy physical labor performed by women."

Conclusion

For many reasons, then, women, especially young women of childbearing age, tend to end up low in importance and recognition in agricultural societies. Their low rank in both their natal and marital households may translate not only into their owing deference to everybody else and everybody else's wishes, but also into others' control over their public demeanor and their life choices. Of course, the degree to which social systems actually determine women's inferiority, denigration, subjugation, or exploitation varies cross-culturally with a number of mediating factors. While systems of deference and familism certainly do not dictate women's secondary status, they lend themselves exceptionally well to patriarchy, which does so dictate for many reasons: male heirship, patrilocality, arranged marriage, and women's socialization to their role. In other words, both deference and familism lay the groundwork for patriarchal control over women, which then arises under the structural conditions I have discussed. As I have emphasized, patriarchy is but the culmination of human potentialities; it is not determined by them.

There is an important third leg to the overall argument I am making, grievously neglected by me here but documented and discussed in the ethnographic context of North India in the excellent chapter by Susan Seymour (this volume). This is the way in which deference and familism are learned: as Wolf (1966, 69) puts it, "by inculcating appropriate behavior patterns in the young." The twin proclivities toward deference and familism are brought to the service of patriarchy by being taught to the young as part of the local cultural model for raising children into virtuous adults. It is only by means of such teaching and learning that deference and familism become culturally distinctive ways of being. Conversely, these proclivities may be minimized or entirely suppressed in the course of child socialization. Thus, many hunter-gatherers suppress domination and subordination, including the proclivity for deference, in the interests of their assiduously practiced egalitarianism.

A final question is left hanging. What happens when the agricultural societies that originally grew and supported patriarchy are supplanted by industrialization, becoming a thing of the past? Patriarchy does not simply evaporate. Partly, this is because the cultural beliefs and practices associated with patriarchy have a life of their own. This may be what Alesina and colleagues (2013) are referring to as the inherent "stickiness" of these beliefs. All cultural understandings can be sticky under the right circumstances, but this is particularly true of a multiply motivated and deeply engrained cultural complex such as patriarchy. As Cynthia Werner's (this volume) discussion of campus rape in the United States today illustrates especially well, elements of patriarchy may prove very difficult to eradicate indeed.

Partly, patriarchy may just find new institutional support in industrial economies, as Alesina, Giuliano, and Nunn also suggest. For example, women's devaluation is reinforced by the capitalist practice of regularly paying them less than men. But partly, too, patriarchy persists because there is no economic and residential system to replace it. Perhaps new kinds of family and workplace relationships, ones that embody gender equality or promote some unique qualities of womankind, will eventually emerge. However, it takes a long, long time for new systems of belief and practice to become established, never mind to represent the dominant expectation about how things are or should be. Such developments come about slowly since they depend on a multitude of changes, both small and large, at every level—including, perhaps crucially, new culturally shared ways of raising children.

Notes

1. Mukhopadhyay and Seymour (1994, 4–5) elect to use the term *patrifocal* and the longer designation *patrifocal family system and ideology*, rather than *patriarchy*,

which they deem to have become overpoliticized and overgeneralized, saying that it is now used "to describe any system of gender hierarchy in which males are construed to dominate." But in keeping with the other contributions to this volume, I reclaim the term *patriarchy*, returning it to what I believe is its original, narrower meaning. My quibble with the term *patrifocal* is that these authors' usage of it is tied to a particular (patrilocal extended) family system, which may well describe patriarchy in India but does not do such a good job of describing it in, say, the United States, where it survives in association with the nuclear family system.

2. Kandiyoti (1988, 282) only hints at the same independent variable when she speaks of "a system in which men controlled some form of viable joint patrimony in land, animals, or commercial capital."

3. These writers come from an array of fields, including evolutionary anthropology, evolutionary psychology, economics, and philosophy. They also employ a variety of methods. Boehm (2012), for example, works from a carefully selected sample of extant foraging societies. Tomasello (2014) summarizes years of his own and others' research on task performance by chimpanzees and other apes compared to that of young human children. Bowles and Gintis (2011) use mathematical modeling. All rely to some extent on ethnographic evidence.

4. Paul (2015, 243) explains the oft-made observation that there are no societies in which women dominate men (the seeming converse of male domination in human societies is relative gender equality) as being due to the fact that so many (though not all) of the cultural strategies for containing men's competition for mates have the side effect that they disproportionately position or advantage men over women in some way or other. No such cultural strategies for women have evolved because none have been needed; women do not generally disrupt the social order to compete for mates.

5. See Paul's (2015, 286–306) interesting critique of Richerson and Boyd's (1998, 1999) readiness to dismiss what they call "runaway" cultural practices that seem to them not to have any adaptive function, in the sense that they detract from reproductive fitness.

6. Wolf is another scholar whose materialist orientation has led him to be neglected by contemporary cultural anthropologists. However, with Goody, he has something substantive to contribute to the understanding of patriarchy.

7. The emphasis on kinship, cooperation, harmony, and generosity, which are common features of hunting-gathering and farming communities, is what likely has led cultural psychologists to lump communities reliant on these two different subsistence economies as collectivist (as opposed to individualist)—a distinction with which some of these researchers have been preoccupied. This tradition was initiated with the publication of a now-classic article by Markus

and Kitayama (1991), who illustrated the hypothesized difference between collectivism and individualism most extensively with the contrast between Japan and the United States. Several valid criticisms have since emerged (see, especially, Ewing 1991; Spiro 1993; Kusserow 2004; and a brief but useful update of the critique by Miller, Goyal, and Wice 2015, 21–22). What has struck me most forcefully is that those who advocate for the collectivist-individualist distinction often stop with this typology, never explaining *why* the world should be so divided. I speculate that what is often lumped together in such appraisals as "collectivism" can better be understood as a collection of disparate cultural strategies that evolved to support and preserve cooperation in human societies, against the ever-present and powerful motivation for pursuing self-interest. These cultural strategies include the hierarchical system of deference I discuss, though those who address collectivism tend to overlook this feature of some of these societies (for an exception, see Triandis 1995). In my view, what is labeled as "individualism" in this dichotomy represents the breakdown of strategies for cooperation in ever more complex and stratified societies.

8. I hasten to add that there is certainly variation, which I am eliding in this brief account. Specifically, there are cases of hierarchy in hunting-gathering societies, and there may be more egalitarian cases in farming societies than my dichotomy suggests.

9. Richerson and Boyd (1999) recognize a tribal level of social organization that unites even hunting-gathering bands in larger political units. They observe, for example, that in one foraging society, "chiefs could only use the respect accorded them to guide the emergence of a consensus; they could not successfully dictate to followers" (263). However, the authors do not clarify the extent to which this kind of leadership may have endured across the transition into farming as a feature of a larger system of deference in post-foraging societies.

10. It is unknown whether deference systems originated in wider authority relationships and filtered down into households, as some researchers argue, or, as I assume, originated in post-foraging extended households and were later adopted by wider authorities. Specifically, early cross-cultural research by William Stephens (1963, 326–39) seems to suggest that household deference was modeled after that owed to higher-ups in the larger society: "the kingdom," by which he means a socially stratified state and which he contrasts with the tribe, "emerges as a kind of pecking-order in which similar deference behavior is repeated throughout many social relationships: wife to husband, child to father, child to father's brother, commoner to noble." However, what Stephens is measuring is the *intensity* of deference behavior or, in his term, how "marked" are these deference customs. Thus, the scale he uses (Stephens 1963, 408–24) treats "son kneels or bows to father" and "son speaks softly to father" occurring together as the most extremely marked (the wife-to-husband scale is similar). He also notes

that there is some tendency for these practices to be more marked in the states than in the tribes in his sample. I, however, am concerned not with whether deference requirements grew more extreme in state societies, but with deference more generally, which I believe emerged in post-foraging households as one cultural strategy for preserving cooperation within them and beyond them in the local community.

11. See Quinn (2006) for an analysis of the instructive case of the Pakistani woman presented by Ewing (1990, 1991).

12. Of course, the other traits implicated in the larger story may be impossible or difficult to measure using the codes supplied by the *Atlas of World Cultures* (Murdock 1981), on which this study depends.

CHAPTER THREE

Growing Up Female in North India

SUSAN C. SEYMOUR

India belongs to an arc of societies that practice what Kandiyoti (1988) has named *classic patriarchy*. This chapter addresses North India, the part of India where the patriarchal family system, or what Mukhopadhyay and I (1994) have called India's "patrifocal family structure and ideology," is most predominant. In her paper "Bargaining with Patriarchy," Kandiyoti (1988, 279) notes, "The cyclical nature of women's power in the household and their anticipation of inheriting [the] authority of senior women encourages a thorough internalization of this form of patriarchy by the women themselves." In other words, women are active agents in the reproduction of their own subordination. Although I agree that the anticipation of motherhood and increased status and power over time is certainly one motivation for many women to help maintain this family system, I argue that the successful early socialization of girls, together with a lack of alternatives, underlies this motivation. First, girls must be effectively socialized into the values and behaviors associated with the patrifocal family system. Later in their maturation, they come to understand their future roles as mothers, wives, and mothers-in-law and that someday they may become senior women in the household with power and authority over younger women.

How, then, are girls socialized into this patriarchal system and effectively made the reproducers of it, both biologically and culturally? What potential for change is there? For my insights and examples, I draw on my longitudinal research on Hindu children, families, and gender systems in Bhubaneswar, Odisha, India (Seymour 1999). Quinn (2005b, 475) has formulated four universal features, or cultural models, of child-rearing that, she argues, "together explain how child rearing everywhere so effectively turns children into valued adults," which I apply to my data on the socialization of girls in Bhubaneswar. These features are experiential constancy, emotional arousal, approval-disapproval, and emotional predisposition.

India has a version of classic patriarchy, namely, a set of predominant kinship and family structures and beliefs that give precedence to men over women, sons over daughters, fathers over mothers, husbands over wives, and so on. While more pronounced among upper castes and classes than lower-status ones and while more predominant in North than in South India, these male-oriented structures and beliefs constitute a sociocultural complex that profoundly affects women's lives. The most significant features of this complex are a patrilocal, extended family residence system (the joint family); patrilineal descent; patrilineal inheritance and succession; gender-differentiated family roles and responsibilities; a gender- and generation-differentiated authority and deference system; family control of female sexuality and reproduction; an arranged marriage system; and an ideology of family honor that rests on "appropriate" female behavior, such as chastity, obedience, and self-sacrifice.

Early Socialization

For reasons that follow from the principles outlined above, sons in North India are preferred to daughters and more celebrated at birth. Due to the selective abortion of female fetuses, made possible with modern technology, and other factors, India has an unbalanced sex ratio.[1] Therefore, to even get to the early socialization stage, a girl has had to surmount this social bias. However, daughters are important to the household economy, especially in lower-status families, and they provide fathers with their most sacred gift: a virgin daughter (*kanyadan*) who can be offered in marriage to another family. This movement of girls and young women in arranged marriages cements kin ties among members of a particular subcaste (*jāti*).

In infancy, girls are treated similarly to boys. They are nursed on demand but not to satisfaction, ritually bathed, held and carried by a variety of caretakers, and always put down to sleep with an adult. There is, accordingly, much physical contact. During infancy, it is not so much gender that is marked as the child's membership in a group. Rather than indicating the infant's sex with color-coded clothing and blankets, what is emphasized is that the newborn is just one more member of a group in which collective family interests outweigh individual ones. She (or he) must learn to value familial interdependence.

Multiple childcare, which promotes multiple attachments and a diffusion of affect among family members, is a critical technique for instilling in infants and young children a sense of interdependence: the need to rely on a variety of

Growing Up Female in North India

people for care and attention and an incipient identification with the extended family as a whole (Seymour 1983, 2004b, 2013). Mothers are discouraged from being full-time caretakers of their infants. In fact, in such families there is a general prohibition on exclusive mothering or other dyadic relationships.[2] Children must learn early on to relate to and be sensitive to a variety of people, including mothers, grandmothers, aunts, older siblings, and cousins. Not all are female, but women are predominant during this stage of life. In extended or joint households, there is a hierarchy of women who manage domestic affairs while men provide economic support, which takes them away from home during much of the day.[3] The following is an example of multiple childcare in action:

> Older Sister (child's unmarried paternal aunt) left the room and returned carrying Bapu, a one-month-old boy. Two neighbor girls (aged 16 and 18) came in and sat down. Older Sister lay Bapu on his back on the wooden platform on which she was seated. Bapu urinated and began to cry. Older Sister ignored him. One of the neighbor girls picked him up and held him for a moment. Then she passed him to the other neighbor girl. They took turns bouncing him on their laps. Bapu's mother came in and took Bapu and held him for a moment. Then she handed him back to one of the neighbor girls and left the room. Bapu did not cry or object to his mother's departure. A moment later Grandmother came in carrying Rabi (Bapu's two-year-old brother), who was half asleep. She told him to greet me, which he did. She smiled and took him out of the room. Several minutes later she returned with him, set him down on the floor, and asked him where his brother was. Rabi pointed to Bapu. Grandmother nodded, picked him up, and carried him out of the room. (Seymour 1999, 81)

Although this example of multiple childcare involved infant boys, it would be the same for infant girls. There would be a variety of caretakers, with the mother appearing only briefly. While this mother's mother-in-law (Grandmother) watched over her two-year-old, several unmarried young women looked after her newborn. This continued until the new infant needed to be nursed and was returned to his mother. The nature of mothering in such households is clearly a group phenomenon, and children learn from infancy to accept, trust, and seek nurturance from a variety of people in the house and immediate neighborhood. The limited verbal interaction in this scenario, it should be noted, was focused on teaching a young child kinship relations. He was asked to acknowledge his baby brother and to greet me, the anthropologist who had the honorific of Auntie (mother's sister). The lesson was *family*.

One of Quinn's (2005b, 478) four universal features of child-rearing is experiential constancy, the "practices that maximize the constancy of the child's experience around the learning of important lessons about what is valued." In North Indian families, the experience of shared childcare teaches infants and young children the importance of identifying with the family as a whole, not just with the mother, and that lesson begins at birth and continues through childhood. This is, as Quinn (2005b, 479) argues, one kind of "habitual, embodied practice" that helps to shape the child's cognitive schemas and "to immerse the child in a cultural world of a certain constant shape, conveying their lesson repeatedly, redundantly, and unmistakably." Co-sleeping with mothers and other kin reinforces that a child should consider herself one of a group, *not* a separate individual.[4] Infants and young children are not even given personal names until they reach their first birthday.

With age, the lessons about interdependence become somewhat different for girls than for boys because boys learn that they are expected to remain with their natal family, if not in the same household then nearby. Even if at a distance, they are expected to contribute financially to the family. When fathers or other senior members of the family die, sons inherit all property and assume responsibility for the family. By contrast, girls learn that they must take their lessons about family interdependence and transfer them to their husband's family at the time of marriage. They must become hardworking, responsible wives and daughters-in-law who initially are subservient to the older women in their husband's household, especially their mother-in-law. (The psychodynamics of this relationship are explored by Marrow, this volume.)

How do girls learn these expectations and appropriate behaviors? If they grow up in a joint family, they observe daily the roles of different generations of women and how those women relate to one another and to the men in the household. In the above example of multiple childcare, different categories of women were present: the grandmother/mother-in-law, who was the senior and dominant woman in the family; an unmarried daughter/aunt and two unmarried neighbor girls who did not have to observe deference to the grandmother; and finally, the children's mother, who only appeared briefly when the grandmother was not present. The children's mother was the first daughter-in-law in this particular household, which made her the principal cook and housekeeper, freeing the grandmother to help with childcare and attend to family rituals, such as the daily puja (paying homage) to certain Hindu gods and goddesses in an effort to protect family members.[5]

Young children witness the gender- and generation-based deference system, such as mothers being given orders by grandmothers. In addition, they observe many kinds of deferential behavior by younger women toward older women and men: lowering the head and pulling the end of the sari over it in the presence of senior women and all categories of older men;[6] escaping to the back of the house when a senior male enters so as to remain unobserved; ritualized bowing to the floor and kissing the feet of parents-in-law; and even drinking the water that was used to wash the feet of parents-in-law. These actions, to children, become habitual practices and instill in them cognitive schemas relating to gender hierarchy and gender segregation in such families.

I once observed the children in one household call to their mother, "Grandfather is coming! Grandfather is coming!" (This grandfather/father-in-law did not reside in the same house as his son and son's family. They were a cow herder family by caste, and the mother of the household handled the milk business while her husband was at work in a neighboring town.) The mother/daughter-in-law quickly retreated to the back of the house so as not to be seen by her father-in-law. However, she had to discuss a business matter with him in the absence of her husband, so she sat on the floor of the rear room with her back to the doorway. The grandfather entered the room closest to hers and sat with his back to that doorway. In this manner, they were able to converse without breaking the rules of sexual segregation and father-in-law/daughter-in-law avoidance. The children not only knew the rules, they helped to enforce them.

Another facet of daily behavior and experiential constancy that teaches children about the status of men versus women is the order of eating. Mothers/wives/daughters-in-law prepare two to three meals a day, which are served first to husbands and then to children; the women eat only when everyone else has been served. At weddings and other special events in more traditional families, the same order of dining is followed. Specialized cooks for such events serve male guests and family members first, then children, and lastly female guests and family members.

Children also learn early on that their mothers and other women are inauspicious (dangerous to others) once a month when they menstruate. They become temporarily untouchable. In more traditional upper-status households, menstruating women do not bathe or brush their hair, and they cannot handle food for seven days. They are temporarily in a "wild" state from which they will emerge and be ritually bathed; they then return to their normal activities. Such restrictions are highly noticeable to young children, who must abruptly distance themselves from their mother and be fed and bathed by others, although nursing infants are exempt. Women, children learn, are very different beings from men and can be temporarily dangerous. This is a dramatic and potentially emotionally arousing lesson in gender differences, especially in more traditional and observant Hindu households. It would be even more emotionally arousing if young children were unaccustomed to having a variety of caretakers.

Gradually, children learn about the Hindu world view concerning human bodies. Bodies are believed to be relatively unbounded and porous containers that are shared or exchanged with others of the right status, especially during such events as birth and marriage and during the sharing of food. Touching and other exchanges with people of the wrong caste are considered dangerous for both men and women. Although all bodies are permeable, those of women are believed to be more so because they are more earthlike: they menstruate and reproduce. Women's bodies are likened, accordingly, to earthen pitchers, men's to brass pots. This greater permeability of women's bodies, especially during menstruation, requires that women follow rules to protect themselves and other family members. Menstruation is a symbol not only of women's greater permeability but also of their innate power (*śakti*), the power to create life but also to harm others. Accordingly, women must be kept safe and must learn to control these innate powers, a topic addressed below. These beliefs help rationalize such practices as purdah (restricting sexually mature women to the house) and sexual segregation within the house. They also help to explain the anxiety felt when girls attend school, a phenomenon that only began in Bhubaneswar in the 1960s when it became a capital city and schooling was provided for children of all ages and socioeconomic statuses. Until then Bhubaneswar had been a small Hindu temple town with only low-caste women leaving their homes to perform certain menial tasks.

Later Childhood: What Girls Must Learn

An old Oriya proverb states, "When a boy is seven years old, he will be given a sacred thread; when a girl is nine years old, she will be given in marriage" (Seymour 1999, 85). For high-status Brahmin boys, the Sacred Thread ceremony symbolically transforms them from children with no responsibilities into students who, theoretically, will leave home to study the Hindu sacred texts (the Vedas) with a guru (Brahmin teacher). Later, they return to their parental homes, marry, and become responsible adult members of the household (the householder stage of life). This ceremony is still practiced by many Brahmin families, but now that most boys attend school, they receive instruction in the Hindu texts outside of school.

When girls were married in childhood, which was the case for several of the grandmothers in my original sample of Bhubaneswar families, the wedding ceremony and transfer to the home of their husband and in-laws served dramatically to transform girls from being daughters in their father's household to daughters-in-law in their husband's household. Marriages at such early ages were not sexually consummated until the girl reached puberty, so she did not immediately become a wife. Meanwhile, there was time for her to adapt to life with a new family and new responsibilities.

Quinn's (2005b, 489) second proposed universal features of child-rearing is emotional arousal. Techniques, she argues, that arouse emotion in children, such as fear-inducing strategies, shaming, or teasing, are effective motivators for desired behavior. Bhubaneswar caretakers use all of these techniques but in moderation. Many of these strategies come together during ritual occasions, such as initiation rites, when the child is taught something culturally important. For Brahmin boys, for instance, the Sacred Thread ceremony marks a change in status in the household, and at the same time sacred knowledge is imparted to them, which is the beginning of longer instruction in the sacred Hindu texts. It is a day of emotional arousal for young boys aged six to nine years. First, their heads are shaved and their clothes are publicly removed, revealing some of the more overt signs of their personhood. Later, they are ritually hand-fed by their mothers and bid farewell. Then they must sit for hours listening to priests, who give them instructions about adult male decorum and sacred knowledge. At the end of the day, they are taken to a temple, dressed in new clothes, and ritually reborn as Hindus. It is a day when they experience shame (the removal of hair and clothing) and fear (saying good-bye to their mothers) before undergoing serious instruction, which is followed by a celebration, new clothing, and crowns on their heads.

In the not so distant past, it must have been even more of an emotional and dramatic coming-of-age ceremony for girls who were married very young. What has perhaps taken the place of that frightening event is a girl's first menstruation. This is the moment when a girl comes of age and, for the first time, must begin following the rules of adult female decorum, including a sense of shame (*lajya*), which I explain below. Although still a highly ritualized occasion in some rural parts of Odisha, the onset of menstruation in Bhubaneswar families is handled less dramatically. There, a girl is not secluded for days, then brought out of isolation, and publicly celebrated. Nonetheless, during menstruation a girl is subject to restrictions that will continue throughout her childbearing years. She should remain separate from other family members; she should rest from all work; she should not touch others or handle food; she should not bathe, comb her hair, or tend to parts of her body; and she should avoid certain foods. It is a dramatic lesson in becoming temporarily untouchable and certainly involves emotional arousal, especially when a girl is teased by younger children. Menon (2002a, 447) notes, "Young boys—five and six years old—will play at trying to touch their unmarried menstruating aunts, to see how far the young women will retreat to avoid contact. Such teasing games usually end in the young women getting irritated and the young children finding the entire situation enormously amusing."

How are girls prepared for this event and for the even more dramatic one of an arranged marriage, potentially to a stranger, and the shift in residence to the household of her parents-in-law? I have already suggested that if a girl grows up in a joint household with women of different statuses, she has witnessed the shifts in behavior required. Even girls in non-joint households have witnessed how their mother's behavior changes when their father arrives home or when a paternal grandparent visits. All girls have witnessed the effects of menstrual taboos. In addition, they have been gradually instructed about shame (lajya), a complex concept in North India, and they have experienced being shamed. These practices fall within Quinn's category of emotional arousal but also within her third category of approval-disapproval, the cultural evaluation of a child's behavior. Quinn (2005b, 497) writes: "Parents and other socializers everywhere exploit the child's desire for love and approval in the interests of their own agendas for molding the child into a culturally desirable adult. The most effective way childrearers have to discourage what is culturally defined as bad behavior, and encourage what is culturally defined as good behavior, is to couple their approval or disapproval of the given behaviors with labeling or other markers of that which is approved or disapproved."

From early childhood, both girls and boys are called *dusta pila* (naughty child) whenever they disobey orders or annoy someone. It is a common expression of disapproval but with few consequences. Over time, however, children, especially girls, learn a more complex term of evaluation: to have lajya.

Lajya is one of the primary moral emotions that middle- and upper-status Oriya Hindus are expected to cultivate, and it encompasses a broader lexical domain than the English word *shame*. It is more accurately translated as "modesty," "deference," "circumspection," "being civilized," "being refined," and "being respectful to elders and superiors" (Menon 2002a, 438–39). The term is not restricted to females, but women carry the burden of displaying lajya in more contexts than men do. The term is an ancient one, attributed centuries ago to Devi, the great goddess of Hinduism, who through self-regulation exemplified the capacity for moral behavior. Women are expected to cultivate lajya so that they can control their innate female power (śakti) for the benefit of their natal family and their family of procreation. They do so through displays of modesty (e.g., heads lowered, eyes averted) and respect (including the practices I have already delineated). Once past childhood, girls are chastised for disrespectful behavior: "Don't touch others with your feet [the dirtiest and most polluted part of the body]"; "Don't expose your legs [considered sexually alluring]"; "Keep your head down when there are visitors present"; "Don't speak to or be seen with strange men." Through such admonitions and the associations girls make with approved and disapproved behavior, they learn what is expected of them as wives and daughters-in-law. These are deeply ingrained attitudes toward the self and others that are cultivated over time and reinforced by daily rituals (experiential constancy), the observance of auspicious days of the Hindu calendar, and frequent recitations of Hindu epics and morality tales, which are cultural models of virtue for both women and men.

Menon has elicited a number of morality tales from Brahmin women who reside in the Old Town part of Bhubaneswar. She refers to them as "canonical scripts that teach young women the virtues and attributes necessary to be a proper Hindu wife" (Menon 2002b, 143). The stories tend to address the disjunction between the natural power of women and their subordinate rank in the family along with the cultural mediations required to transform their powers for benign ends. For instance, one story addresses the popular goddess Kali, who is depicted in an Old Town temple icon standing upright with her tongue protruding and her foot placed squarely on the chest of her supine husband, the high god Śiva.[7] On the face of it, this is a shocking reversal of roles. The story, then, is about how such an event could have occurred. Briefly, the explanation is that Kali had been in her warrior state and had killed demons; she had grasped a bloody decapitated head and then lost control and stepped on her husband while he lay on the ground. As soon as she realized what she had done, she stuck out her tongue and bit it, saying, "Oh! My husband!" She was filled with lajya. Having recognized her transgression, she regained self-control. For local Brahmins, the protruding tongue symbolizes Kali's shame and her acknowledgment of her subordinate position with respect to her husband (Menon and Shweder 1994; Menon 2002b).

Marriage constitutes the culmination of all this training for girls. Until she is safely married, a sexually mature young woman is considered highly vulnerable. Her bodily fluids are dangerous and must be channeled into her family of reproduction. Sexual relations and pregnancy outside of marriage bring serious dishonor to her natal family, enough so that honor killings still occur in North India. The control of female sexuality is, therefore, critical to the maintenance of the patrifocal family system and to the caste system of which it is a part.[8] Since it is girls who move between families, enabling interfamilial ties to be created, and who produce the next generation for their in-laws, it is they who can potentially disrupt the whole status system. By imposing restrictions on their behavior, beginning with their first menstruation, the society teaches girls and women to guard their sexuality and their family's honor.

Even low-status girls internalize many of these attitudes and values although they do not have the same burden of upholding the honor of high-status families. For example, in an effort to help their families financially, low-status girls and young women engage in informal tourist work on the main ghat of the sacred Ganges River in Varanasi (Huberman 2012). Higher-status girls would not be allowed to appear in such a public setting, crowded with foreign tourists and Indian families cremating relatives. These girls, however, are praised for contributing to their family's welfare. Nonetheless, they are informally supervised by kin and neighbors and cease working when they reach puberty. Huberman (2012, 40) states that many of the girls are aware that "they walked and talked a very fine line between critiquing traditional gender norms and notions of femininity, and reinscribing them."

The Transition to Wife and Daughter-in-Law

Much of a girl's upbringing prepares her for marriage and the transition to the roles of wife and daughter-in-law in her husband's household. From infancy, she learns that individual desires and goals must be kept subordinate to the welfare of the family and that, however important females are, they are subordinate to the senior males of the family, who hold authority. They also learn that their sexuality is dangerous and that they represent the purity of their natal patriline. To be given in marriage as a chaste woman to a suitable family symbolizes, accordingly, their natal family's honor. Moreover, most young women and men in North India continue to submit to marriages arranged by their father and other kin. They have learned to trust their parents and to distrust marriage based on romantic love and self-choice. As one highly educated and employed young woman said, "My parents have left me free. . . . But I have left the responsibility to them [of finding a suitable husband]. I don't want to take any such project on for myself because I know my parents are very capable in this matter" (Seymour 1999, 197).

This young woman's family was unusual in giving their daughter the choice of finding her own husband, but she did not feel comfortable with that choice. Generally, self-chosen unions are considered individualistic and antisocial in character even in a large, contemporary urban center like Kolkata (Donner 2008). Furthermore, the cultural models that children acquire do not make the husband-wife relationship central to adult life. For example, most North Indians do not understand the high divorce rate in the United States. This was brought to my attention early in my first fieldwork in Bhubaneswar (1965–1967), when two Old Town adolescent girls queried me about divorce. "Why," they asked, "would anyone want to leave one's husband or wife?" I tried to explain that husbands and wives are sometimes very unhappy with one another. They responded, "But you're part of a joint family." The idea that the husband-wife relationship could be central to one's happiness made little sense to them. As a woman, they explained, one's relationships are primarily with other women, and the source of one's unhappiness is more likely to be other women than one's husband (Seymour 1999, 59).

Early multiple attachments have taught male and female children to identify with a variety of other people in the family, not just with their mother or father. In addition, they have been taught to distrust dyadic bonds, which if they grow too strong can threaten the harmony of the larger family. They gradually learn the distinction between *prem* (unselfish love) and *kam* (a dangerous form of love that includes the selfish lust and desire for another person). To choose one's own spouse based on kam is dangerous. With only 3 exceptions, all of the children in my original sample of 130 from 24 Bhubaneswar families have had arranged marriages, with greater and lesser veto power.[9] Some young women married someone they had never seen while others had seen a photo of their prospective spouse; others had a chance to meet the young man under supervised conditions.

Both the wedding and the transfer to her husband's family can be more or less traumatic depending on the age and education of the girl, her opportunity to meet her prospective spouse and his kin in advance, and the degree to which she is welcomed into her new household. Brides know that they enter with the lowest status, a new daughter-in-law in the hierarchy of females, but they also enter with the prospect of providing more labor for household work and the promise of bearing children, especially sons.

Most new brides whom I met over the past fifty years made the transition successfully. (Below, I discuss the ones who did not.) When I returned to Bhubaneswar in 1989 to systematically discuss with mothers and grandmothers their transition in status from daughters to daughters-in-law, among other things, they regularly responded, "I was a child in my parents' home; here I am a daughter-in-law. Here I have responsibilities. I take care of the entire family. I make the household decisions" (Seymour 1999, 97). Their responses make it clear that they not only navigated the difficult transition to a new family and negotiated the power hierarchies within that family, but they also became the senior domestic managers of often large, complex households. They made such comments with pride. They were now mature, even elderly women who had moved from the low status of new daughter-in-law to the much higher status of mother and mother-in-law, and they had produced and reared children.

Change

When I initially began research in Bhubaneswar in the 1960s, it was to examine change in a place that was being transformed from an ancient Hindu temple town to a new capital city.[10] When India gained independence from Great Britain in 1947, there was some rearrangement of political entities, and several new states were formed. Odisha (formerly Orissa) was created as a new linguistically based state, which meant that a capital city and a state government had to be established. Bhubaneswar became the site of that new city of administration (known as the New Capital), which was built next to the old temple town (known as the Old Town). My project was to sample families from each side of town and to compare family organization and child-rearing practices in an effort to examine change.

My sample of households consisted of 12 families from the Old Town and 12 from the New Capital, with 130 children under the age of 10. In each part of Bhubaneswar, the households were stratified: by caste in the Old Town and by the father's position in the state government in the New Capital. I have been able to follow 23 of these 24 families for more than 50 years (since 1965) and have seen dramatic change. The original two-year study provided rich ethnographic data, timed samples of caretaker-child interactions, and many insights into the roles of women and gender relations. Although I found many interesting contrasts between Old Town and New Capital families and between higher- and lower-status ones, two years did not provide enough time to see substantive change. Longitudinal research has made that possible.

As previously mentioned, one of the principal forces of change was the establishment of schools throughout both parts of Bhubaneswar, which enabled many children to get a formal education for the first time, and all middle- and upper-status girls and boys in my sample attended school. By contrast, most low-status children did not because they were needed at home to help with chores and to care for younger siblings in the absence of parents who worked outside the home. In 1965–1967, parents were uncertain how much schooling they would allow their daughters to have because of the burden of marriage and dowry. For girls, marriages needed to be arranged with young men who were both older and more educated than they were in order to maintain the requisite gender hierarchy. The families of older, more educated men could demand bigger dowries, a financial burden for the parents of daughters. In addition, many families, especially those living in the Old Town, were anxious about what might happen to their daughters' social reputations when they were away from the supervision of kin. Girls schools had been established to address this concern, but worries remained about what might happen to daughters when they walked or were transported to and from school.

When I returned to Bhubaneswar in the 1970s, most girls were still in school with their brothers. By the mid-1980s many families were in a state of crisis because they now had educated daughters, many of whom had not only completed high school but had also attained college degrees. Finding suitable grooms for their highly educated, older daughters, some of whom were desirous of careers outside the home, had become a major challenge for parents, and this was the primary topic of conversation during that visit. I returned to Bhubaneswar in 1989 specifically to interview mothers, daughters, and grandmothers in each family about the changes that schooling and other facets of life in the New Capital had produced. In many instances, I had all three generations of women together exchanging their views on change in women's lives and in gender roles (Seymour 1999).

Here, I highlight some of the issues that pertain to this book's topic, the psychology of women residing in a highly patriarchal family system. In the early stages of life, all middle- and upper-status girls had been socialized into family life in ways congruent with what I reported above. In the Old Town, most grew up in joint households in caste-based neighborhoods. In the New Capital, they grew up in truncated extended families because fathers had been assigned to government posts in Bhubaneswar and not all family members could move together. Socialization experiences were subtly different between these two populations, but attitudes about the patrifocal family and ideology were similar on both sides of town.[11]

At the time of marriage, there were no rebellious daughters. They all anticipated arranged marriages and seemed to look forward to their lives as wives and mothers in patrifocal households. However, not all daughters had to reside with in-laws because new economic opportunities took their husbands away from Bhubaneswar. The one thing that many daughters *did* want was to complete their education, something to which most mothers and grandmothers were sympathetic because they wished that they had had the opportunity for more schooling. New Capital mothers and fathers were more supportive of their daughters' higher education than their more conservative Old Town counterparts were. All but one New Capital daughter completed college, and many of them completed postgraduate degrees, whereas in the Old Town most girls completed high school but only five attended college. Nonetheless, this represented a dramatic change from their mothers' generation, which had little or no formal schooling. Old Town girls, accordingly, were married at a somewhat younger age (18–20 years) than their New Capital counterparts (20–26 years) were.[12] In a few instances, marriages were arranged with the understanding with prospective parents-in-law that the bride could complete her education following the marriage. Marriage negotiations also included consideration of a daughter's current or potential employment.

One area of major change was what these educated young women wanted in marriage. Many wanted a more companionate relationship with their husband and less gender hierarchy in the home, although all accepted the reality of living, initially at least, with parents-in-law. One New Capital mother-daughter exchange about husband-wife relationships suggests these subtle changes in attitudes:

Mother: "Give-and-take is what makes a good relationship."
Daughter: "Mutual understanding. Both husband and wife must want to work together."

I ask what happens if there is a difference of opinion between husband and wife.
Mother: "The wife should give way."
Daughter: "No. There is no reason why the wife should give in any more than the husband."
Mother: "The husband's voice should come first."
Daughter: "I disagree." (Seymour 1999, 232)

In my interviews, I observed variations in the degree to which a husband should have full authority or should have a consultative relationship with his wife. One New Capital daughter responded to my inquiry about husband-wife relationships as follows: "I think it's adjustment—adjustment with one another—with your husband. Both should adjust—the wife 80 percent and the husband 20 percent. There is more making decisions together. Still the major decisions lie with husbands" (Seymour 1999, 233). Another New Capital married daughter, who had not completed college, responded: "It would be different if I were employed. Then they [employed women] are economically more independent. They have more of a say in decision making. Women like myself and my mother are very dependent. We cannot assume an equal role on that account. We must tend to the home and the children. The husband has the final word" (231).

These were transitional women, women who were much more educated than their mothers and who were trying to forge somewhat different relationships with husbands in a highly patriarchal society. Unlike their mothers and fathers, the difference in age between husband and wife was significantly reduced, as was the difference in levels of education. Nonetheless, they had grown up in a society where men were expected to be dominant and where they were expected to adapt to their husband's and in-laws' ways. One daughter, however, rebelled, and two others left their marriages when their husbands became involved with other women, something they would not have been able to do in an earlier era. In the latter two cases, their natal families took them back in although it cost them significantly in family honor. Yet several other women had husbands who moved out of their joint family in order to set up a nuclear household where husband and wife could be free from oppressive parents and parents-in-law. This, at the individual level, was a form of resistance to the constraints of joint family life.[13]

The one rebel in my sample of girls was Gitali Panda (a pseudonym). At age 26, she had entered a traditional arranged marriage: she and her husband had not met before the wedding ceremony. He came from a highly educated family in a neighboring town. Gitali had a master's degree and was employed before marriage. Upon marriage, she moved into her husband's household. At the time of our 1989 interview, she had left her husband and in-laws and was residing in Bhubaneswar with one daughter while their other daughter remained with her husband and his family. Gitali's parents had retired to their natal village, but they frequently visited her in Bhubaneswar. Gitali also had a married sister in Bhubaneswar who was very supportive of her. In response to my question about husband-wife relationships, Gitali said:

> It should be one of commonality, of cooperation. Women and men should have the same rights. The only difference between them is physical, although women are more sensitive. They consider everything for their children. There were two major problems with my marriage. My husband and I never had any time together. [This was partly due to work schedules, but her husband also chose to spend his evenings away from the house.] . . .
>
> The second problem was that he [her husband] wanted to be very dominant—to order me around, not discuss things together, not have a cooperative relationship. My father-in-law had liked my personality and had selected me because I had a strong personality, and he hoped that I would set right his unruly son. But my husband was dominated by his mother for his first twenty-nine years and feared being dominated by a wife, so he tried to be very dominating [with me] from the beginning. He expected me to carry out his orders. . . . My father-in-law is very considerate, but he has no voice in the family. My mother-in-law is very dominant. My husband is very attached to her. He's like a child. When I began living separately, he had to have his mother's permission to visit me. . . .
>
> Women feel that they should sacrifice, that they would lose respect in society if they leave their husband. I don't feel so. I don't care [what society thinks]. Sincerity is what's most important. I am sorry that I was not born to participate in the fight for independence. I would have been a follower of Gandhi. . . .
>
> In my day I was too fast. I was out of step with society. (Seymour 1999, 235–36)

Gitali is clearly unusual in this part of India, where women generally submit to the authority of their husbands and in-laws even if they want a more companionate marriage. She was able to leave her husband because she was employed, had her own salary, and had the support of her natal family. Nonetheless, it was a courageous act in a town where there were few single working women. Where did her courage come from? In part, it came from receiving mixed signals as a child. Her mother supported her educational and personal interests even when her father did not. For instance, her mother secretly allowed Gitali to have dance lessons, something her father had opposed. It was also a family that had experienced tragedy. Her brother had committed suicide when their father opposed his academic career interests. After that event, the father was much more amenable to his two remaining children's (both daughters) ambitions. Although both daughters agreed to arranged marriages, both also pursued graduate degrees and careers. In order to complete her graduate education after marriage, Gitali's older sister had lived matrilocally with her parents rather than with her parents-in-law, another unusual facet of this family.

My interviews made it clear that it took understanding mothers-in-law for young educated women, especially women with careers, to adapt successfully to their husband's family. (See Marrow, this volume, for a discussion of the responsibility of elders to understand the mind and heart of juniors in the family.) When the mothers-in-law expected their new daughters-in-law to enter the family as low-level workers, things did not always go well. As already mentioned, in at least five instances in both the Old Town and the New Capital, sympathetic husbands moved out with their wives and set up separate households. The idea of a companionate marriage, which might conflict with the ideals of the patrifocal family system, had begun to emerge.

Some Concluding Remarks

Kandiyoti's (1988) focus on the cyclical nature of women's power in patrifocal households, such as the ones I have described for Bhubaneswar and North India more generally, is not an adequate explanation for the endurance of this family system. Instead, we must examine the early socialization of girls, including how they have been reared to identify with the family as a whole and to subordinate their personal desires to the well-being of the larger group. In addition, they have internalized, from early childhood, powerful Hindu beliefs about the nature of women and men, which have had indelible effects. Furthermore, as Quinn (2005b, 500–501) argues, female children have been "predispositionally primed" for all these lessons.[14] They have been reared from infancy to be sensitive to others, what I have called the "diffusion of affect," so that when instructions about lajya are introduced, for instance, girls are prepared to internalize rules of decorum and beliefs about the effects that their behavior can have on family honor. "Shaming begins, and begins to have its effect on the child, long before the child is able to appreciate the relationship of the feeling of shame to right conduct, or understands how to act in order to avoid or ameliorate the experience of being shamed" (Quinn 2005b, 501). Ultimately, girls also internalize the importance of submitting to an arranged marriage, moving to their husband's household, and adjusting to the roles of daughter-in-law, wife, and mother. They are motivated to do all of these things because of their early and ongoing socialization, and they know that they may or may not achieve a position of power and authority in their husband's household. Their future status depends on how many other daughters-in-law there are, how long their mother-in-law lives, and what position their husband has in the family. It is not easy just to walk away from all of this, as Gitali did. Furthermore, there are heavy external pressures not to do so.

Nonetheless, change is occurring. Higher education produces not only women who are older and more educated at the time of marriage, but women who are potentially more independent-minded with personal career goals. Education has also produced men who want more educated and companionate wives. This makes for qualitatively different relationships between husband and wife and between mother-in-law and daughter-in-law. However, if things work smoothly, the joint or extended family provides a variety of people to help care for children and enhances a woman's ability to combine career and motherhood. Can the patrifocal family be transformed into something different, a place with less gender hierarchy and more shared power between men and women and among women of different generations? I have evidence that this is happening, but it will be neither an easy nor a universal process.

When I visited Bhubaneswar in 2013, I had an engaging conversation with one of my "grandsons," the son of a New Capital daughter from my original sample. He is a young man studying computer science in Bhubaneswar, and he spoke with passion about issues of gender inequality. He suggested that to produce substantive change for women in India, women, who do most of the caretaking of children, must begin to socialize *boys* differently. They should, he said, teach boys from early childhood that they are *not* superior to women and that they should not tolerate beliefs and practices that encourage gender inequities, an idealistic, subversive idea.

Notes

1. India's 2011 census indicated that the gender imbalance was at its highest level since records began being kept after independence in 1947. In the ten years since the previous census in 2001, the gender ratio declined from 927 girls aged six and under to 914 for every 1,000 boys (Baklinski 2011).
2. This is because dyadic relationships (e.g., mother-child, husband-wife), if allowed to become too strong, can threaten the unity of the joint family.
3. In low-status households, where most women work outside the home, gender relationships are very different. Clearly, these women cannot observe purdah restrictions; there is less sexual segregation in the home; and husband-wife relationships are less hierarchical.
4. There is a lot of variation in co-sleeping patterns in Bhubaneswar. Nursing infants sleep with their mothers. Older children may sleep with mothers, fathers, grandmothers, or others. Everyone may sleep in the same room. In larger New Capital homes, fathers and grandfathers often have separate rooms for sleeping.
5. Most homes have a room or space dedicated to icons of Hindu deities, which are worshipped on a daily basis, especially by wives and mothers who feel responsible for the well-being of their husbands, children, and other family members.
6. This was a practice that, at first, made it difficult for me to identify women in joint households. Young married women moved about homes with saris covering their bowed heads so that I could not see their faces. I learned to identify them by the jewelry they wore, especially toe rings.
7. Śiva is the reigning god of Bhubaneswar's temple town.
8. In her review of the cross-cultural literature on the management of sexuality, Broude (1981) finds that patrilineal, patrilocal societies tend to be restrictive regarding premarital sex for women whereas matrilineal, matrilocal societies are not.
9. The three exceptions were sons who, while studying or working abroad, fell in love with Western women and married them without familial permission. In each case, this created a crisis in their natal families.
10. I was part of the interdisciplinary Harvard-Bhubaneswar India Project, initiated by Professor Cora Du Bois in 1961, to study sociocultural change in Bhubaneswar, Odisha, India.
11. Socialization experiences for most low-status girls were quite different because by the age of six to seven years, they became responsible workers who performed household chores and cared for younger siblings.

12. The normative age of marriage for girls in Bhubaneswar rose in one generation from 12–13 years to 18–26 years.

13. As I have argued elsewhere (Seymour 2006), the concept of resistance has become ubiquitous in contemporary cultural anthropology, but there has been a lack of understanding of the underlying motivations when people take actions that are inconsistent with what they have learned is expected and appropriate behavior in their society. In the cases that I cite here, I know the underlying motivations of the actors but do not have space in this chapter to expand on them.

14. Emotional priming is the fourth of Quinn's (2005b) proposed universal features of child-rearing.

CHAPTER FOUR

To Make Her Understand with Love
Expectations for Emotion Work in North Indian Families

JOCELYN MARROW

In the previous chapter, Susan Seymour presents an account of child socialization in Odisha, India, that explains how the systems of honor and deference distinctive to classic patriarchy are learned. She focuses on the repeated, affect-laden, prescriptive, and proscriptive lessons for behavior taught in Old Town and New Capital Bhubaneswar to girls, beginning in infancy and continuing through early adolescence. Much of the behavior that girls learn promotes the prestige of the familial collective through modesty and deference. In this chapter I extend Seymour's insights about the "stickiness" of deference behaviors by focusing on why women, particularly young married women, are psychologically motivated to fulfill them. My discussions with middle-class, vernacular-speaking North Indian women about communication in the family provide a glimpse of how the attachment and affiliative needs of subordinates—here, young women—are met by participation in North Indian patriarchal family structures.

I describe how people are psychologically motivated to participate in North Indian family structures qua subordinates. Ideal communicative processes in adult junior-senior family member dyads, according to my interviewees, are sought by juniors because they provide (1) a sense of belonging and acceptance, and (2) the support of strong, admired others. How these motives support healthy development across the life course has been the subject of US psychoanalytic theory. Here, I employ self psychology to articulate the psychodynamic mechanisms involved in hierarchical relationships from the perspectives of subordinates. Self psychology is a psychoanalytic theory of human development and flourishing articulated first by Heinz Kohut in the United States during the middle of the twentieth century. According to self psychology, three basic psychological needs of individuals are to belong (twinship), to participate in a close relationship with another whom they hold in high esteem (idealization), and to be appreciated and recognized (mirroring) (Kohut 1971). When discussing relationships among adult juniors and seniors in extended, joint families, my middle-class, vernacular-speaking interviewees' descriptions of ideal communicative processes bore a strong resemblance to the first two of these needs (twinship and idealization).

Using data from ethnographic fieldwork and interviews, I describe the focal concept of *samjhaana*, which in Hindi means "to make one understand," and how it was deployed in discussions about resolving the emotional distress of intimate others. At first, these discussions surprised me because they did not include paying close attention to the feelings of the distressed other as important to resolving their distress. Instead, what resolved distress was enhancing the junior's sense of unity with the superior and providing highly directive support. As a psychodynamic psychotherapy trainee working in Chicago in the late 1990s, I was well acquainted with self psychology, and I noticed that the emotion work on behalf of an emotionally upset subordinate seemed to fulfill two of the basic needs of the tripolar self as posited by Kohut.[1] Therefore, I turn to psychodynamic theory to suggest how the North Indian communicative model motivates subordinate family members to participate qua subordinates. I conclude with a discussion of the limits of psychoanalytic theory (a US ethnopsychology) for explaining interpersonal processes in vernacular-speaking North India and elsewhere.

Mona's Distress

I met Mona, a 29-year-old middle-class homemaker, in 2002, when she was a patient of the Department of Psychiatry at a university hospital in Uttar Pradesh, India.[2] Mona had experienced periods of unconsciousness for which a medical cause could not be found. As I became better acquainted with Mona over the next one and a half years, I learned that her conjugal family life was miserable in an ordinary, chronic, and uneventful kind of way. Her husband had continued to carry on an affair with his elder sister-in-law (*jethi*), which had begun before Mona's marriage to him. The two couples resided in the same household, and the sexual relationship between her jethi and her husband had always been part of Mona's marriage. Mona's husband's uncle, who also lived in their household, was hardly a source of moral leadership; he exposed himself to her regularly. Mona's two other sisters-in-law, residing separately, refused to share their significantly greater material prosperity with Mona and her household, and they accused Mona of pretending to be ill.

In an effort to understand how Mona and other junior women might communicate their distress to others in their family, I asked whether elders should try to understand (samjhaana) the heart/mind (*man*) of the juniors in the family.[3] Mona replied with bitterness to my inquiry: "Yes. They *should* understand, but they do not understand. They leave all the compromising up to the junior family members.... The younger members also have feelings and desires [*man*]. But everything is for the elders. It is only by chance that these individuals are younger and those are elder. But everyone should be equal."

Without a thorough understanding of Mona's motivations, a feminist reading of her answer might proceed as follows: Mona describes how an imbalance of power ("everything is for the elders"), which is morally wrong ("everyone should be equal") in an almost Rawlsian way ("it is only by chance"), structures a family system that is insensitive to subordinates ("leave all the compromising up to the junior family members") and that fails to attend to their needs ("the younger members also have *man*"). This reading of Mona's answer might argue that her distress is a result of a pervasive familial milieu in which she has been victimized by inequality. She has been dominated, restricted, demeaned, and abused. It might be speculated that Mona has eschewed the paternalistic and patriarchal model of North Indian family life in which elders (and men) have more power, authority, and rights than juniors (and women). We might read her statement as a political one that is subversive of this paternalistic and patriarchal order.

This interpretive move would be consistent with much of the nonpsychological theorizing about inequality in the anthropological corpus (Seymour 2006). However, Mona's invocation of individual equality is in tension with other thoughts and behaviors she expresses. Mona is strongly attached to many individuals she honors as elders, and her attachment to them is structured by a cultural system of relating that is, in its best instantiations, benevolently paternalistic.[4] Taking into account how Mona is motivated by her attachment to her family members, I suggest that Mona's answer ought to be understood as a complaint about her husband's and specific elders' failure to meet expectations ("They *should* understand, but they do not understand. They leave all the compromising up to the junior family members"). Her verbal endorsement of egalitarianism among family members ("everyone should be equal") refers to an equality of needs and desires ("the younger members also have *man*. But everything is for the elders"), instead of an assertion of equal status, rights, and responsibilities. Mona's psychological distress is best understood as related to the massive failure of her husband and elders to meet their responsibilities as benevolent patriarchs toward her.

Samjhaana: A North Indian Model of Emotion Work

From 2001 to 2004 and for a brief period in 2013, I conducted research in Varanasi, India, about the family and community contexts of mental illness and women's emotional distress. In 2003, I undertook a systematic exploration of the meanings of a focal concept I had heard again and again when people spoke of how they help emotionally distressed others. The Hindi word signifying this concept is *samjhaana*. Literally, *samjhaana* means "to make understand," as in "I made her understand [*men ne usko samjhaaya*] she needed to consider her children's future when she wanted to kill herself." As I listened to acquaintances, friends, and mental health professionals practicing in Varanasi describe the emotion work they do with those who express suffering, it became apparent to me that they practiced an asymmetrical communicative model in which making one's juniors understand is central to effective and satisfying relationships for both junior and senior intimates. Hierarchical, unequal intimate relationships in vernacular North India are familial: father and son, mother-in-law and daughter-in-law, older brother and younger brother, older sister-in-law and younger-sister-in-law, husband and wife. This model is extended to nonfamilial relationships: doctor and patient, teacher and student, employer and employee.

The vernacular North Indian model of intimate communication stands in contrast to the US model of intimacy, which is undergirded by the politically liberal assumption that equality is a basic good. In the US model, the process by which both individuals in relationship have their interior psychological life validated and reflected by the other is the same. Ideal dyadic communicative processes involve each partner expressing their unique, private, and idiosyncratic feelings, preferences, and ideas. The other party demonstrates love, care, and support by listening carefully and trying to understand the expressed point of view as if it were their own; he or she empathizes (Rogers 1989, 226). Feeling that one's unique inner life is understood by the other creates a secure bond between individuals (Eagle 2003, 38).

Engaging in careful listening to junior family members in order to understand their perspectives is not a crucial component of mutually satisfying communication among my vernacular-speaking North Indian interlocutors. For them, the most beneficial communicative act toward a status inferior is telling (*making* her understand). In relationship, subordinates and superiors accept that telling, rather than listening, is more important to good care of the subordinate. Understanding the hearts/minds/desires of junior family members is not an affective good for its own sake.

The data collection I undertook to explore the model of communication undergirded by vernacular North Indian processes of making understand and being understood began with observations of and unstructured interviews with families at the Department of Psychiatry. There, I observed and spoke with people about managing the emotions and behaviors of others in the family, and with professionals who reflected on the interpersonal causes of distress or well-being for families and individuals. After nearly two years of ethnographic work, I interviewed twenty individuals recruited through Varanasi friendship networks who did not have a psychiatric patient as a member of their household or immediate family, but who were of similar class status as the patients and families who had led me to wonder about this communicative dynamic. Interviews were loosely structured around what it means to understand and what it means to make someone understand in the family setting. Interviewees were not segregated from other household members, and most interviews involved the participation of multiple family members, even though one person served as the primary interviewee. Interviewees were divided almost equally between junior (daughter-in-law with no married sons and co-residing elder in-laws) and senior family status (mother-in-law or head of household), and all but one of the primary interviewees was a woman. This selection bias likely came about since women were most likely to be present in the home when I visited in the late morning or afternoon and because our hosts assumed that the conversation would proceed most comfortably with my female research assistant and me if the primary interviewee was a woman. Interviews lasted from one hour to four hours, and I allowed interviewees to wander across subjects and discuss what seemed most important to them on the broad topic of communication in the family. Interviewees conversed easily and at length about making others understand; it was very salient.

The descriptions of communicative processes across role statuses in this chapter are both "ideal types" (Joseph 2005, 86) and "cultural models" (Quinn 1996, 397) serving as aspirations for feelings and behavior, rather than faithful accounts of interactions between elders and juniors. As such, they provide templates for communicative processes and emotions that may be uneasily inserted into the contradictory and multidimensional circumstances of actual relationships. As Mona asserted, elders sometimes do not fulfill their responsibilities for the well-being of junior members as the model prescribes. When expectations based on the model are not or cannot be fulfilled, it is not surprising that the people involved experience pain.

Complementarity in Telling and Listening

The ethnographic literature on emotion and love in India demonstrates that there are distinct "feeling rules" (Hochschild [1983] 2003, 94) for emotional expression based on differences in status (Appadurai 1990; Derné 1995; Gold 2006; Inden and Nicholas 1977; Lamb 2000; Marriott 1976; Orsini 2006; Roland 1982; Shweder 1991, 2003, 2008; Trawick 1992; Wadley 2002). Similarly, the communicative model represented by the concept of making one understand (samjhaana) involves a complementary, not reciprocal set of expectations, expressions, and responsibilities.

In the vernacular North Indian communicative model of samjhaana, elders and juniors inhabit complementary roles with respect to the type of work they perform managing others' behaviors and emotions. The work of elders is to shape the emotional experience, expression, and behavior of juniors by making them understand, while juniors do not have a symmetrical responsibility to make the seniors understand. Pintu's mother's explanation of the role of seniors in making junior family members understand is typical of my interviewees' responses:[5] "I am [the] elder, but I also make some mistakes. My 'guardian' [English word] is my husband. . . . He is above me; he is my 'guardian.' If there is a mother-in-law, then the mother-in-law will make me understand. If there is a husband, an elder brother-in-law, or an elder sister-in-law—to whoever's words I give weight—then that person will make me understand."

Pintu's mother explains that the junior must feel respect for the elder who is trying to persuade her of a particular point of view; there must be a relationship of trust. The junior must trust that the senior has the best interest of the junior in mind. Pratima's father reassured me that in these relations of intimacy, "if I will make you understand[, for example], then I will make you understand for your benefit. He [the elder] won't deceive you by making you understand wrongly." Gollu's mother shared a very similar understanding of the value to juniors of elders' utterances: "Because they are [an] elder, they are good. If they say something, they are saying it for your betterment: Do this work. Do this. Do that."

When I asked the same interviewees, "In the family, should elders understand the mind and heart of junior members?" the answers surprised me because no one suggested that, by itself, listening to the junior member is loving or supports their growth. Three people said it was not important for family elders to understand their juniors because the juniors are ignorant and likely to be wrong. Pratima's father was particularly eloquent regarding how it is not in the juniors' interest for the elder to attend carefully to the juniors' desires. He argued that juniors' inclinations are uninformed because of their innocence. Referring to his preteen son, he said, "He is innocent, is he not? He is unknowing, is he not? He cannot recognize good and bad, now can he?" Likewise, Rika's mother explained to me that younger members of the family do not "have the benefit of experience. This is why we accept what they say less. 'Experience' [English word] gets the most importance."

The work of juniors, according to this communicative model, is to listen to their seniors and act accordingly. Beena Auntie, for example, explained the relationship between seniors' and juniors' roles this way: "Making them understand is my duty. Doing [*karm karna*] is their [juniors'] duty." All my respondents asserted that the juniors should carefully attend to their elders. There were a number of reasons given by interviewees regarding why juniors find it emotionally satisfying to attend to seniors in this way. The most compelling emotional reason was to become similar to the elder; elders share their *man*, perspectives, beliefs, and desires so that the junior may become more like the elder. Elders' invitations to share their habits, thoughts, and perspectives demonstrate their love for juniors.

Young married women, especially, are motivated to participate in a communicative system that brings their beliefs, behaviors, and habits into harmony with those of their conjugal family in order to become a bona fide member of that family with all the rights and entitlements enjoyed by its members. By listening and taking in the perspectives and exhortations of their elders and by transforming their own thoughts and behaviors in accordance, newly married women strengthen their claim to full membership in their conjugal families.

The Contours of Emotional Expectations in the Indian Family

The ideal North Indian family is extended, joint, and virilocal. This means that an ideal household includes at least three generations of kin, with the men of the family marrying exogenously and bringing their wives to live with them;

the women born in the household migrate from their natal homes to live with unrelated families of the same caste after marriage. While this living arrangement may not be actualized in a majority of cases, it remains an aspiration for many, if not most, middle-class North Indian families.

Although Indian law was amended in 2005 to provide daughters with a share of parental inheritance along with their brothers, less than 10 percent of women in North Indian states inherit anything (Sircar and Fletschner 2014). The survival—and, in fact, spread—of the dowry system despite its illegality for more than fifty years in sovereign India demonstrates the persistence of the patrilineal-patrilocal complex that Quinn (this volume), following Kandiyoti, argues is responsible for motivating women's participation in systems of deference to men.

During my fieldwork, hierarchical roles and responsibilities among Indian family members were valued positively and described as a major difference between South Asian and non–South Asian families. For example, when asked to describe the Indian family to British professionals, the first response from among a group of local psychiatrists claimed that the family was "an institution with rules, hierarchy, and a leader." In this hierarchy, elder family members are superior to junior family members, men are superior to women, and within any generation, elder sons, elder daughters, and elder daughters-in-law have authority over younger sons, younger daughters, and younger daughters-in-law, respectively.

Vernacular-speaking Banarsis people regard the constructing of the self of junior adults as open to the participation of their elders. My interviewees spoke of how good or bad *samskaar*,[6] received in the form of utterances, food, caresses, and even blows, makes and remakes subordinates bodily, affectively, and psychologically. Ethnographic writing about the selves of North Indian people in the 1970s–1990s emphasized the importance of the participation of others in their construction. Writers coined a number of terms during this efflorescence of theory about South Asian bodies and psychologies to describe the permeability of the person: dividuality, we-self-regard, interdependence, fluidity. Dividuality refers to the way bodies exchange material and intangible substances to become more like one another the longer and closer they remain in contact. Marriott's (1976, 1989) paradigmatic example is people who eat from the same pot and become more similar to one another by ingesting the same food. We-self-regard is psychological; it describes the extent to which feelings, behavior, and the well-being of family members interpenetrate the pride and well-being of other family members (Roland 1982). Interdependence is also psychological, referring to the tendency to define oneself in relationship with others, rather than to think of the self as an independent motivational center of traits, preferences, and values (Markus and Kitayama 1991). Fluidity refers to the extent to which identities are dependent on the formation and dissolution of social alliances (Cohen 1998; Daniel 1984).

The vernacular North Indian model of emotional management represented by the concept of samjhaana is built on two assumptions that provide fertile psychological conditions for patriarchal and paternalistic social forms (Joseph 1993a, 459–60). First, social life is and ought to be structured hierarchically. Second, people are psychologically and bodily permeable to shaping and reshaping by affectively important others. A strong sense of interdependence, we-self-regard, or dividuality stabilizes hierarchical family forms; that is, family roles are anchored by the desire of people to seek the participation of other family members in the building of self and personal identity. Selves are responsive to and actively seek the involvement of others in self-fashioning. The honor, fate, and fortune of North Indian people depend on the honor, fate, and fortune of family members, lineage ancestors, and future generations.

Psychological anthropologists writing about India have recognized the processes by which juniors seek to absorb, psychologically and materially, the qualities of admired superiors or elders as attempts to share in those qualities (Appadurai 1990; Roland 1982). Material incorporations of the qualities of superiors include eating the leftovers off the husband's plate and the ritual of drinking the water in which the mother-in-law's feet have been washed (Menon 2013; Shweder 2003). The psychological qualities of superiors, when assumed by the subordinates, may lend the latter self-confidence, dignity, and moral certainty. Marked with the attitudes, values, habits, and ideas of their betters, junior people may share psychologically in the honor and success accumulated by the seniors over a lifetime of toil, sacrifice, and achievement. Status inferiors may assume the powers of their superior as their own in an incorporative move that enhances their own self-regard (Roland 1982). South Indian employees, for example, may incorporate psychically the "big man" of an organization, lending the impression that the boss's personality pervades every aspect of the organization (Mines 1994).

Components of *Samjhaana*

In the next sections, I describe important aspects of the model of samjhaana as explained by my interviewees. First, samjhaana only occurs properly in the context of an ongoing relationship in which the senior provides love, care, and nurture to the junior. A large part of this care is in the form of directives regarding how the junior ought to act and what they ought to do. The senior is thought to possess a deep knowledge of the needs and desires of the junior, which the senior has gained through their wisdom, their experience of the world, and their own experiences as a junior person. Finally, the act of samjhaana involves an attempt on the part of the senior to bring the junior closer by inviting the junior to become more similar to the senior.

THE NEED FOR LOVE

To provide love—to speak and behave lovingly toward junior family members—is to demonstrate sensitivity to their needs. Juniors want the love of their elders first and foremost, according to my interviewees, and elder family members must understand this. For example, Mrs. Thakur explained that when a new bride comes to a conjugal household, the young woman misses the love she received from her natal kin. Her mother-in-law must be cognizant of the fact that the new bride misses her natal kin and that she wants love from her new family: "At least she should get a little love from the mother-in-law."

THE INVITATION TO BECOME SIMILAR TO THE ELDER

The model of samjhaana, as described by my interviewees, involves an opportunity to assimilate the qualities of the elder who is providing understanding. In the following, Mrs. Tripathi gives an example of how a mother-in-law might go about making her new daughter-in-law understand how to behave in her new marital home. In the back-and-forth of this imagined communicative sequence, Mrs. Tripathi demonstrates how the new daughter-in-law is invited to become part of her conjugal family:

> The daughter-in-law is a daughter that comes from another house, and she doesn't know about your family, what is liked, what people do, how she ought to live. So you should tell her about your family beforehand: how she ought to live, that she ought to do this and that.
>
> If she accepts it, then this is good. If she is completely against, if she doesn't like you [and says]: "This family is not okay for me!" then you should tell her, "Son [*betha*], it is harmful for the family if you do this."

Having made her understand with love [*pyaar se*], if she accepts . . . it is a good thing. If she doesn't, then you can make her understand with a little harshness [*sakht se*] or by scolding her. If after all this, she still doesn't understand, then it gets a bit difficult.

You should let it go. She will understand by herself after one year, two years, three, four, or five years, either because she is older or because of her experience. If we take care of her, she will come to understand: "I have not adjusted to this family. What I am doing shows that there is some lack in me. I must change all of this."

First, Mrs. Tripathi asserts that the daughter-in-law should be held in the same esteem as one's own child ("the daughter-in-law is a daughter"). However, since she "comes from another house," the elder must tell the young woman about the preferences, values, and idiosyncrasies of her new family ("she doesn't know about your family, what is liked, what people do, how she ought to live"). Because she is a stranger, the mother-in-law does not know how she will react to this overture ("If she accepts it, then this is good. If she is completely against . . .").

If the first attempt at making her understand leads to rejection of her conjugal family ("this family is not okay for me!"), the mother-in-law should make clear her loving invitation to pull the bride into the heart of the marital family ("made her understand with love") by referring to her with an endearing term that affirms she is prized ("Son"). If this does not work, the mother-in-law may try to make her understand with "a little harshness or by scolding her."

In spite of these efforts to cause the junior to identify with her conjugal family, she may continue to remain other, and Mrs. Tripathi advises that the in-laws must let it be this way ("you should let it go"). At some point, she will be older and wiser and will have undergone a great deal that will teach her what is good and what is bad ("she will understand by herself . . . either because she is older or because of her experience"). Even so, if she is ever to assimilate to her new family ("she will come to understand: 'I have not adjusted to this family'"), her in-laws must continue to offer the love ("take care of her") due to a daughter of the house.

The invitation to the new daughter-in-law to become psychologically part of her conjugal family, as outlined in this imagined communicative sequence, is likely to be perceived as deeply loving and satisfying. For newly married women residing in their marital homes in the first few months or even years of marriage, the feeling that she is loved as part of the family may be tenuous. Women may feel and be regarded as other (*paraayi*) in their marital homes. They desire to assimilate and become "one's own" (*apni*) to conjugal kin, to be considered not as a daughter-in-law but as a daughter of the house (Raheja and Gold 1994).

My interviewees reported that the early months and years of residence in their father-in-law's place were difficult. They did not feel cared for and loved, like a full member of the conjugal family. For example, Rika, who married into a large joint family in a village, felt that she was not treated the same as her husband's flesh and blood: "I used to think, 'Why do *I* always have to make the sacrifice?' Everyone [in my conjugal family] used to say, 'Don't do this. Do that. Don't do this. Do that.' At that time, it was trouble.... At the beginning, I thought that my husband didn't love me. It was always, 'sister, sister, father, father.'" Rika subsequently developed a strong, loving relationship with her husband and his kin and became a central member of the family, but not until she felt she had proved her devotion repeatedly through her service and sacrifice.

KNOWLEDGE OF NEEDS AND DESIRES

Elders' greater experience of the world enables them to anticipate the needs and desires of junior members. These seniors have had the experience of being young; they have "also gone through that stage," in the words of Maya Auntie. They rely on the wisdom built on a lifetime of experiences combined with their memories of what it was like to be a young family member in order to project themselves into the minds and hearts of their junior kin. Mrs. Thakur explained: "The elder person will understand [the junior person] because they have seen a lot of the world. Because they are [an] elder, they know and understand things we cannot see. There is a big difference between their age and our age. The main thing is that they have had much experience of good and bad things."

Elders call on the events and feelings of their lifetime when attempting to grasp the perspectives of their juniors; they rely on a broad temporal dimension of past knowledge and experience (Throop 2008). This is in contrast to a narrow temporal dimension, which would restrict the understanding of the other to their specific utterances and behaviors. Narrowly attending to young people's expressed needs and desires, according to Pratima's father, who is quoted above, would be an error in judgment. Although elder family members may not expect or encourage junior family members to verbalize their needs and desires, seniors should know and, in fact, anticipate what juniors want and need. Pintu's mother explains: "It was the elders' responsibility to think about the quality of our lives."

If elders fail to discern the minds of their junior family members through this projective process, they risk defaulting on their responsibility to provide sensitive love and care to them.

THE BEST COURSE OF ACTION

Finally, according to the model, understanding their elders benefits junior family members because it guarantees that the juniors are informed regarding the most moral, effective, and appropriate actions. Elders, as Gollu's mother and Pratima's father assert (see above), are "good," and heeding them will benefit junior family members. Elders' increased experience of the world, according to Rika's mother, Maya Auntie, and Mrs. Thakur, has allowed them to experiment with means and ends and determine the best way to accomplish important aims. Finally, elders have had the benefit of a long moral apprenticeship to *their* elders. By listening to the elders and being made to understand, juniors receive knowledge regarding effective and appropriate action. As Beena Auntie says, it is her duty to provide guidance to her juniors, who ought to use it as the foundation of their behaviors.

A Psychodynamic Explanation for North Indian Patriarchy

The model of intimate communication represented by the vernacular North Indian concept of samjhaana involves the following features:

> It is complementary, with elders tasked with making juniors understand and juniors expected to act accordingly.
> It invites juniors to share in the superior qualities of elders.
> It involves elders in a projective process of imagining the perspectives of their juniors.[7]
> It entrusts elders with providing guidance to juniors because they are wise, morally astute, and experienced.
> It is an act of care of the junior.

As described earlier in this chapter, there are two counterintuitive features of this approach. First, the model does not privilege attending to the expressed thoughts of juniors as an affective good. Rather, a sensitive and responsible elder makes use of projective interpersonal processes in order to understand what the junior needs and desires without the junior family member being required to articulate it. Because the elder was once a junior, they are able to reflect on their youthful subjectivities with the wisdom of age and surmise what their junior's needs might be.

Second, instead of encouraging the junior family members to become autonomous and separate from their elders and their families, this approach invites adult juniors to become similar to their superiors psychologically and materially. Since the cultural model assumes that people who inhabit superior role statuses are wiser, perfect, and more moral than those who are subordinate to them, juniors' attempts to ascertain the desires and intentions of their seniors are the first steps in a process leading toward assimilating the best qualities of those superiors. Ideally, by coming to know and understand the ways and minds of their elders, juniors will cultivate similar qualities and inclinations in themselves. As Varanasi elders encourage their juniors to partake of the elders' qualities, they hasten the development of a connection with important goals and a sense of acceptance by others.

Psychoanalytic theory may assist in explaining why the communicative model of samjhaana feels psychologically compelling to vernacular-speaking North Indian subordinates. In particular, the invitation to idealize and become similar to elders during the work of samjhaana may psychologically motivate the juniors to participate in this communicative process. There is thus a partial alignment of the model of samjhaana with theories of psychological motivation described in self psychology.

For Kohut, the psychoanalyst who developed self psychology, the self is a heuristic for understanding psychological motivation, rather than an essence. It is a "center of initiative and perception" (Kohut 1971, 177) from which emanate needs and desires and in which experiences are organized. Kohut's (1984) work with patients in psychoanalysis led him to posit that there are three basic psychological requirements that must be fulfilled by important others throughout life. In order for a person to be psychologically healthy, they must be recognized and appreciated for who they are (mirroring), they must have closeness with someone they admire (idealization), and they must feel that they belong to a social unit and are similar to others (twinship). According to this theory, all individuals are psychologically motivated to seek others who provide appreciation, inspiration, and an experience of attunement and alikeness (Fosshage 2009, 7). These psychological needs continue throughout life (Goldberg 1998, 244; Morrison 2009).

Self psychological theory provides an explanation for why junior family members might be motivated to participate in the model of samjhaana as subordinates. The expectation that juniors will idealize and become more similar to familial elders promises to fulfill juniors' attachment and affiliative needs. Two essential features of the model of samjhaana are strikingly similar to two of the psychological motivations underpinning the model of the tripolar self of Kohut: the need for idealization and the need for twinship.

The need for twinship is about the "sense of [being] a human being among human beings" (Togashi and Kottler 2012, 333). It involves feeling that one belongs to the group and that one is connected to others in meaningful ways. The invitation to become similar, which Varanasi seniors hold out to their juniors, including the semiotic and material rituals of assimilation that they perform over and over again in mundane daily life, helps the juniors foster connection with the elders and with the larger group. For example, above I quoted how Mrs. Tripathi's daughter-in-law is addressed as part of the family—"daughter" and then, even better, "son"—affirming that the daughter-in-law was emphatically "her own" and not other. As a second example, Soni Devi told me that the elder should feed the junior from her hand, thus making her similar to the elder by imbuing her with the senior's substances, while satiating the junior's desire for tasty food.

Idealization, in the view of contemporary psychoanalytic theoreticians, is "the support of strong affirming others from whom we derive much of our own strength" (Morrison 2009, 76–77). It involves using the affective and experiential resources of another (whom the subject deems as abundant in those resources) to meet one's needs. Likewise, intrinsic to the model of samjhaana is the view that the senior has a wealth of experience, wisdom, and affection to bestow on the junior and that the latter wishes to be enhanced by these resources. The junior's admiration of these resources, combined with the generous gifting of them by the senior, provides inspiration and a clear purpose to the junior.

The third basic psychological motivation posited by Kohut is the need for mirroring. Feeling recognized, appreciated, and understood (mirrored) is as important for psychological health as the need to belong (twinship) and the need to feel close to someone in whom we have confidence (idealization). Yet juniors' needs and desires to be recognized, appreciated, and understood were conspicuous in their absence from explicit theorizing by my interlocutors. It was not mentioned by my Varanasi interviewees as important to how samjhaana (making understand) and *samajhna* (understanding) works. A few interviewees even explicitly stated that it was not advisable to attempt to draw out juniors by trying to understand their needs and desires. With the exception of mirroring, my interlocutors' model of satisfying intimate communication was so evocative of Kohut's model of healthy psychological motivation that I could not help but wonder why it was missing.

It seems likely that the explicit valuing of hierarchical differences in vernacular Indian societies makes the idea of providing subordinates with admiration, appreciation, and understanding hard to conceive. Mirroring, to my interviewees, is the affective good that seems appropriate for status superiors, since those with higher status are expected to be worthy of admiration: their generosity is worthy of appreciation, and their thoughts are worthy of understanding. Writing about emotion and self in South India, Appadurai (1990) describes how being admired by a status superior would seem patronizing and only embarrass the subordinate. More recent observations of relationships among working-class children and parents in Varanasi reveal that parents do not compliment their children, although they may heap very high praise on their efforts and qualities when they are not present (Huberman 2012, 95–98).

Yet the junior member of every dyad is the senior of another family member. The daughter-in-law may not hear expressions of admiration and appreciation from her mother-in-law or even her own husband, but her teenaged nieces and nephews and even her husband's younger brother are likely to affirm her efforts and attractiveness, contributing to a vitalized and expanded sense of herself. In this way, family dyads are not exclusive. Just as the infant and young child rely on multiple caretakers in joint families (Seymour, this volume), adults in the family system rely on multiple others to meet their emotional needs, reinforcing interdependence.

Mona's Answer

The first time I met Mona (featured in the vignette that opened this chapter), she was undergoing an intake interview at the Department of Psychiatry. In the middle of the interview, the young resident conducting it asked if she would feel more comfortable speaking about her problems if her husband were out of the room. She responded, "It is not like that. I never hide anything from my husband." In the ensuing discussion, she explained the reason for her recent suicidal gesture. At that time, she said, she had not been sleeping well because her elder sister-in-law's children were making a lot of noise at night. She had served dinner to her husband, who scolded her for not putting any salt in the vegetables. That night, she broke up two mosquito coils and angrily swallowed them with water. She explained with indignation, "If I do something wrong, then my husband should hit me, but if I don't do anything wrong, he shouldn't scold." She repeated this statement two or three times for emphasis.

Further, she had recently had an operation to remove her thyroid. When she was in the hospital after the operation, her husband's uncle told her mother, "Please take this woman and her two children. She has brought this illness from her natal home, and he [her husband] is spending too much money on her. I will get him remarried." Mona was shocked and saddened after hearing this comment because this uncle, who co-resided with Mona and her husband, had always treated Mona's husband like a son and Mona like his daughter-in-law. Mona told the resident conducting the intake that whenever she thought of this, she became very angry that her husband had not said anything to his uncle in her support.

At this time, Mona did not mention the sexual transgressions of her husband and uncle; only later, when she had built a rapport with her doctors and with me, did she discuss them. Yet even in this first interview, she drew attention to how the elders in her household were failing to fulfill their responsibilities to her. Her husband scolded her when she had not done anything wrong, and her husband's uncle threatened to abandon rather than care for her, which was his responsibility toward her.

Mona emphasized that she was not protesting her familial superiors' right to discipline her. She repeated several times that if she were to do something wrong, her husband should correct her. However, she appealed to the intake worker and to me to recognize that she was being disciplined unfairly. She had no wrongdoings to "hide" from her husband, and yet he and his uncle had reneged on their responsibilities to treat her as their own and care for her.

Mona consciously accepted the patriarchal contract in which she is a dependent subordinate to be nurtured and to be disciplined by her elders when appropriate, and she evidenced a psychological commitment to the communicative model of samjhaana. I came to know Mona well over one and a half years during which I visited her at her home and at the hospital when she was twice readmitted. I want to highlight two examples demonstrating how the model of samjhaana structured Mona's emotional life.

During Mona's first inpatient hospitalization, I learned that she considered a physician she had been consulting for palpitations as one of the only people in Varanasi who truly cared about her. This physician was of the same *jāti* (community and subcaste) as Mona, and that fact made her feel close to him. Mona had become attached to Dr. Singh over the course of her consultations with him; she told me that she thought of him "as a father." To her, this meant that she should try to follow his advice. Dr. Singh's response to her disclosure that she wanted to kill herself left her feeling cared about and loved. I asked what he had said that made her feel good. "Dr. Singh made me understand not to kill myself. He said I should think about my children and what would happen to them after I die."

During a visit many months later to Mona's husband's home, she revealed a diary that she had begun during one of her inpatient stays. Suggesting that the patient keep a diary is a common therapeutic intervention with emotionally distressed women by the psychiatrists at the hospital where she sought care. The doctors advised literate, married women patients who had limited social contact outside their conjugal families to write about their complaints, problems, and suffering as a way of venting and managing distress. When Mona showed me the notebook, she explained that her doctor told her that if something came into her mind, for example, if she felt hurt about something, she should talk about it with someone, but if she could not tell anyone, then she should write it down. Dutifully, Mona had filled the notebook with writing. There was an essay describing and praising the hospital's doctors. Another essay lauded the natural beauty of the hospital grounds. In between were sentimental quotes from popular film *gazals* (romantic poetry and songs). There was no writing pertaining directly to Mona's concerns.

Both examples demonstrate Mona's psychological investment in the communicative model in which elders provide love to their juniors by making them understand, and juniors, in turn, idealize their elders and do not wish to nor ought to need to share their thoughts about their suffering. In the first example, Mona described herself as "loved" because Dr. Singh advised her lovingly. Note that Mona did not evaluate how closely Dr. Singh listened to her complaints. In fact, it was not clear how much Dr. Singh knew about the mistreatment Mona endured in her conjugal home. In the second example, the writings in Mona's diary suggest that praise and understanding are the affective goods to be delivered to seniors (in this case, she was writing with the expectation that her psychiatrist would read the notebook), despite her clear understanding that the doctor wanted her to write of her troubles.

Coda: On Ethnopsychology

The psychodynamics of twinship and idealization help explain why the dual offering of a sense of belonging and of the provision of supportive direction are motivating to North Indian subordinates. While there is a partial overlap of the model of emotion underpinning samjhaana and the model of the tripolar self, the third pole of the self—mirroring needs—is not described as part of North Indian subordinates' striving in relationships with their seniors.

Being affirmed and recognized, or mirrored, is central in US ethnopsychologies to developing and maintaining a healthy self. Even cursory attention to self-help and self-improvement books, blogs, advice columns, and talk shows in the United States demonstrates ad nauseam how important having the affirmation of others is to an individual's self-esteem and self-efficacy. Psychoanalytic theory in the United States is merely a particularly sophisticated, thoughtful, and well-articulated example of US ethnopsychology because it cannot help but be limited by the time, place, and culture in which it was developed. Kohut worked out his theory of the self in the 1960s and 1970s with data from the psychoanalytic treatment of US patients. No doubt, the extent to which the patients treated by Kohut longed for affirmation of their goals and accomplishments spoke to the struggles experienced by his (mostly) young, white, educationally elite, middle-class patients in urban US social environments in which independent initiative and autonomy were expected and valued. As such, Kohut's work remains somewhat consistent with the classical psychoanalytic models of motivation focused on drives and strivings for autonomy, to which he was reacting (Lessem 2005). Since the time of Kohut's research and writing, psychoanalytic discussions of psychological motivations have subsumed mirroring needs as belonging to a larger set of strivings for attachment and affiliation. (Examples from psychoanalysis are Lichtenberg 1989 and Eagle 2003. An example from neuroscience is Panksepp 2004.)

Just as US ethnopsychologies fit their social environment, so too do North Indian ethnopsychologies; the model of samjhaana outlined here is an example. Sustaining young, married women's participation in extended, joint family living requires economic, social, and emotional motivators. Innate human dispositions for attachment and affiliation within a patriarchal system characterized by an interdependent lifestyle find their fulfillment through the active participation of subordinates qua subordinates. In the extended, joint family household, women's accommodation to patriarchy is mediated through more senior women. While young, married women build intimacy with their husbands in private, they maintain distance from their husbands in front of other family members and in public. Therefore, much of young women's intimacy is with senior women. Deference behaviors (taking direction from elders, adopting their values, and avoiding drawing attention to the self) are more than merely prescribed, they are emotionally rewarding.

Notes

1. *Emotion work* is a term introduced by Arlie Hochschild ([1983] 2003) to refer to efforts to change the feelings of another person.
2. All names used in this chapter are pseudonyms.
3. *Man* is a Hindi word that refers to the seat of feelings and desire. Speakers sometimes touch a place on their chest above their sternum when referring to the will of their *man*. It is usually translated as heart/mind in the anthropological literature written in English.
4. Thanks to Rick Shweder for suggesting the term *benevolent paternalism* to describe the system of expectations and desires that structure interaction across familial status hierarchies.
5. In general, people do not address their social betters or social equals by their given names in the communities where I have collected data. Instead, it is more respectful to use a circumlocution. Teknonymy is the practice of referring to an individual in relation to his or her offspring. I addressed the interviewees with a teknonym. Although all names in this chapter are pseudonyms, I preserve the form of address I used with each individual.
6. Here, the meaning of *samskaar* is similar to what is meant by the concepts of psychological influence, mental imprint, or even education. Samskaaras in Hinduism refer to life cycle rites that change the nature and substance of the person from that of one status (for example, unmarried) to another status (married). Likewise, samskaar received from an elder may change one's habits, thoughts, and behavior.
7. In projective processes, individuals attribute their "own feelings or ideas to another" (Hollan and Throop 2008, 386).

CHAPTER FIVE

Perspectives on Gender Roles and Relations across Three Generations of Maya Women in Southern Mexico

ADRIANA M. MANAGO

In this chapter, I reflect on my work studying how Maya women's understandings of gender are changing in Chiapas, Mexico. In 2007–2010, I interviewed first-generation professional Maya women who had migrated to the Mexican city of San Cristóbal de las Casas (Manago and Greenfield 2011), first-generation Maya college students who had migrated to San Cristóbal for school (Manago 2012), and first-generation high school girls, their mothers, and their grandmothers in the nearby Maya community of Zinacantán (Manago 2014). My goal in reviewing these studies is to bring attention to the psychological underpinnings of cultural change and continuity when there is an erosion of classic patriarchy, a form of patriarchy tied to patrilineal, patrilocal, rural subsistence agricultural ecologies as defined by Kandiyoti (1988) and Quinn (this volume). The ways in which women resolve value conflicts amid sociocultural change are a potentially fruitful area for discovery. In revisiting my interview data, I found that women accommodate existing familistic values to varying degrees in their self-schema as they adapt to urbanization, professional work, and formal education. In the process, new patriarchal bargains are forged. For example, the high school girls I interviewed expanded familistic values to incorporate new education roles outside the home into their self-schema. In order to gain the freedom to pursue these roles, daughters assumed responsibility for controlling their sexuality in the service of family honor, thus engaging in a new kind of patriarchal bargain with their parents.

Sociocultural Change and Gender in Chiapas

The theoretical model I use to study intergenerational perspectives on gender roles and relations in Chiapas is Greenfield's (2009) theory of social change and human development. According to Greenfield, when a community shifts from a small-scale, rural subsistence farming economy based on kinship networks to a large-scale, urban, and high-tech market economy with greater elaboration of personalized social networks and attenuation of kinship networks, pathways of development veer away from socialization that promotes family interdependence and toward socialization that encourages greater individual independence. Greenfield uses German sociologist Ferdinand Tönnies's ([1887] 1957) terms, *gemeinschaft* (community) and *gesellschaft* (society), to describe sociocultural change as a spectrum between these two anchors of contrasting sociological prototypes. The theory grew out of Greenfield's (2004) longitudinal research demonstrating greater physical separation and independence in trial-and-error learning in weaving apprenticeships as families in the Maya hamlet of Zinacantán became increasingly involved in commerce from the 1970s to the 1990s. Greenfield's theory plus survey studies (Inglehart and Norris 2003) show associations between economic development, individualistic values, and gender egalitarianism in a variety of nations. This work laid the foundation for the main premise of my own research in Chiapas: when women migrate to urban centers and become involved in commerce and formal schooling, they are drawn to individualistic values prioritizing personal choice, individual rights, and equal opportunities for women and men. Although Greenfield's theory is useful for understanding shifts that occur under particular sociodemographic conditions, it lacks a framework for exploring the continuity of values across generations, which also seems to occur even under conditions of sociocultural change, such as those happening in Chiapas. One way to study continuity in values is to examine women's lives across generations, as I do in this chapter.

Since the 1970s–1980s, the subsistence agricultural way of life in Chiapas has been in rapid decline largely because of Mexico's neoliberal economic policies (Rus 2009). As a result, indigenous Maya families have moved into wage labor and commerce in Mexico's market economy, and some are migrating to urban centers, such as San Cristóbal and Tuxtla Gutiérrez, creating shantytowns at the peripheries. Men are traveling farther away from home to pursue commercial and wage-earning endeavors in Mexican cities and across the border. Women are spending more time outside the domestic sphere, participating in commerce and transforming woven textiles, which traditionally clothed the family, into artisanal products to sell to tourists. With a cash economy has come television and movies, which transmit Western values.

Political and educational institutions are also effecting change. The Mexican government has expanded the number of middle schools and high schools in rural areas, which bring mestizo teachers, language, curricula, and norms to indigenous communities. Mexican schooling prepares youth for participation in a market economy and implicitly assumes that girls and boys are equivalent learners, practices that contradict apprenticeship styles of learning with same-gender models in subsistence agricultural roles. Enrollment in middle and high schools has increased, especially since the early 2000s. This is due in part to a national program called Oportunidades, which began in 1998 to give stipends to rural women when their children continue their secondary education. The Mexican government established the Intercultural University in the city of San Cristóbal in 2005 to provide indigenous youth with pathways to adult work roles in a market economy. In addition, the Zapatista movement in Chiapas has attracted NGOs, religious groups, political activists, and feminist scholars from around the world, which come bearing gender-egalitarian ideologies along with desires to help (Marcos 2005).

I am one of those feminist scholars who went to Chiapas bearing the proverbial gifts of gender-egalitarian ideologies in my Trojan horse. I use this admittedly strained metaphor of a beguiling but problematic gift to highlight the value conflicts that come with a gemeinschaft-to-gesellschaft shift. Certainly, I see many of these sociocultural changes, such as women having more opportunities to earn their own money and advocate for themselves, as progress. However, I also see loss in the deterioration of interdependent familistic values. My background is not Greek, but Italian; my parents were raised in a rural village in southern Italy, completed only a few years of elementary school, and migrated to New England together after marriage. My personal experiences negotiating intergenerational value conflicts have sensitized me to tensions between individualistic and familistic value orientations. In my own gender identity development, I came to prioritize personal achievement, exploration, independence, and career over marriage, children, stability, and close family ties.

Cognitive developmental psychologists, such as Susan Harter (2012), consider gender identity as a content area within the self-concept, which consists of self-schemas, defined as descriptive and evaluative beliefs about the self. Schemas are higher-order mental structures sometimes, but not always, organized around metaphors, stereotypes, and standardized sets of beliefs, and they are composed of networks of associations that organize information in memory and that function as interpretive frameworks for processing the vast complexities of social life. Schemas are also imbued with constellations of value assumptions about idealized standards of human conduct. What we see as important and desirable influences how we evaluate our actions and ourselves. Cognitive anthropologists (e.g., Strauss and Quinn 1997) have adopted the concept of a schema from psychology in order to theorize about cultural schemas, which represent the internalization and generation of cultural understandings from salient dimensions of shared social practices.

According to Harter (2012), the self works as a coherence creator, making meaning of past experiences and setting intentions for the future in order to maintain consistency between the self-concept and cognitions about behaviors. Inconsistencies create negative emotions that the self seeks to resolve in some way. The notion of the negative drive state, which occurs when cognitions about behaviors contradict self-schemas, derives from cognitive dissonance theorists (e.g., Aronson 1968). These theorists argue that individuals use one of two processes to reduce this negative drive state. They either engage in a compromise by making minor adjustments to address the current situation, or they engage in the more costly cognitive work of altering their self-schemas to incorporate new knowledge and values. Claudia Strauss (in Strauss and Quinn 1997) elaborates on the compromises people make when they internalize, but do not integrate, inconsistent beliefs. Beliefs may exist in the form of separate but dynamically interacting schemas that cause unconscious and unresolved emotional conflict, or they may be compartmentalized as separate, disconnected schemas in the neural network. Harter (2012) argues that in the transition from childhood to adulthood, work and social roles multiply, increasing the potential for inconsistencies between behaviors and self-schemas. Persistent contradictions lead to increased radical alterations in the self-concept.

The middle-aged professional Maya women I interviewed in my first research project experienced a tremendous amount of conflict in their transition to adulthood. The four women provided audio-recorded accounts of their lives, which included migration to the city of San Cristóbal, family abandonment, and eventual work as actresses in an all-female theater troupe called Fortaleza de la Mujer Maya (FOMMA; Manago and Greenfield 2011). This organization is supported by Western feminist scholars and activists who seek to empower indigenous women and families through the arts, literacy programs, and workshops that encourage women's commercial enterprises. A common theme in the FOMMA women's narratives was that they all had to support themselves financially in the city after various forms of loss in their family support systems due to domestic violence, divorce, family abandonment, or the death of a husband. They described their experiences in moving to urban settings, learning how to write and perform their own plays, and making their own money as salient challenges that made them more autonomous, self-reliant, self-confident, and then, eventually, outspoken about the maltreatment of women. Moreover, the FOMMA organization provided an ongoing source of belonging and social identity, which likely facilitated the women's identification with individualistic Western discourses and gender-egalitarian world views.

It would be overly simplistic to describe the FOMMA women's identity development during times of conflict as a process of substituting familistic values for individualistic ones. Instead, familistic values, presumably learned in childhood, were reformulated to emphasize gender equality. The FOMMA women accommodated familistic values within their self-schemas so that their self-concepts as mothers became consistent with gender egalitarianism. In the following quote, Petrona de la Cruz Cruz invokes the revered role of the mother in the family but does so in order to stress the importance of equivalent gender roles and female-male relationships based on companionship rather than family duty: "We can't achieve equality out[side] of our homes, because respect, equity, the ideal man, the ideal woman are formed at home.... I tell my son ... you need to learn how to cook ... and to wash your clothes ... because the day you get your wife she won't be your maid, she will be a mate for you.... That's why it is said that mothers are the source of education, of their homes and of love" (Manago and Greenfield 2011, 11).

These women did not jettison familistic values but, rather, reformulated commitments to family gender roles to make them compatible with gender equality. In the face of conflict, they engaged in the cognitively arduous work of altering self-schemas to integrate new values. The women reconciled contradictory forces in their lives and found new meaning and purpose in the value of mutual love and respect between women and men rather than hierarchical ascribed gender roles.

Yet at the time of my interviews, the FOMMA women did not identify as feminists. There was likely a variety of reasons for the hesitation. *Feminista* in Spanish has a ring to it reminiscent of *machista*, a word associated with hypermasculinity, aggression, and domination of women. *Feminista* may connote a feminine version of machista: women's domination over men. Indeed, the term *feminist* has a negative connotation in many different social contexts, including in the United States, where social psychologists find that the word triggers feelings of threat (Fiske, Cuddy, and Glick 2007). Perhaps identification as a feminist involves greater orientation to the West or requires a stronger rejection of familistic values, which are perceived as inimical to equality feminism. According to Deniz Kandiyoti (1988), women oppose feminism because they are unwilling to give up the stability and social security of family. This seems to have been the case with the women I discuss next.

The Patriarchal Bargain

Kandiyoti (1988) argues that a central mechanism in the perpetuation of classic patriarchy is women's compliance with their subjugation through a patriarchal bargain. Classic patriarchy is a particular form of gender hierarchy that appears in patrilineal and patrilocal social structures in rural subsistence agricultural ecologies of North Africa, the Middle East, and South and East Asia, a list to which Quinn (this volume) adds preindustrial Europe, the United States, and other colonized areas. Classic patriarchy includes bride-price or dowry systems in which women do not have rights to land or resources outside their relationships with men. Both Kandiyoti and Quinn argue that an important aspect of classic patriarchy is a particular form of female collusion in which women support the legitimacy of men's authority in exchange for stability and security. Kandiyoti further suggests that women internalize the rightness of their subjugation during adolescence and young adulthood because they are promised respect and authority later in life through their reproductive capacity: when they have sons, they will have power over new wives entering the household.

Women may be so invested in this system that they will seek to maintain classic patriarchy even as it is unraveling (Kandiyoti 1988). When agricultural forms of living erode, one of the first things to happen is that young men become less dependent on property inheritance, which means that they are no longer subject to elder males' authority. Thus, men's incentives to stay close to and support the family weaken before women's do. The disintegration of a patriarchal system that has maintained men's obligation to family represents a loss of economic security and emotional stability for women, who become worse off when men's power and control are no longer tempered by their commitment to family well-being. Kandiyoti (1988, 284) writes that this loss is crystallized in the conservative antifeminist backlash: "The familism of the antifeminist movement could therefore be interpreted as an attempt to reinstate an older patriarchal bargain, with feminists providing a convenient scapegoat on whom to blame current disaffection and alienation among men."

Indigenous women in Chiapas may resist equality feminism as a solution to conflicts in a disintegrating classic patriarchy when they are unable to accommodate prior familistic values in their new self-concepts. The new equality does not register intellectually with the interdependent familistic value frameworks through which previous generations raised them to interpret the world. Indigenous studies scholar Sylvia Marcos (2005, 87) asserts that "there is nowhere a concept of equality" in the gender ideology rooted in a precolonial Maya cosmovision. In this cosmology, gender role equivalency is incompatible with reverence for the yin-yang harmonious duality found in nature and, accordingly, the interdependent complementarity of female and male. From this world view, personal needs do not exist separate from the collective because, as Marcos (2005, 93) writes, "the intersubjective nature of men and women is interconnected with the earth, sky, plants, and planets." For this reason, Western feminists and indigenous feminists are doomed to miscommunicate, the former valuing equality defined in terms of the rights of equivalent, independent individuals negotiating relationships based on personal choice, the latter valuing a unity of opposites who are interdependent with everything in nature, such that personal needs are subsumed within the collective's well-being. In contrast to Western feminists, who fight for *igualdad*, indigenous feminists in Mexico fight for *paridad* (a closer approximation to notions of unity and balance).

The maintenance of a cosmovision of interdependent unity is apparent in the autobiography of a middle-aged indigenous woman called Antonia (a pseudonym), who lives about a 45-minute drive into the rural highlands north of San Cristóbal in the municipality of San Pedro Chenalhó (Eber and "Antonia" 2011). Antonia's autobiography begins with how she was raised in the 1960s and 1970s to be a *batz'i antz* (true woman), who prepares food from the corn that men provide, who respects the authority of her father and husband, and who stays close to home to take care of children and manage domestic chores. Although her husband no longer cultivates corn and Antonia now earns money for the family, she continues to shoulder the responsibility for housework and childcare, circumstances similar to those documented by Arlie Hochschild and Anne Machury (1989) in the United States. Antonia refers to values for an interdependent gender division of labor to define herself and her family relationships.

Importantly, she did not experience family trauma and loss in an urban environment, as the FOMMA women did, but continues to live with her husband and children in the rural highlands.

Nevertheless, societal changes in her rural community have strained Antonia's ongoing commitment to complementary and interdependent gender roles. Her municipality, Chenalhó, became an EZLN (Ejército Zapatista de Liberación Nacional) stronghold after the 1994 uprising in San Cristóbal, and women's rights are central to the EZLN agenda, which includes both Western and indigenous ideological influences. The Zapatistas' Women's Revolutionary Law includes women's right to take leadership roles in the community, to work and earn a fair salary, to go to school, and to be free from obligation to enter into marriage. Antonia began to participate in the Zapatista movement as an adult woman through her membership in the Word of God Church, a progressive branch of Catholicism associated with liberation theology. She also has taken on leadership roles in women's weaving cooperatives. Given her experiences, Antonia articulates an indigenous feminism that includes participation in the public sphere, an amendment that shapes the arc of her ideology in the direction of individual rights and equivalent gender roles: "It is necessary for a man to respect his wife, and also for a wife to respect her husband. They must be equal. A man must not mistreat a woman. He must not beat her. Not only men should have the right to leave the house. Women should have this right too, in order to do good things. We have the same blood, men and women" (Eber and "Antonia" 2011, 35).

Whereas Petrona accommodated familistic values in order to integrate new professional roles and gender equality with motherhood, Antonia's autobiography reveals ongoing conflict. She laments how her leadership roles outside the family took her away from her children. She also says that her outspoken nature strained her ability to fulfill batz'i antz ideals of deference to the collective's harmony and well-being. Deference to a collective authority structure is an important value principle in the Zapatista movement, encapsulated in the phrase *mandar obedeciendo* (in leading, we obey), adopted from the Tojolabal Maya (Marcos 2005). Even members at the top of the hierarchy obey the will of the collective because personal and collective goals should coincide. Antonia's endorsement of equivalent gender roles conflicts with her assumption that obedience to the collective through adherence to ascribed gender roles is the glue in a cohesive family. In contrast, Petrona resolved this conflict by redefining family relationships in terms of personal desires for companionship, rather than obedience to ascribed roles. Although Antonia endorses female leadership and work outside the home, she has not radically altered deeper cultural values that stress obedience, which constitute her conceptualization of human relationships and her purpose in life. Rather than redefining, reintegrating, and resolving, Antonia compartmentalizes the contradictions, such that one set of self-schemas is activated at home and another set is activated in her public leadership roles. Yet her autobiography also suggests that the contrasting self-schemas are linked in her self-concept, causing unresolved emotional turmoil.

Societal changes that influence normative transitions into adult roles could stimulate more widespread accommodation of different values in self-schemas. Thus, the introduction of secondary schooling during adolescence and young adulthood is significant. First-generation high school and college students may be working through value tensions between home and school contexts during identity development. In their quest for reconciliation between the two self-schemas, they renegotiate the classic patriarchal bargain with their parents.

Renegotiating the Patriarchal Bargain

When I interviewed twelve first-generation college students in the city of San Cristóbal, I asked them about differences between their generation and their parents' generation and about differences between life in the village and in the city (Manago 2012). I wrote a case study of Susana, who was the first person in her community to attend college (she commuted daily from her village to the city). She describes how postponing marriage and children for schooling led her to value a life based on personal fulfillment and choice:

> [I: Why don't you want to get married now?] Because I want to study, I want other experiences, I don't know exactly. I'm free to go out at any time, to wake up at any time, late, early, I don't have a schedule, that is, I get phone calls, let's go, and well, there's nobody to ask permission to go out, just my parents, [I say] "I'm going out." [They ask] "What are you going to do?" [I say] "I'm going out, I'll be back later." And so, I see it with my [married] sisters, my aunts. . . . you have to prepare the food, if you don't have a gas heater, you have to heat the water, and washing and ironing, oh, when I want to iron, I iron, and when I don't I just put on my

clothes and go out, that is, I have this freedom to do what I want. (Manago 2012, 695)

In this quote, Susana talks about her personal independence and family obligation in apparently contradictory ways ("there's nobody to ask permission to go out, just my parents"), suggesting that she is in the process of working through conflicts between personal choice and family obedience. At other points in her narrative, she combines independence and family obligation in a more logically consistent manner: she says that she works hard in school so that she can eventually help her family with money. In this case, Susana reinscribes family obligations into new work roles outside the family, roles that at the same time afford her greater freedom and personal choice. She is redefining the meaning of being a dutiful daughter to make it consistent with her personal choice. Although Susana is similar to Petrona in that she accommodates familistic values in her self-schema, Susana does not fully challenge the underlying premise of obedience to the family. Rather, she participates in a new kind of patriarchal bargain in which obedience is maintained but in a different mode. In the following quote, Susana describes a kind of patriarchal bargain in which her father gives her greater freedom to pursue her educational goals in exchange for her agreement to control her sexuality in service of family honor:

I didn't destroy my right, what my dad gave me, that is, it's something of my dad's legacy. . . . He gave me that freedom, and then they ask my dad, "Is your daughter still studying? Yes, but how does she do it?" "I don't know, ask her; me, I don't know, I just give them the freedom." "Oh, but you don't get mad at your daughter?" [My dad says] "Why would I get mad at her when she does her duties too, when she obeys me?" [They say] "Yes, because your daughter thinks about things very well, not like the other girls, the other girls will get married, they go to secondary school, they go to high school and get . . ." The parents' shame is that girls get pregnant, that is why there are not many girls studying, because most of them get pregnant in the schools. (Manago 2012, 698)

Susana's commentary is reminiscent of Khurshid's (this volume) description of the way in which Pakistani *parhi likhi* (educated) women distinguish themselves from and justify their increased power over uneducated women, who are thought to lack self-discipline. Parhi likhi women participate in the perpetuation of new forms of hierarchy based on education, never challenging a key assumption about family control over female sexuality. Similarly, Susana constructs herself as remarkable in her ability to be both free and dutiful, thus distinguishing herself from other girls, who become pregnant in schools. She achieves freedom by obeying her father's call for her to take more personal responsibility to restrain her sexuality. As a result, she perpetuates the cultural notion that women's sexuality *should* be constrained to serve the collective's goals: procreation and family reputation.

In Chiapas, some indigenous families are loath to send their adolescent daughters to secondary school because norms that allow casual, mixed-sex social interactions in school jeopardize family control over marriage and sexuality. Antonia's eldest daughter was 14 years old when she began a relationship with a boy in middle school, which seemed to lead to a tacit agreement to marriage outside of proper family consultation and customs. The situation was tremendously upsetting to Antonia, who was consequently torn about whether to allow a second daughter to continue schooling. She feared her second daughter would also have difficulty avoiding unsafe and inappropriate relationships, even though she recognized schooling as a route to greater financial wealth and family security.

I heard many concerns about the dangers of mixed-sex relationships in 2009 when I interviewed eighteen grandmothers, mothers, and adolescent daughters attending the high school in Zinacantán Center, which had been inaugurated ten years earlier. Their interviews once again demonstrate the persistence of cultural values for family control over women's sexuality through girls' assumption of personal responsibility for sexual self-regulation.

Intergenerational Conceptions of Gender Roles and Relations in Zinacantán

Zinacantán is a Tzotzil-speaking, largely Catholic, and non-Zapatista-affiliated community about a 25-minute taxi ride west of San Cristóbal. Grandmothers in my interviews grew up in the 1950s and 1960s when the municipality was primarily a peasant farming economy and mixed-sex relations in adolescence were regulated through gender segregation and formalized marriage rituals. Anthropologists who conducted ethnographies in Zinacantán at this time (e.g., Vogt 1969) described mountain hamlets of patrilineal and patrilocal extended family compounds sharing a single source of maize. At about 17 or 18 years old, a young man would begin to look for a wife with the sponsorship and advice of his father and a group of "askers," respected elder men in the community. Yearlong ritualized visits, gift giving, and manual labor for the new bride's family ensued; finally, the young woman would move into the home of her husband's family. There, she would obey older women in the household and fulfill the important role of providing tortillas to her husband. Men represented the family in the cargos, a series of village-wide positions of prestige in which men move up the local hierarchy with age and financial contributions to religious festivals.

Mothers in my interviews grew up in the 1970s and 1980s, a time when more families moved into Zinacantán Center, formerly the spiritual center, now a populated commercial hub with paved roads, shops, a Mexican high school, and frequent taxi service to San Cristóbal. During this time, wage work encouraged some young men to bypass the traditional bride service, and elopements increased (Flood 1994). Many of the mothers in my sample said they had "escaped" with their husbands; their husbands did not submit to the formal marriage proposal process. Men in Zinacantán have become particularly successful in developing greenhouse floriculture businesses, growing and transporting flowers to nearby cities. Zinacantán's close proximity to San Cristóbal makes it popular with tourists interested in women's woven textiles, which are sold in the center of town and out of families' homes. Weaving is a viable way for women to earn their own money while maintaining traditional feminine ideals. The church, elaborately decorated with locally grown flowers, and religious festivals, such as the running of the horses, are also spectacles for tourists. We might say that the local culture has become commodified in Zinacantán. Indeed, tourism helps to preserve Zinacantán's traditions.

Daughters in my interviews were the first generation to attend the new high school in the community. Thus, they were also the first generation to postpone marriage for schooling and to engage in casual cross-sex interactions during adolescence. As a volunteer in the high school, I observed girls and boys interacting in class, outside of class for group homework projects, and during breaks and social gatherings, such as school-sponsored dances and parades. I also observed them walking home from school, sometimes in mixed-sex groups of friends. (School starts after lunch and concludes at 8:00 p.m., so they walk home at night.) The teachers told me that a few parents were upset about romantic pairings in the school, and there was gossip about a student getting pregnant in one of the greenhouses.

The interviews I conducted included a series of eight vignettes that I developed from my ethnography. The vignettes functioned similarly to gossip and served as prompts for grandmothers, mothers, and daughters to talk about gender roles and relations. For example, in the vignette *Who Makes the Tortillas?* a woman named Maria wants to work for her sister-in-law in San Cristóbal, but her husband will not allow it because she would be abandoning her ascribed role of serving him fresh tortillas in the morning. The majority of both mothers and grandmothers endorsed this ascribed gender role, siding with the husband simply because it is women's job to make the tortillas, and ultimately, *el hombre manda* (the man commands). In contrast, two-thirds of the adolescent girls, like Gabriela (all interviewee names are pseudonyms), sided with Maria, stating that working women can increase the family's resources and well-being: "It is good what the woman says because she can look for work. . . . It is better that they help between them. . . . The husband shouldn't worry, nothing is going to happen, she is only going to work."

Adolescent girls in Zinacantán, like Susana, are resolving conflicts in their identity development by expanding family obligations to include new kinds of work roles for women. Only two girls went a step further to challenge the notion of family obedience by objecting to the husband impeding the wife's will. This is the more extreme example: "I think it is bad when men prohibit women from doing what they want, like prisoners or slaves. Already we pay attention to the man [*ya le hacemos caso al hombre*] but not like this. If the woman wants to leave to work and help the family with money, the man should respect that. . . . The woman is right because she wants to help her husband" (Emma, adolescent).

Most adolescent girls endorsed equivalent gender roles without making arguments about women's personal autonomy and rights, perhaps because that stance conflicts too strongly with the notions of family obligation they were raised with. Instead, most took the less cognitively and socially costly route, supporting equivalent gender role activities within traditional interpretive frameworks, arguing that Maria's behavior was ultimately in service of her family's well-being and therefore justified.

The vignette *Grandmother Walks Behind* provoked expressions of a more radical revision of the obedience value among adolescents. The story is about a young male university student who goes home to his village, where his grandmother insists on walking behind him on the way to the store, according to traditional customs. He disagrees and says that women and men are equal, so they should walk side by side. For many of the grandmothers I interviewed, this vignette evoked memories of adherence to norms as a practical matter in daily life: "Who knows if it is good or bad, but before we didn't do this. That's why we always say, it doesn't seem good walking together. That's why I sometimes say, 'we are blocking the road,' that's what the elders used to say. If we walk side by side, other people can't pass by" (Guadalupe, grandmother). Mothers acknowledged changes in the custom but did not voice negative reactions to physical instantiations of gender hierarchy, for example: "The way I see it, both are fine, men first and women behind, or men behind, it almost seems the same to me" (Manago 2014, 879).

The high school girls were more likely than their mothers and grandmothers to vehemently oppose overt displays of hierarchical relations between women and men and emphasize emotional bonds. They said walking side by side was the correct point of view because it is more conducive for talking and shows greater kindness to the grandmother. Adolescents prioritized intimate psychological connections in social relationships and referred to internal emotional characteristics, such as compassion. A few adolescents, like Carola, reacted particularly negatively to suggestions of men's superiority over women: "We have now lost that custom, now we walk together. It is humiliating when the man walks ahead and we behind. I like how it is now, we go together. Before, even if they were recently married, they wouldn't walk together, making it seem like they don't love each other."

Differing responses across generations suggest that women's commitment to the family through outward displays of deference are giving way to new cultural sensibilities in which the next generation of educated women locate their family commitment through internal attributions. Commitment in the past was physically manifested in the ways women walked behind men and adhered to ascribed duties, such as tortilla making. Adolescent girls, similar to Petrona at FOMMA, seem to be moving toward a focus on internal emotions, such as love and companionship, as explanations for family closeness. This kind of accommodation to familistic values may be a useful way to resolve conflicts during changes in gender roles.

An intergenerational shift in the emphasis on internal feelings is also apparent in the responses to a vignette called *Novios*. In this story, two high school students want to break off their intention to be married, which is upsetting to the parents, who say the couple should keep their promise. Again, adolescents tended to respond to the vignette by emphasizing the emotions of the youth in the story. Here is one typical example: "What the parents are saying is bad. We know our feelings, not other people. They shouldn't order us to do something we know isn't right" (Irene, adolescent).

In contrast, grandmothers, such as Maruch, emphasized obedience to elders and traditional customs for partnering: "[It's] better [to do] what her mom says. [It] is possible that her daughter would not be able to find a husband, but if she behaves well, she will find a husband. Sometimes, when girls stay single, bad comments start to arise.... What can be done, if the girl has been already asked for marriage? There's no other way, there's no other way if he already asked for her hand in marriage and her parents gave permission. It is better that way." The grandmother's statements "if she behaves well, she will find a husband" and "when girls stay single, bad comments start to arise" allude to assumptions that women are vulnerable to community gossip and doubts about their virtuousness when their sexuality has not been appropriately contained in terms of familial relationships. Community gossip continues to shape girls' experience of gender relations, even as romantic love gains prominence over family obedience in marriage partnerships.

The mothers I interviewed departed from the grandmothers' views in that many prioritized the love between the couple. The following quote represents one mother's reasoning that emotions should be prioritized over strict adherence to formal rules: "For me sometimes this is okay since they have gotten to know each other. It can be that they do not like each other, and it is better to know other people.... If they are forced to get married without love, at the end that can be a problem" (Eliza). Mothers' emphasis on romantic love as an important component of a healthy marriage is consistent with Merielle Flood's (1994) assessment that love pairings increased in Zinacantán in the 1980s, when men began to engage in wage labor (and when the mothers in my sample were first partnering with their husbands).

In the *Just Friends* vignette, a girl and a boy socialize in school and walk home together but say they are just friends. Grandmothers sometimes objected to their socializing but were likely to add that their views were no longer relevant to contemporary circumstances, since women had become more mobile and competent in public spheres. Here is one example of a grandmother making such a proviso: "Even if we forbid them to talk to boys, we won't know, we won't see it.... It is because they want to be intelligent, they want to know other places, they want to work. Before, we didn't have anything because we were ignorant, we didn't know anything, we didn't know where to go" (Edith).

This grandmother's quote underscores how mixed-sex relationships in the high school extend beyond the realm of household or village elders' authority. Indeed, some mothers commented that they had to adjust their parenting style because family surveillance and physical separation between the sexes, like when they were growing up, are no longer feasible. For example: "I think it is fine. Even if you scold them 'why did you talk to that boy?' what are you going to do if they are already accustomed to it? You can't scold them, we can't say anything because they are accustomed to it now. Now it is a decision [for] each of them, the only thing is that they need to know how to take care of themselves" (Pascuala, mother).

As this mother points out, with the introduction of secondary schooling, more of the burden for managing safe mixed-sex relations has been placed on adolescent girls themselves. Girls embrace their personal responsibility for sexual gatekeeping because it gives them access to public institutions. The adolescents I interviewed reported that they managed this responsibility by limiting their interactions with boys to schoolwork. That is, the majority of the girls responded to this vignette by stating that it was acceptable for girls and boys to discuss homework but that they should not walk home together after school. Schoolwork marked the boundary of the contexts in which mixed-sex interactions should take place: "My parents have realized that they barely have education and that now we need to do homework with boys, because we are integrated, and my parents know that's how things work. They give me permission as long as I am only doing my homework" (Rosa, adolescent).

Through their adherence to a scholastic work ethic, adolescent girls, like the college student Susana, renegotiate the patriarchal bargain rather than resist family jurisdiction over their sexuality. Attention to schoolwork demonstrates to their community and to themselves that they are virtuous and in harmony with familistic values even as they are pursuing more freedom in public institutions. There, surveillance over female sexuality persists in the form of community gossip: "I don't like when people gossip that girls only go to school to find a boyfriend [*novio*]. Well, there are some girls that go to school just to find a boyfriend, but not all. Some really do want to study, if they want something they go after it. You can tell who wants to move forward in life. They apply this to everyone, but it is not all of us" (Margarita, adolescent).

Rosa's and Margarita's comments suggest that an academic work ethic is a culturally recognizable way of demonstrating that they are not involved in independently negotiated romantic relationships with boys. Ironically, adolescents' emphasis on internal attributions for behaviors sets them up to thoroughly internalize the assumption of family control over female sexuality into their self-schemas as sexual gatekeepers. Margarita attributes her virtuous behavior not to family obedience, but to internal motivations and ambitions to pursue professional goals, thereby reconciling familistic values with personal choice and freedom. She supports the value of equivalent gender roles and simultaneously upholds her side of the patriarchal bargain to maintain family honor through sexual restraint. When she distinguishes herself from girls who "go to school just to find a boyfriend" and those who do not want to "move forward in life," she is reinforcing the assumption that it is undesirable for women to pursue sexual relationships outside the confines of family control, but she places the focus on women's internal desires to get ahead in a market economy. In this way, family control over female sexuality is one of the "sticky" aspects of patriarchy (see Quinn, this volume).

Perhaps the most overt demonstration of continued family control over female, but not male, sexuality in the public sphere is in the clothing practices in Zinacantán. The boys wear Mexican contemporary dress—jeans and stylish shirts—whereas the girls maintain the traditional clothing customs, wearing the very modest *traje*, which is woven and embroidered by women in Zinacantán. The traje, which includes a long skirt covering the ankles, a loose blouse, and a huipil (shawl), immediately identifies the social and ethnic identity of the girls as Zinacantec and marks their bodies as constrained by traditional Zinacantec values for female virtue through chastity. (I noticed when trying on the outfit how it restricts free body movement.) Moreover, the contemporary trajes are far more colorful and elaborately embroidered than they were in the past (see Greenfield 2004), perhaps exemplifying a particularly creative "intensification of [a] traditional modesty marker" (Kandiyoti 1988, 283). Khurshid (this volume) also describes how educated Pakistani women maintain modest clothing in order to preserve family connections and influence, thereby perpetuating female chastity values. In wearing the traje and emphasizing their personal desires with regard to family obligation and the maintenance of family honor, adolescent girls in Zinacantán reconcile contradictions in gender role activities while maintaining connections to their families and familistic values.

Why Is Control over Women's Sexuality So Sticky?

The persistence of family control over women's sexuality may be understood by looking more deeply at the process of renegotiating the patriarchal bargain. When the college student Susana and the Zinacantec high school girls assumed increased responsibility for family honor through demonstrations of purity via a scholastic work ethic, they also began to attribute their adherence to family duties to internal motivations, and in the process they deeply integrated sexual gatekeeping into their gendered self-concepts. Sexual gatekeeping is a cornerstone of the sexual double standard schema, likely rooted in a classic patriarchy of subsistence agricultural communities.

Janna Kim and colleagues (2007) have extended Adrienne Rich's (1980) dimensions of compulsory heterosexuality to identify the sexual double standard in US media and in young people's descriptions of their sexual experiences. A central code comprising the sexual double standard is the notion that men are *inherently* sexual initiators and women *inherently* sexual gatekeepers. Men are entitled to act on their sexual needs because they are construed as biologically driven to sexual voraciousness; women are passive partners and are expected to limit the sexual advances of men because they are construed as less biologically driven by sex and more vulnerable to the consequences of sex. The cultural schema likely remains persuasive because it is rooted in facts (i.e., women get pregnant, men do not). I saw evidence that sexual gatekeeping is well established in Zinacantec high school girls' self-schemas. In the following quote, the adolescent Margarita describes mixed-sex relationships in terms of the need for girls to protect themselves from risk: "Now, men are very different. A lot of them are liars, they are only playing. I want to know him for a long time, and then after I will get married."

The shift from family obedience to sexual self-regulation provides conditions ripe for ongoing social constructions of the sexual double standard and the perpetuation of patriarchal gender relations. The sexual double standard schema is based on the premise that human sexual behavior is rooted in essential differences between women and men, an assumption Margarita also alludes to ("now, men are very different. A lot of them are liars"). Internal attributions for behavior shore up the sexual double standard, which is prominent not only in popular conceptions and in commercial media in the United States, but also in some widely disseminated Western scientific theory (e.g., Buss and Schmitt 1993). With cultural shifts to personal responsibility and internal attributions for behavior, gender essentialism can become even more entrenched as an insidious way that patriarchal values for family control over female sexuality remain compelling.

Essentialist assumptions that promote beliefs of innate sexual differences that are fixed and inevitable hinder new renderings of human sexuality that acknowledge women's pleasure and personal control over their own bodies. Future work should consider how young women in a variety of cultural contexts resolve cognitive conflicts and social stigma surrounding female sexuality in order to illuminate both change and continuity in the ways that patriarchy perpetuates itself under a new guise of girls' gendered self-concepts.

CHAPTER SIX

Contested Terrains of Female Education in Rural Muslim Pakistan

AYESHA KHURSHID

Girl Rising (Robbins 2013), a documentary film about girls' education in developing nations, is a narrative of empowerment through education that inspires resistance to oppressive patriarchal traditions. The film, narrated by Hollywood celebrities, focuses on the changing fates of nine girls from diverse countries and captures how these girls are overcoming poverty, bonded labor, sexual abuse, early marriage, and patriarchal customs through education. Particularly moving is the story of Amina, a child bride from Afghanistan, who persisted in her determination to attend school despite early marriage, childbearing, and cultural restrictions on women's movements and opportunities for education. In the final segment, she is shown leading a group of young girls to school in the rural countryside of Afghanistan. They shed their burqas (garments that fully cover women, including face and hands) to reveal their smiling faces as Amina declares, "Look into my eyes. Do you see it now? I am change." There are no men or boys in sight as more and more girls appear on the dirt roads and hills of Amina's village. Amina's determination is depicted as a wind of change that reaches every woman, inspiring them all to follow her lead. *Girl Rising* presents education as the way to empower women against traditions that have oppressed them and as a means of challenging the patriarchal institutions of family, community, and local culture.

Girl Rising's strong imagery of women's education as an empowering tool that unites women in their struggles against patriarchal norms echoes mainstream discourse on women's education, especially for Muslim countries (Gee 2014; Monkman 2011; Stromquist and Fischman 2009). In this discourse, empowerment is assumed to result when women distance themselves from their families, communities, and Islam, the patriarchal institutions seen to confine and restrict their access to new roles and opportunities (Abu-Lughod 2009; Kandiyoti 2005; Mahmood 2005; Najmabadi 1998; Scott 2007). This education-as-empowerment narrative operates on two central assumptions: first, it presents women's education as a universally empowering tool and process (Herz and Sperling 2004; Schultz 2002; Tembon and Fort 2008); and second, it hypothesizes a sisterhood among all women who share the experience of being oppressed, especially in Muslim societies (Abu-Lughod 2009; Mahmood 2005). In this view, educated Muslim women are to become agents of change who will work to empower *all* women by challenging patriarchal norms. This individualistic and market-oriented approach to women's education and gender empowerment undergirds the programming of many international agencies and has been incorporated into state educational policies.

In this chapter, I show that these assumptions about women's empowerment are never adopted wholesale; rather, they are remade and adapted to local cultural contexts and the complexity of women's lived experiences (Khurshid 2015; Merry 2006; Subrahmanian 2005; Unterhalter 2007). I draw on ethnographic data collected with thirty-two women teachers working at four girls' schools in the suburbs of Islamabad, Pakistan. The majority of these teachers were the first girls in their low-income and rural communities to attend high school and college and to hold jobs outside the home. My ethnographic analysis reveals that the participants view themselves as confident and empowered women who are capable of taking on new roles and responsibilities without disrupting the core values of their families and communities. The participants view their ability to negotiate new roles while maintaining the harmony in their families and communities as a trait of *parhi likhi*, an Urdu term for educated women. The women teachers employ the term *parhi likhi* not merely to refer to their educational qualifications. Instead, this self-description indicates the acquisition of a set of manners and behaviors associated with educated women, a professional or middle-class status, and a distinction from uneducated women (*unparh*). In rural and low-income contexts with low literacy rates, being a parhi likhi woman thus includes the ability not only to take on new roles but also to align these roles with preexisting gender norms.

I explain this interplay between new and traditional roles first through showing how new educational opportunities for these parhi likhi women have led them to challenge certain patriarchal practices that limited their mobility and access to employment. My ethnographic analysis reveals that the participants do so by creatively combining the newer language of rights and choices with local conceptions of family honor and gendered domestic roles. In addition, I explore the reasons that education has not led these same women to challenge patriarchal practices within the family, including the idea that they should be primarily responsible for maintaining the household and that they should accept parentally arranged marriages.

This new form of patriarchal bargain (Kandiyoti 1988), similar to the one discussed in Adriana Manago's chapter (this volume) on Maya women, involves trading public participation for fidelity to traditional family roles for women. For the parhi likhi participants in my study, this patriarchal bargain constitutes a conditional access to participation in public life, which implies certain shifts in gender norms regarding women's education and employment, along with a simultaneous reproduction of domestic and sexual roles for women. My ethnographic analysis echoes the feminist scholarship (Chisamya et al. 2012; Subrahmanian 2005; Unterhalter 2007) that has problematized women's education and gender empowerment as universal notions through showing how the impact of women's education is shaped by preexisting social, political, and economic hierarchies.

Research Methodology

The data I am using here emerged from a larger case study of a women-centered, transnational development organization that I call the Institute for Education and Literacy (IEL).[1] The IEL has chapters in major cities across the United States (where it is headquartered), Canada, and the United Kingdom, with staff who are primarily female volunteers from the Pakistani diaspora. The IEL also has offices in Islamabad and other regions of Pakistan with a combined paid staff of 60–70 people, mostly women from urban, middle-class backgrounds who are generally education or development professionals. The organization manages more than 200 girls' schools with more than 16,000 students in low-income communities throughout Pakistan. It has recruited and trained more than 600 women from the same communities to work as teachers.

Initially, I conducted sixteen months of ethnographic research from 2008 to 2010, focusing on the experiences of IEL staff, teachers, and community members in Pakistan. I concentrated on interviewing teachers at four IEL girls' schools located in the suburbs of Islamabad, where I lived during my data collection process. This geographical access helped me ground participants' experiences in the particular economic, social, and cultural contexts of their villages.

While all of the schools are in the Punjab province, the communities differ greatly in terms of their caste, kinship, and even language structures.

I met the majority of the thirty-two participants during a training workshop held at IEL's Islamabad office in 2008. I approached the teachers at the end of the session to request their participation in the study, and everyone whom I contacted agreed. I believe that my positionality as a Pakistani Muslim woman with an urban, middle-class background and as a researcher based in the United States shaped my relationship with the participants. There were significant power differentials between the women I interviewed and myself based on educational, class, and rural-urban hierarchies, as well as on my association with the development organization that recruited, trained, and employed them. Although IEL staff introduced me to the teachers, the participants were not forced or even asked by the IEL staff to participate in the study. However, I believe that the local culture of hospitality, especially toward outsiders, played a large role in shaping how the participants welcomed me into their schools and their homes and their generosity in sharing their time and experiences with me.

With each participant, I conducted two and sometimes more semi-structured interviews, lasting 60–150 minutes per session. The interviews were in Urdu, the national language of Pakistan, and I then transcribed and translated the audio recordings into English. The open-ended questions focused on a broad range of topics, such as personal history, family relationships, the women's work as teachers, their perceptions of women's education, and the role of women in their community. I explored issues brought up by the participants in detail, especially during the second interview. Most interviews took place at their schools when they were not teaching, and some took place in their homes. I also took detailed notes during participant observation in classrooms and during formal and informal meetings with other teachers, IEL staff, parents, and community members.

I approached each interview transcript as an independent conversation focusing on participants' particular understandings of women's education and of their relationships with family and community. Emergent themes were coded during the first stage of analysis. Gender empowerment, one of the main themes from the first stage of analysis, was used to recode the data to examine how the participants define and enact these rights.

Contextual Background

The IEL is an international development organization that recruited and trained the women participants in my study to work as teachers at its schools serving different communities all over Pakistan. The organization views education as the key to empowering women and defines gender empowerment as an individualistic and market-oriented notion. Many of the participants learned the language of rights and choice from their own educational experiences, from media discourses, and from the international development discourse that shapes the IEL's teacher education and curriculum development policies. For example, the organization's leaders and staff envisioned the participatory nature of teacher training workshops as a way to motivate and encourage the teachers to form and voice their opinions in their families and communities. In teacher trainings and curriculum support materials, the organization emphasizes the notion and value of individual rights. The organization accommodates local cultural values, however, even when some of those values contradict the IEL's primary focus. The group's leaders and staff rely on the support of influential community elders, all of whom are male, to support the functioning and management of their schools. Farzana, the CEO and founder of the organization, expressed this philosophy explicitly: "We want to reach the full potential of our students and teachers. It is a gradual process, an incremental change, but we have to be patient. For example, our teachers have to unlearn so much before learning new things, such as speaking correct English, how to dress up, how to present themselves. But they are phenomenal women. You know, getting jobs is important . . . but it is also important [for women] to develop in other ways, to be able to give back to the family and the community."

The need to educate women so that they become useful members of their families and communities, as promoted by the IEL, reflects the public discourse about women's education in Pakistan. These views have been largely shaped by the nineteenth-century Islamic revivalist movement, which was led by urban, middle-class Islamic scholars of India.[2] That project focused on constructing a modern Muslim community in response to the British colonization of India. Muslim reformists presented science and Islam as two compatible paradigms that should inform Muslims' daily lives (Metcalf 1994; Minault 1998). This discourse popularized the idea of modern education for Muslim men and women as an Islamic duty. Although the movement was most influential for urban, educated, and middle-class Muslims, it produced the discourse that connects modern education for women to the revival of the Muslim community. These ideas remain central to the education discourse in Pakistan as the state mobilizes Islam, rather than notions of Western modernity, to promote girls' education.

The Muslim reformists argue that education trains women as good Muslims and as productive members of their families and communities by instilling wisdom, piety, and discipline in them. Unlike the unregulated and sexually promiscuous *unparh* women, *parhi likhi* women are seen as capable of taking on leadership roles in public domains without compromising the core values of their families and communities (Metcalf 1994; Minault 1998). This *parhi likhi* subjectivity is relational, and *parhi likhi* women enjoy certain privileges that are not available to *unparh* women. The *parhi likhi* subjectivity of the women participants in my study is grounded in the nexus of these two narratives of women's education and gender empowerment, which promote education through highlighting the *lack* in women who are not educated. Thus, when *parhi likhi* women from urban and middle-class backgrounds are allowed to enter into public spaces to receive education and to educate girls, *unparh* women are presented as unfit not only for public but also for domestic roles. In other words, *parhi likhi* women are positioned as the agents of reform who are ready to take on new roles while maintaining the gender order at home (Minault 1998).

This contextualization also explains how being *parhi likhi* became synonymous with being wise, pious, and a productive member of the family and community for the participants in my study (see Khurshid 2015). In their roles as teachers, *parhi likhi* women are valued for their service. Grounded in Islamic traditions that place high value on education, the communities view the work of teachers as the "work of prophets," and not only is their type of employment outside the home valued, but these women also gain a more privileged position inside the home in terms of participation in some family decision-making processes. All the female teachers who participated in my study came from rural Pakistan where they resided in patrilocal households. Kandiyoti (1988) describes the "belt of classic patriarchy," which includes Pakistan, as an area where the family forms and social systems derived from an agrarian base are characterized by male domination, a preference for sons, restrictive codes of behavior for women, and the association of family honor with female virtue. Mann (1986) elaborates that in these areas, power is held by male heads of household, and there is a clear separation between the public and private spheres of life. Moghadam (1992, 37) writes, "The patriarchal extended family gives the senior man authority over everyone else, including younger men, and entails forms of control and subordination of women which cut across cultural and religious boundaries." Men are entrusted with safeguarding family honor through their control over female family members. Such control includes restricting women's mobility in public spaces; monitoring their behaviors, mode of dress, and contacts with others; and arranging appropriate marriages for them.

Notions of family honor and the need to maintain the family's reputation resonated strongly with my respondents, many of whom willingly accepted arranged marriages and expressed strong desires to honor their fathers and families by behaving as proper Muslim women. The chapters in this volume by Susan Seymour and Jocelyn Marrow and the work of Suad Joseph (1993a) explicate many of the psychological processes involved in socializing children to live in hierarchical, extended families and how these shape particular forms of subjectivity in patriarchal systems. An issue that needs to be further explored is why exposure to education leads women to espouse a rights discourse and engage in behaviors that challenge restrictions on public mobility and employment but does not extend to questioning patriarchal authority within the family.

Education and Rights: Challenging Patriarchal Norms

Salma, a 28-year-old principal, shared how education had expanded her horizons by enabling her to have a paid job outside of the home: "What would my life have been like had I not been educated? Sitting at home, putting up with whatever was given to me. I work very hard, but at least my work is appreciated." Shama, a 30-year-old teacher, said that it was the experience of meeting new people and learning new things that made her feel confident and independent. The women in her village spent their days taking care of domestic chores but had to rely on the male members of their families for everything occurring outside the home. However, as a parhi likhi woman, Shama transformed some of these gender roles by having a paid job and doing things in the public sphere that had been open only to men. For example, she traveled to the city without being accompanied by a man to visit a doctor or for a shopping trip. She distinguished herself from the unparh women, who were neither allowed by their families nor felt confident to take on such roles.

Being educated enabled the women participants to speak up and thus reshape some of the traditional gender hierarchies that had excluded women from the labor market and from the public sphere. Salma explained, "Educated women become aware of their worth. You know why some people are against women's education? It is because educated women start raising their voice[s] . . . they start fighting for their rights. . . . That is alarming for many people."

Salma saw herself as a living example of how educated women speak up for their rights. She decided to take the teaching job against her husband's and in-laws' wishes. In this rural context, women primarily perform domestic chores and sometimes participate in agricultural activities. It is rare for a woman to take a paid job outside of the home. However, Salma refused to give in to the "unreasonable" demands made by her husband and in-laws. Education had made her aware that it was her duty to provide schooling to the girls in her village. Because of gender-segregation norms in this rural context, girls and boys were expected to be in single-sex educational facilities after elementary school, and there was no locally available school for girls. Those who wanted to continue their education had to walk long distances in mountainous and rural terrain in varying weather conditions to attend secondary school in a nearby village. Public transportation was infrequent and expensive for most families. The public spaces were exclusively male, and women had to be accompanied by a male relative on their commutes. However, it was not possible for male family members to accompany their daughters, sisters, and nieces to school on a daily basis. Therefore, most of the girls dropped out after finishing elementary school.

Salma and her sisters were among the few women in the village to receive high school and college educations. Their family had lived in the city because of their father's job, and they had easier access to educational institutions. The family moved back to the village when Salma married her cousin. Because Salma felt that education had equipped her to live a resourceful and dignified life, she wanted to make the same knowledge and skills available to the girls in her village. Thus, she readily accepted the job offer when the IEL opened its school seven years before our interviews. Salma's husband and in-laws, however, did not approve of her working outside of the home, which they saw as inappropriate. In a context where women are not visible in public spaces, they were uncomfortable with the idea of Salma commuting to school on her own. They also felt concerned that she would not be able to fulfill her responsibilities as a wife, daughter-in-law, and mother. Salma felt confident that she had made the right decision by taking the job even though it was not an easy process. She shared the following:

> My husband and in-laws were giving me a really hard time about the job [when Salma was offered the teaching position at the IEL school]. They

kept fighting with me the whole month. I did not know until the last day if I would actually be able to work. I got up really early on the day I was supposed to start my job, said my *fajr* [morning] prayers, and then asked myself if I really wanted to do it. And then I said, "Why not?" This is my right and my choice. And is it not my job as a Muslim to educate others? And then I left for school without telling my husband and in-laws. Now they are fine with it, but it was hell for me in the beginning.

Importantly, Salma's quote reveals the way she conceptualized her decision to work as a teacher as a reflection of her rights and responsibilities as a Muslim, which for her took precedence over her husband's and his family's wishes and local cultural practices. By accepting a job outside the home, Salma challenged the patriarchal norms that prescribe particular roles for women and give their family complete authority over their choices. She used a creative combination of the language of rights (learned from her exposure to higher education and the IEL training workshops) and Islamic teachings to rationalize her decision. She felt justified in modifying this cultural norm because it meant providing education to the girls in her community.

The use of Islam to challenge the local patriarchal norms that restrict women's access to education was the dominant theme that came up in my interviews with women and their families. Safia, for example, shared how she convinced parents to send their daughters to school by telling them, "Our Prophet [Mohammad] was a teacher. The first verse of the Quran [that was] revealed to him asked him to learn and teach. We are his followers." Fatima, a 38-year-old woman, shared how her father responded to the objections raised by his brothers about sending Fatima and her sisters to school after grade five: "My father would tell my uncles, . . . you ask me to not send my daughters to school, but my Prophet [Mohammad] PBUH [peace be upon him] orders my daughters to seek knowledge even if they have to go to China [quoting a saying of the Prophet Mohammad]. Now, should I listen to you or do what my Prophet PBUH asks me to do? My uncles would not utter a word after that."

Despite these justifications, actions like Salma's defiance of her husband were still viewed by many as violations of the gender norms, which define a wife's obedience as a measure of her respect for her husband and his family. However, Salma believed that her insistence on working was not a sign of disrespect for her husband and in-laws but was instead a reflection of her standing up for the "right" cause. She explained, "Education enables you to distinguish between right and wrong. . . . We start thinking, start looking at things in a different way and want to improve them. We start questioning and asking 'why?' and 'how?' . . . [This is] why and how [education] becomes the catalyst for change."

Salma believes that she as an educated woman is able to judge that it is her duty to provide education to the girls in her community. She claims the status of a good wife and daughter-in-law even as she refuses to listen to her husband in this particular case. She sees this as evidence of her ability to distinguish between right and wrong, instead of as a reflection of disrespect for her husband. She, as a parhi likhi, can determine when it is appropriate to raise her voice. She said, "I see [uneducated] women from my village fighting and cursing over things such as whose cattle entered into whose fields. Now, this can be resolved very easily if they communicate with each other and make some permanent arrangements. But no, they will fight and curse the whole day just to prove their point." Salma sees such fights and disputes as a reflection of ignorance rather than as arguing for the right causes. She believes that parhi likhi women do not indulge in such "petty" fights but speak up for the "right" issues. She sees her stance against her husband and in-laws as the right cause because it means providing education to the girls in her community. She does not see her defiance as something that weakens the institution of family. Instead, she sees her work as something that will help girls become productive members of their families.

Salma's dispute with her husband was public knowledge in a tight-knit rural community. However, she enjoyed a respectable status in the community, and people often asked her to help them with their children's education and, at times, with filling out forms for property or employment-related issues. She was often the only woman participant in community meetings with representatives of state and development organizations. Her natal family, especially her father, strongly supported her decision to work as a teacher. In other words, she did not face any hostility or even opposition from her own family or the community even as she violated the obedience code for women. In Salma's opinion, this acceptance was because people recognized that she was fighting for the right cause. Further, she did not engage in shouting matches with her in-laws, like other women do. She was always respectful toward them even as she decided to do what she wanted to do. Salma's status as an educated woman meant that she was trusted to make the right decision even when it meant modifying the commonly held gender beliefs and practices.

Other women participants shared Salma's perception that education had equipped them with the knowledge and skills to take up new roles. Just like Salma experienced, these new roles often challenged deeply ingrained gender beliefs and practices. For example, at the age of 23, Noreen, an IEL teacher, took her first trip outside her village without a male relative as an escort. Although Noreen called it "traveling on my own," she was actually accompanied by a woman friend as she journeyed to visit the nearest doctor in a town 20 miles away. Noreen was filled with excitement as she described her trip to discuss her recurring cold with the doctor, and she told in detail how she and her friend waited for public transportation by the roadside, got off the bus at the right place, saw the doctor, bought medicine, and returned home. She took this trip with her friend because she did not want to wait for her father or brother to take a day off from work to go with her. Commonly in these rural villages, women had to wait for weeks to see a doctor if a man could not take time off from work. The success of her trip was a source of great pride for this young teacher at an IEL school serving low-income students. She had accomplished something that most women in her village were not allowed to do. She felt that her education had given her the confidence and knowledge to be more independent. Noreen questioned the gendered practices that restrict women's mobility by asking, "How can I be qualified to educate our next generation but not to visit the doctor on my own?"

Both Salma and Noreen used the language of rights and choice to conceptualize their decisions regarding employment and public mobility, which challenged the local patriarchal norms. Yet in other cases, these women embraced and sometimes actively supported dimensions of the local patriarchy. For example, Salma's decision to take up a role in male-dominated public spaces does not mean she disagrees with the role of women as the primary caregivers at home. She believes that her husband, his family, and other community members accept and even appreciate her work as a teacher because it does not translate into her overlooking domestic responsibilities. She takes pride in fulfilling her multiple roles, even when it means emotional and physical exertion for her. After returning home from work, she cooks, cleans, takes care of her son and other family members, and entertains guests—everything that women who do not have jobs do. Salma's case is by no means unique. Rabia, a 32-year-old teacher, for example, explained how her performance of the double work shift was a privilege despite the heavy physical and emotional toll it took on her: "I am so tired at the end of the day that my whole body aches. But I still feel satisfied that my life is more than cooking and cleaning. I am the youngest of my siblings, but my brothers seek my advice when they need help with something. That makes me feel proud of my education."

The complex lives of these women included work outside the home, which most women around them did not do, along with primary responsibilities at home, which all the other women did. The participants in my study realized that they had to prove that their education and employment did not affect their domestic and family roles in order to continue to gain family and community approval for their new activities. However, they did not see their domestic and family responsibilities as evidence of gender inequality even when their dual roles became mentally and physically exhausting for them. Instead, they took pride in their ability to perform multiple roles, which proved their worth and distinction as educated women. The teachers felt that their perfection at domestic roles reinforced the value of education for girls. People looked at their work and realized that girls' education was useful not only for women but also for their families. For example, Rabia stated, "I do everything that women who stay at home do. No one can claim that I am not interested in domestic work or am not good at it just because I am parhi likhi or because I work [outside the home]. People look at me and say, 'This is how women should be.' I educate their children but do not ignore my home."

Ignoring domestic responsibilities was not an option for parhi likhi women like Rabia. The patriarchal bargain that they had made with their families and communities in order to take on new roles included their embracing the gender norms in the domestic sphere. Bilquise, a 36-year-old woman, elaborated on that theme: "My husband will perhaps not say much if things are not the way they are supposed to be, but my in-laws would get so very upset. They would blame my job, my education, and how all of it has gone to my head."

The women participants were acutely aware that their education and job would be held responsible for their less-than-perfect work at home. This would negatively affect their ability to continue their jobs and would diminish the community's perception of the value of education for women. Paradoxically, in Pakistan as in many other parts of the world, women's participation in the labor market further reinforces their adherence to traditional roles as homemakers and primary caregivers. These processes highlight how women's domestic roles remain a particularly sticky part of patriarchal systems even as women enter into spaces that have been historically occupied by men.

Family Honor and Self-Regulated Sexuality

Noreen, the 23-year-old participant discussed earlier, was pleasantly surprised when her father did not get upset about her commuting to the hospital in a nearby town on her own and without his permission. She explained, "My father did not get mad at me because he trusts me. He knows I am educated and will not do anything wrong." When I asked what she meant by doing anything "wrong," she smiled and looked at me as if the answer was self-evident before replying, "This is not a city where women are smart enough to do everything on their own. Here, women can be so naïve. They are not educated to know the difference between right and wrong. I bet my cousins would not stop giggling on the bus if they were traveling on their own."

Noreen used the example of her female cousins, who are not educated, to explain what she means by "wrong." Such "naïve" behavior, she believes, attracts undue attention in public spaces and maligns the name of the family. She does not trust her cousins to be in public spaces without a male relative because their behavior could potentially cause a scandal. On the other hand, Noreen feels justified in leaving home without the permission of her father and without the company of a male member of the family. Her restraint and reserved mannerisms in public spaces convey the message that she is not interested in male attention or extramarital relationships. She believes that education has enabled her to take up new roles in a respectable manner that protects the honor of her family.

In these contexts, women are seen as carriers of family honor and are expected to protect it by behaving in a modest way, giving no hint of sexual impropriety. Even gossip about the possibility of such improprieties in encounters with others could damage the reputation of a woman's family and ruin her prospects for marriage. Traditionally, family and community members were responsible for monitoring women's behaviors especially when they entered public spaces, and much of the resistance to women's education and employment was rationalized in the name of protecting family honor. However, these gender norms started shifting as Noreen and other women became educated and obtained professional employment. Community members valued the service that parhi likhi women were performing and assumed that they had acquired the middle-class manners and values that made them capable of restraint and self-control. Thus, educated women did not need male escorts to monitor their behaviors or to ward off unwanted attention in public spaces. In other words, these parhi likhi women, much like the Maya students analyzed by Manago (this volume), were viewed as having the awareness and capacity to regulate their own sexuality. Noreen's unparh cousins, on the other hand, were still viewed as needing surveillance since they could not be trusted to behave appropriately, having not acquired education.

Noreen accepts the patriarchal norms that present women as carriers of their family's reputation and therefore subject to family surveillance and protection. However, she sees herself and other educated women as exceptions whose presence in public spaces does not threaten family honor. She believes that educated women have the right to take up new roles and opportunities. However, she is not in favor of extending the same rights or choices to women who are not educated. This reflects the general perceptions of the participants: they employed the language of rights and choice as well as self-regulated sexuality to justify their presence in public spaces. Thus, while these shifts in the gender norms of public mobility have produced new opportunities for educated women, they also reinforce the status of women as symbols and carriers of family honor.

The women participants embodied the success that global discourses of women's education promise: they had access to jobs, public mobility, and increased status in family decision-making. They felt empowered, confident, and resourceful, and they greatly valued education for making these opportunities available to them. However, these successes were achieved by fashioning a new form of Kandiyoti's (1988) patriarchal bargain, which trades public participation for fidelity to traditional family roles for women in their day-to-day lives, and by taking on the self-regulation of their sexuality.

Arranged Marriage and Family Loyalty

Salma's experience demonstrates how the participants strategically engaged with the patriarchal system through identifying the spaces and opportunities to exert their rights without facing hostile resistance. While she refused to give in to the unreasonable demands of her husband that she not work outside the home, she had acquiesced to her father's decision to marry her cousin despite having strong reservations about him. She had realized that her refusal would malign her father's name in the community because he had already given his word. Talking about her marriage, Salma said: "How could I refuse my father's wishes? He has educated us [the sisters] against the wishes of the family. He did everything for us. So I knew that I had to do this [accept the marriage proposal] for him. I proved [to the community] that my father was right in educating us. Today, people want to educate their daughters because they look at me and say, ... 'We want our daughters to be like her.'"

Salma felt responsible for protecting the honor of her father, especially since he had given his daughters opportunities that were not available to other women at that time. Salma did not view her marriage as something that was imposed on her. Instead, she took pride in the fact that she brought honor and respect to the family and said that she did not regret her decision even though her marriage turned out to be turbulent. Her acceptance of the regulatory role of the family regarding marriage validated her status as an agent who could protect family honor.

Arranged marriage persists in much of Pakistan because it is seen as a symbol of the unity and cohesion of families and the communities of which they are a part. These marital arrangements are also an effective tool to control the sexuality of the younger generation, especially women. In a context where a woman's sexuality is seen as a potential threat to family honor and the social order, a woman choosing a potential spouse could be seen as evidence of her loose character. Families are at times open to their sons expressing interest in particular women as potential spouses. However, a woman's expression of such a choice is a violation of the honor code. Safia, a 29-year-old woman whose parents arranged her marriage to her cousin, spoke candidly about the fact that her husband is nine years older than she is and said that it did not bother her: "We do not marry outside [our] community; our families arrange our marriages. At times, men get to choose who they want to marry, but not women. But our [women's] minds are made up right from the start. We have not had any problems so far. . . . No one has said no."

Safia, who commuted a long distance every day to teach and who saw herself as a reformer in the community, did not relate women's empowerment to marital choice. Like Salma, her lens for understanding this issue was the relationship of affection and trust with her parents, not individual rights:

> Our parents have been so good to us. They listen to us, have given us everything, and never asked for anything in return. They have made good decisions for us, decisions about marriage, education. . . . My [extended] family is seen as an example in the village. We [were] the first ones to go to school, to college, to work as teachers. My elder sister was the first woman

in our community to attend college. My father used to say, "My daughters [will] set an example for others," and we did that. We upheld our family's name through our values and virtue.

Safia spoke of her father's struggle to send his daughters to college as evidence of his ability to make good decisions, including choosing spouses, for his children. This is another demonstration of how the women participants felt that they had made a good bargain with their families. All the participants expressed a deep sense of gratitude to their parents for educating them. They spoke of their arranged marriages as embodiments of their trust and affection for their families, not as symbols of their oppression. Their willingness to obey the authority of their parents also validated their status as trusted agents, who were then extended other opportunities and roles that had historically been available only to men. Mariam, a 24-year-old teacher, summarized this position by stating, "We know that Islam has given us the right to choose our husbands, but we do not feel the need to practice this right. The parents who have educated us can also make the best decisions for us when it comes to marriage." Rabia, the teacher mentioned above, was the only participant who referred to her relationship as a "love marriage." She said, "We liked each other, and our parents agreed to it." Her parents had endorsed this arrangement, however, because her prospective husband was her first cousin, and he was the one who openly expressed his interest and sent his parents to Rabia's family to propose the arrangement. Rabia, like the other participants, did not see her love marriage as the result of her exercise of rights or as stemming from her empowered status.

The question of importance, then, is why the women in my study did not contest the rights of their father to arrange their marriages, especially since human rights groups in Pakistan have taken up a number of high-profile legal cases to support women who married against their family's wishes (see Jahangir and Jilani 2003), and international media and policymakers employ these cases to evaluate the modernization of the social, legal, and political institutions of the country. However, despite being exposed to these discourses through the media and through their interactions with different development agencies, the women participants did not approach marriage as a site that validated or violated their rights.

This reveals that the women participants—despite seeing themselves as confident, independent, and empowered—did not challenge certain gender norms. Suad Joseph (1993a, 1996) has argued that the family is the crucial site both for the reproduction of the social order and for the socialization of individuals and satisfaction of their needs for affiliation, affection, security, and love. Under conditions of socioeconomic uncertainty or political instability, families are often the only stable resource for the meeting of physical, social, and emotional needs. Moghadam (1992, 45) reports that rural Pakistani women still remain dependent on the domestic group for their economic survival and social status, even when they are able to get one of the scarce jobs outside the home. On one hand, women may feel able to ask permission to attend school or to work as teachers, especially since these activities can be justified with reference to Islamic values; on the other hand, their dependence on the family and their role in supporting family honor may make it seem impossible to deny parents the authority to make decisions about the central institution of marriage.

The chapters by Seymour and Marrow in this volume, however, suggest that the process is more complex psychologically because these young women have been socialized into deference structures inherent in the extended family. Suad Joseph (1996, 18) has also argued that patriarchy works because it becomes part of the psyche. She finds that patriarchy in some Arab societies is linked to a "connective" or relational notion of self, "a sense of self that is embedded in relationships" as opposed to the individualist, autonomous, bounded, and contractual self valued in the West (Joseph 1993a, 453–54). Patriarchal connectivity, in particular, Joseph (1996, 18) says, emerges in settings where there is a fostering of selves with "fluid boundaries who defer to male[s] and elders and understand gender and age privilege in kin and religious terms." While Joseph describes the type of self that enacts deference as a naturalized desire, she also contends that we lack complete understandings of the complex psychodynamic processes involved in creating these selves.

Marrow (this volume) proposes the importance of a communication model built on intrapsychic processes, which operates within the patrilocal extended family to foster such relational understandings. Specifically, juniors are invited to share in the superior qualities of the elders, involving, Marrow contends, the psychodynamic process of idealization, defined by Morrison (2009, 76–77) as "the support of strong affirming others from whom we derive much of our own strength." Marrow notes that idealization involves using the affective and experiential resources of another, whom the subject deems as abundant in those resources, to meet the junior's needs. Because the senior has a wealth of experience, wisdom, and affection to bestow on the junior, the latter wishes to be enhanced by these resources. The junior's admiration of these resources, combined with the generous gifting of them by the senior, provides inspiration and a clear purpose to the junior.

While my research did not attempt to uncover or analyze the psychodynamic processes at work in rural Pakistani families, the interviews quoted above, where young women describe their willingness to go along with their father's selection of spouse, give hints of idealization at work. Salma, for example, asked how she could go against her father's wishes when he had gone against the community to educate her. Safia talked about her parents being good to her, providing for her, and making wise choices for her, and she viewed her father's decision to educate her as a prime example of why he could be trusted to select her marriage partner.

For many of these young women, it was usually their father or a male elder who became convinced of the value of education for girls. However, the journey to education was full of hardships. The participants often had to walk miles on their own to get to a high school for girls in a nearby village. They faced harassment on their way to and from school. Rabia shared that after she completed grade five, her father decided to send her to a boys school because there was no school for girls beyond elementary level in her village. She was made to feel like an outsider everyday because she was the only girl. The walls of her school were full of graffiti containing her name. In a context where a woman's reputation is based on her invisibility in public spaces, this was a traumatizing experience for her. She said, "I wanted to quit school. I was the first woman in my community to go to school and then to college. I felt so ashamed when I saw my name written all over the walls of my school. I had done nothing wrong but still felt that I had maligned my family's name." She survived this ordeal because of the support and encouragement from her father. She shared how her father stood firm in his resolve because he saw education as an Islamic right and responsibility.

Many of my respondents spoke affectionately of their father's efforts on their behalf and of the gratitude they felt. Importantly, going along with parental choices in marriage was seen by these young women as a way to protect the family honor and, in essence, give back to their elders. They spoke of their arranged marriages as embodiments of their trust and affection for their families, and they displayed some of what Marrow (this volume) refers to as a clear sense of purpose when they talked about how their willingness to go along has contributed to a preservation of their family's strength and honor.

Conclusion

Whereas control over marriage and the expression of sexuality remain particularly sticky issues for rural Pakistani women, they and their families felt confident in challenging gender norms regarding access to education, jobs, and male-dominated public spaces. The fact that a majority of the girls in these communities now attend high school is a huge shift from the late twentieth century, when very few girls went beyond elementary school. My respondents were often the first and, in many cases, the only women in their communities to hold a paid job outside the home. They commuted to and from school on their own, something that was taboo until recently. In the process of this change, their families shifted the duties of behavioral and sexual monitoring to the parhi likhi women themselves, who were circumspect about their public conduct as they sought to demonstrate their modesty and adherence to gender norms while pursuing employment and public travel away from home.

Public sites were fraught with conflict but remained spaces where differing points of view were allowed to enter the discourse. The active role of state, nongovernmental, and international development organizations shaped this shift. Groups like the IEL began using the language of individual rights and choices to promote female empowerment, and the young women who later became the first teachers clearly internalized and adopted some of these ideas. At the same time, even when some family or community members opposed the idea of education for girls, they could not challenge its status as an Islamic duty. In other words, Islam as a set of beliefs and practices took precedence over what the participants saw as local cultural norms, and my interviewees effectively used Islam to counter opposition to women attending school or working outside the home as teachers.

This mobilization of Islam to modify local patriarchal norms that restricted women's access to education, the labor market, and public spaces problematizes the mainstream perception of Islam as inherently oppressive toward women. This global discourse approaches the patriarchal family, the community, and kinship structures as mere reflections of Islam rather than as complex products of social, political, and historical processes (Kandiyoti 2005). The lived experiences of the participants in my study highlight how, in this particular case, Islam was employed to challenge the local patriarchal structures.

However, this argument is not a commentary on the universal role of Islam. Instead, I approach Islam as a set of flexible resources (Predelli 2004) and a "dynamic tool kit" (Bartkowski and Read 2003) that can be used to activate, reinforce, and subvert gendered boundaries in different contexts. For example, the women I interviewed recognized that choosing a spouse was their Islamic right, but they decided not to exert it. In contrast to education, employment, and public mobility, choice in marriage was closely tied to their relational sense of self as junior members of the family, their affection for elder members, particularly their fathers, and their desire to help preserve family honor. In this case, local cultural practices and the primacy of family loyalty prevailed over strict adherence to Islamic teachings.

As these newly educated, parhi likhi women began to increasingly enter public spaces and take up new opportunities, they often did so by fashioning a new form of Kandiyoti's (1988) patriarchal bargain. They traded public participation for fidelity to traditional Islamic family roles and took on the self-regulation of their sexuality. How these bargains are constituted is highly variable across cultural contexts. Manago (this volume) shows that young Maya women have pursued education and public mobility by refashioning the definition of women's work to include hard work at school, not just the undertaking of domestic chores. Yet these young women, like those in my study, assume the burden of self-regulation of their sexual behavior. Guin'ee (2014) and Jeffrey, Jeffery, and Jeffery (2008) have found that educated women in Nepal and India take on additional responsibilities toward their families in order to strengthen their bonds with them while Adely (2009) reports that educated girls in Jordan regulate their sexuality in order to be seen as "ideal Muslim women." Research from Jordan, Israel, and Afghanistan (Hertz-Lazarowitz and Shapira 2005; Holland and Yousofi 2014; Weiner-Levy 2006) documents the efforts of educated and professional women to adhere more strictly to community norms of modest dress and behavior in order to avoid conflict with their families and censure by others. All of these studies provide insight into the complex processes through which education impacts gendered cultural norms and the lives and identities of women in different societies.

The film *Girl Rising* mobilizes the post-9/11 narrative that casts Muslim women as the other, as passive victims oppressed by their culture and in need of rescue. In this chapter I have problematized a narrative that positions cultures in Muslim societies as static patriarchal regimes that stand in opposition to the universally empowering institution of women's education. My ethnographic analysis reveals that in this particular context Islam and the local culture were not always synonymous. In fact, Islam was employed to challenge the patriarchal practices that restricted women's access to education, employment, and public mobility. Ironically, the patriarchal norms and women's education at times overlapped in shaping the gender roles and identities of the participants as educated women. This overlap reveals the shifts in patriarchal systems as complex and multidimensional: they not only restrict but also empower educated women. Women are active participants in patriarchal systems who strategically claim their rights as they stand in tension with and shape the power hierarchies in their contexts. Instead of a linear narrative of women's access to education, labor markets, and public mobility, the lived experiences of the participants in my study highlight women's education as a contested terrain shaped by the intersections of multiple discourses.

Notes

1. I use pseudonyms for the organization and the research participants.
2. India was divided into the two sovereign states of India and Pakistan at the end of British colonial rule in 1947.

CHAPTER SEVEN

Moving beyond Notions of Resistance and Accommodation
Understanding How Women Navigate Conflicting Models of Marriage in Rural Mexico

HOLLY F. MATHEWS

In 1982, I interviewed Rosa, a 25-year-old married resident of Santa Ana, the rural Mexican town in which I began fieldwork on gender roles in the late 1970s.[1] Born in 1957, Rosa married at age 17, moved in with her husband's family, and had her first child at 18. In discussing her marriage, she said:

> Rosa: I made a mistake in my marriage [*Me equivoqué en casarme*]. It was the biggest mistake of my life. I have suffered so much with my husband and my in-laws. My own family does not know how he wastes our money on drinking and how I have to beg others to help feed my children. Did my mother-in-law ever help us? No, she always takes his side. Others will tell you that I am a good wife and mother, but she would never say that.
> Holly: Why did you get married?
> Rosa: Well, truthfully, I didn't want to, but what choice did I have [*qué alternatívas tenía yo*]? My father knew the family, and he said that I should marry Raul. We only met two times. I really did not know him. But he was the one I got [*pero el era lo que me tocó*]. It was my destiny [*era mi destino*], and I endure it [*lo aguanto*] so my children can finish school and make their own futures [*hacer sus propios futuros*].

In the summer of 2014, I interviewed Rosa's youngest granddaughter, Alma, a secondary school graduate who had just turned 18 and discovered she was pregnant. In talking about her future plans, she said:

Alma: I always thought that after I finished school, my *novio* [boyfriend] and I would "elope" [*nos vamos*] to the States. There, we would get jobs and make enough money to get a house and start a family by working together to make a good life [*una buena vida trabajando juntos*]. I am not like the women of before [*no soy como las mujeres de antes*]. I am not one to be pushed around [*dejada*]. I only want to marry a man who treats me well [*por las buenas*] and wants to be with me. But there are no jobs here, and it is very difficult and very expensive now to cross the border. All the men are leaving, but the women cannot. Some girls are afraid that if they don't find someone, they will be "left-behinds" [*quedadas*]. When my boyfriend, Antonio, was preparing to leave and he wanted us to have sex [*estar juntos*], I thought it would bring us closer [*para acercanos más*]. I did not think I would get pregnant, but maybe it will be okay. I will move in with his parents, and he will send us money. I have the hope that when he returns, we will marry.

On first examination, it may seem that the more things change, the more they stay the same. Despite the passage of three decades and despite being better educated than her mother and grandmother, Alma has ended up in the same circumstances. Yet her discourse clearly reveals evidence of emerging new values and aspirations. Why do women in some areas still appear to comply with or accommodate to practices they view as oppressive while others are espousing new values? How do shifting ideas about marriage and gender roles relate to self-understandings, behavioral goals, and the choices women make?

In this chapter, I draw on schema theory from cognitive anthropology and psychology to explore the ways that contemporary young women in rural Oaxaca navigate between an older schema of marriage based on respect and deference and rooted in an agrarian-based, collectivist system (see Quinn, this volume) and a newer schema of companionate marriage emerging as the basis for rural life becomes more individualistic. The former, which I label the respect (*respeto*) schema following the conventions adopted by Jennifer Hirsch (2003), is characteristic of marriages traditionally arranged by parents and entails spousal relations based on male dominance, gender role complementarity, sex segregation, and adherence to duty.[2] The latter, which I label the trust (*confianza*) schema, is based on the idea of free choice in marriage and emphasizes the importance of mutual understanding and gender roles characterized by emotional intimacy, mutual support, and cooperation in family duties. This Mexican version of companionate marriage, however, is distinctive from such models found in other societies in its continued emphasis on the importance of motherhood for women and a shared understanding between spouses that men are the heads of the household and as such bring respect to the home.

Untangling Women's Various Responses to Patriarchy

One of the defining features of classic patriarchy is women's accommodation to it. Some scholars view this as complete acquiescence, implying a lack of agency on the part of the women involved. Others see it as a partial adaptation to an exploitative system that women may still attempt to manipulate. The reasons for women's variable responses are complex. In her chapter in this volume, Susan Seymour documents that young girls socialized within deference structures accept such behaviors as natural and normal. Jocelyn Marrow's chapter shows that the North Indian emotional model of intrafamilial relations causes young women to desire to be like and to be liked by their elders. Saba Mahmood's (2005) research on women in the Egyptian mosque movement posits that their enactment of sequences of disciplined practices and actions creates their desire to be pious Muslim women, which is displayed partly through submission to their father and husband. Alternatively, as Ayesha Khurshid (this volume) illustrates, women may acquiesce to patriarchal controls because they fear gossip and punishment if they do not, while Kandiyoti (1988), Wolf (1974), and Joseph (1994) suggest that within the boundaries of the institutional constraints they face, women do attempt to strategize actively to secure their own best interests. In so doing, however, they often become more committed to the very structures that oppress them.

In much of the feminist literature, accommodation is counterposed to its assumed opposite, resistance, which Seymour (2006, 305) defines as "intentional, and hence conscious, acts of defiance or opposition by a subordinate individual or group of individuals against a superior individual or set of individuals." While women may organize public protests or strikes to oppose patriarchal practices, the acts of resistance most typically documented occur under the radar of the more powerful. James Scott (1985) labels these the "weapons of the weak," and they include the more passive strategies of foot-dragging, dissimulation, gossiping, and so on, which often do nothing to change the existing power dynamic. Additionally, women in structurally powerless positions may express anger and distress through psychodynamic processes of possession and illness. Because such behavior is indirect and unconscious, women are not held accountable for their actions (Bourguignon 2004).

Underlying this dichotomy is the issue of what constitutes female agency in patriarchal systems. If women acquiesce to practices that are inimical to their interests, do they lack agency (defined as the intention or capacity to act)? The continued framing of women's choices in terms of this simplistic dichotomy between accommodation and resistance renders feminist scholars, as Mahmood (2001, 209) writes, "insufficiently attentive to motivations, desires, and goals that are not necessarily captured by these terms."

The same conundrum can be found in the philosophies guiding international development programs targeted toward women, which seem to posit a linear path to women's empowerment worldwide (Malhotra and Schuler 2005). These programs often assume that education will produce individualistic values and a greater desire for autonomy, leading women to enact changes to make their gendered relationships more egalitarian (Worthen 2012, 368). Yet time and again, such assumptions have been proven wrong (Kabeer 1999; Mahmood 2005; Worthen 2012). As a result, Adriana Manago (2012) argues that change is better viewed as a gradual process involving the negotiation of pathways through old and new values.

Schema theory provides a mechanism for analyzing and understanding alternative gender scripts in a cultural group. Strauss and Quinn (1997, 48–88) define *schemas* as mental representations used to organize and simplify knowledge about the world, which are built up from experience and stored in memory. Quinn (2005a, 38) writes, "To the degree that people share experiences, they will end up sharing the same schemas—having, we would say, the same culture (or subculture)."

On the other hand, all people have experiences that are only partially shared with others or that are completely idiosyncratic. Thus, schema theory predicts that women's responses to patriarchal ideals and practices are often varied and complex even when they grow up in the same cultural tradition. The data presented in this chapter illustrate how rapidly shifting political and economic circumstances may favor women's allegiance to one cultural model over another or to different components of the same model as their shared life experiences change across cohorts. Other women may embrace new ideas but be unable to act on them in a world devoid of opportunities, causing them mental anguish and anxiety. For example, some of my respondents deny that conflicts exist, others languish in limbo unable to navigate their new circumstances satisfactorily, while a few forge integrative compromises that facilitate limited changes in behavior. Quinn's (1996) analysis of US schemas of marriage shows that when certain contradictions are confronted by many people over long enough periods of time, shared task solutions may emerge to resolve them. This has not yet happened in Santa Ana, where the pace of change has been unpredictable and faster than people's abilities to adapt. As a result, conflicts and contradictions abound as women and men struggle to make meaning in an insecure world.

Description of the Research Community and Data Sources

I began fieldwork in Santa Ana, a rural town of approximately 2,000 people in the southern arm of the valley of Oaxaca, Mexico, in 1978 and have returned to collect data on five occasions, most recently in the summer of 2014. Originally inhabited by Zapotecs with the later addition of a resettled Mixtec barrio, the community initially exhibited a a preference for village endogamy, patrilocal residence after marriage, and inheritance by the eldest son, who continued to reside with his parents. Many lands were held in common for subsistence use by different barrios and for village projects (see Wolf 1957). Families were pressured to participate in a civil-religious hierarchy of offices known as the cargo system, which involved ever-increasing expenditures of resources and time in exchange for prestige and eventual political influence (see Mathews 1985). By the 1950s, some lands had been privatized, and more villagers were growing cash crops for sale in addition to food for consumption. In the 1960s, a primary school opened locally, and by the 1970s, regular bus service to Oaxaca City reached the village and a Mexican government health post had been constructed.

I spent two years, 1978–1980, living with a local family and conducting ethnographic research on gender roles and gender ideology. Between 1982 and 1984, I did a set of life history interviews with 32 women and analyzed 60 versions of the classic folktale of La Llorona (the weeping woman) to illuminate alternative schemas of gendered human nature and marital roles (Mathews 1992, 2005). In the summers of 1994, 2000, and 2014, I conducted 24 open-ended interviews with young women, ages 17–23, about their lives and their perspectives on marriage. In the summer of 2014, I held a focus group with 9 young men, ages 15–19, to discuss their views on marriage and their plans for the future All interviews were conducted in Spanish, audio recorded, transcribed, and translated.[3] These transcripts were then analyzed to reveal the taken-for-granted models of the world that respondents employed to structure their discourses, including the sequences of reasoning they used in making sense of their lives.

I reconstructed marital schemas in Oaxaca in order to uncover the implicit assumptions being used by respondents to connect their reasoning about how other people should or did behave to their own desires, motivations, and intentions. It became clear that two overarching cultural models—respect and trust—structured people's discourses about marriage and gender relations. While most people articulated some aspects of these two cultural models, they varied greatly in the degree to which they found them influential. People also voiced other statements that were not linked with the models but that were important ideas circulating in the greater community. For example, some of the recent converts to Pentecostalism talked about God creating man to be the head of the household. This statement of belief was not yet linked to the respect schema as a justification for men's role nor was it integrated in any way with the trust schema. Yet as aspects of this belief system gain currency, we might expect other shared models to emerge and influence behavior.

In any community, there are various sources of information circulating, but not all arise from common experience and not all are widely shared in a systematic way. The two overarching models of marriage that I uncovered are closely linked to higher-level life goals for each sex, and they specify norms and expectations for appropriate gender-role behavior in the community. I describe these norms and expectations briefly below before examining in more detail how women navigate between them in making decisions about their own lives and in evaluating those of others.

What Makes Cultural Models Compelling: The Respect Schema

To understand why people behave as they do, we not only need to know the cultural schemas that are available to them, but we also need to figure out why and how some schemas become more compelling than others. Roy D'Andrade (1992, 24) proposes that motivation is experienced as a desire or wish, which is followed by a feeling of satisfaction if it is fulfilled or a sense of frustration if it is not. Cognitive schemas have the potential to instigate action because they often function as goals generating such desires and wishes (29). On the other hand, not all schemas have the same level of goal direction. Higher-level schemas, such as those for love, work, and success, often comprise a person's most general goals and might be thought of as master motives capable of instigating action autonomously (30). Quinn (1992) finds that one important way cultural schemas, even midrange ones like the schema for marriage, become master motives is by supplying people with self-understandings (see also Markus and Kitayama 1991). For example, for many of Quinn's (1992) American informants, a sense of themselves as a good wife in a successful marriage is at the core of their being. Instead of being motivated by some abstract conception of the components of marriage, these women have an inner sense that they would be lesser people if they were not trying to be good wives.

Quinn (1992, 92) also suggests that specific goals become linked to self-understandings through the course of experience, especially early life experience, and the extent to which the seeming naturalness and rightness of certain understandings are acquired during socialization. Strauss (2017, 9) further proposes that the cultural models people find most compelling may be those learned from particularly trusted sources, such as a parent; those that are associated with emotionally salient experiences, especially early in life; and those that are well learned in childhood and are reinforced in subsequent experiences. Ideas, therefore, can become powerful by being so deeply internalized that people are hardly aware that they hold them and do not consider any alternatives to them (Strauss 2005, 203). This was clearly true for the respect schema of marriage from the late colonial period through the early 1960s in Santa Ana. Everyone internalized its goals and felt compelled to behave in accordance with the norms. And those who did not were penalized by community gossip and family punishments.

Components of the respect schema, derived from a system of arranged marriage and patrilocal residence (Mathews 1992, 1995), can be found in Rosa's narrative at the beginning of this chapter. By the terms of this schema, women are expected to marry, which enables fulfillment of their most important life goal: to become mothers. Not only are children markers of adult status and the means by which daughters-in-law begin to gain status in the husband's household, but children also provide women with valued companionship, household help, and security for old age. Men in this schema are also expected to marry, but they value above all the achievement of success as measured in public respect as the head of an honorable family and public status achieved through cargo participation. Marriage in this model is a means to an end for both sexes. After marriage, spouses lead largely separate lives, with each sex performing its gender role's responsibilities.

When I first started my research, most couples did not know each other well before marriage and did not expect to be friends afterward. Women who married as virgins had little preparation for sex and referred to intercourse as "when he uses me" (*cuando el me usa*), viewing it as a marital obligation they had to fulfill whether they wanted to or not (*hay que cumplir si una tiene ganas or no*). Descent and inheritance were traced through males, and men acquired split images of women beginning in childhood (see Seymour, this volume). They revered their mother but feared the sexuality of their wife, who had to be controlled so as not to compromise male honor. Raised to distinguish between "women of the streets" (*mujeres de la calle*) and "women of the home" (*mujeres de la casa*), men sought sexual liaisons with the former but marriage with the latter: decent, virtuous women who had limited knowledge of or interest in sexual activities. Men and women had little opportunity to interact before marriage, and they spoke of marriage as destiny (*el destino*). For women, who had to move to the home of a virtual stranger after marriage, it was also a cross or burden to bear (*una cruz, un cargo*), and the wife had to make do with the one she got (*el que te tocó*). Women spoke of learning to get along (*saberse llevar*) and of enduring much suffering (*aguantar mucho sufrimiento*) because this system implied that they bore the burden of making their marriage work and of upholding family honor (see Hirsch 2003, 88–89; Horowitz 2012; Napolitano 2002, 159; Stephen 1991, 2007, 1–2).

In my previous work (Mathews 1992), I showed how this schema of marriage connected to more general assumptions of gendered human nature. In the 1970s, for example, parents generally believed that male infants were weaker and more sickly (*debil*) than female infants. Therefore, male babies were nursed longer and held and comforted more often than females were. This differential treatment carried over into childhood as young girls were put to work doing chores at an early age while young boys had more leisure time and were urged to eat and rest. In an interview conducted in 1979, Eulalia, then age 36, spoke about how her mother had prepared her for a life of suffering. She said that her mother would not let her go to school beyond third grade because she wanted Eulalia to learn to do housework properly. From a young age, she also had to care for her siblings. Once she reached age 10, she was not allowed to leave the house to play or visit friends. She told me: "My mother would beat me if I did anything wrong. She never spoke nicely to me. All she ever did was scold me [*regañarme*]. She never gave me gifts or bought me clothes like she did for my brothers. When I cried or complained, she said she did not want me to be indulged [*consentida*] because I would never survive with my mother-in-law [*sobrevivir con mi suegra*]." Stories of harsh childhoods were common in my interviews with older women, who described ambivalent and sometimes emotionally painful relations with their mothers, which were rooted in their perceptions of unfair treatment in comparison to their brothers.

As historian Steve Stern (1998) has demonstrated, this respect schema of marriage has existed since the colonial period and engenders a specific type of patriarchal bargain (Kandiyoti 1988). A good wife works hard in the household, is circumspect in her behavior, is sexually faithful, complies with her husband's wishes, grants him public deference, and sacrifices her personal desires for the good of the family. A good husband works hard outside the home, provides materially for the family, makes sure that his children are respectful and behave appropriately, and treats his wife with respect in public. As my examination of La Llorona folktales (Mathews 1992, 148) demonstrates, conflicts occur when one spouse fails to meet the terms of the pact, but the legitimacy of the schema itself is not questioned. Thus, men who mistreat their wives in public; men who gamble and drink, diverting resources from the family; and those who acknowledge mistresses and illegitimate children in public are identified in the tales as problematic types, prompting their long-suffering wives to try and correct these behaviors and restore the terms of the patriarchal bargain. Alternatively, wives who are lazy, who wander the streets and gossip or flirt, who refuse to have sex with their husbands, or who fail to take care of the children prompt husbands to take corrective actions (145). Stern's (1997) examination of court cases throughout the late eighteenth and early nineteenth centuries documents numerous examples of men and women in Oaxaca seeking redress against their spouse for violations of the specific marital obligations entailed by the schema but notes that they never questioned the fairness of the patriarchal bargain itself.[4]

Shifting Views of Marriage and the Trust Schema

The newer companionate schema of marriage—trust—which is based on notions of mutual understanding and support, began to emerge in Santa Ana during the 1980s. The introduction of electricity gave people access to popular soap operas (*telenovelas*) that portrayed modern, middle-class conceptions of marriage and intimacy. Educational opportunities increased with the opening of a secondary school in a nearby town, and by the end of the decade as the economy worsened, young men were migrating to the United States and returning seasonally with stories of how people's lives differed on the other side (see Horowitz 2012). In the early 1990s, more young women began taking jobs in Oaxaca City as maids with middle-class families, and they too began to see different ways of organizing marriage. Generally, the trust schema became associated in the minds of young people with modernization, education, and the values of the Global North. They saw it as a more progressive and less old-fashioned way of living and came generally to associate this view of marriage with upward social mobility. At the same time, members of the older, parental generation resisted these new ideas and attempted to reinforce traditional values through the use of behavioral controls and gossip.

The trust schema emphasizes the importance of marriages based on mutual understanding. Therefore, individuals should choose their own partners, making courtship important (see Hirsch 2003, 81–83). Young couples need to spend time getting to know one another well (*para conocerse bien*). Interestingly, the word *conocer*, which means "to know," as in to meet or become familiar with someone, is also a euphemism for being involved with someone sexually, implying that courtship also involves more physical intimacy than was permitted in the past. In describing what they want in a husband, many of my younger informants emphasized they were looking for a man who would treat them well by talking with them, taking their opinions seriously (*que me toma en cuenta*), and sharing thoughts with them (*compartir los pensamientos*). Yet they still wanted men who were hard workers, who were serious, and who would treat them with respect. As one young woman described it, "En el principio, lo físico es importante, pero despues quiero alguien que me vale por mí misma [In the beginning, physical appearance is important, but later I want someone who values me for who I am]." Young women recognized that to attract these spouses, they had to be more sexually open (*abierta*) and willing to show affection. They also considered the decision to have sex, which they now labeled "making love" (*hacerse el amor*) or "being together" (*estar juntos*), before marriage as one that should be made jointly with a serious boyfriend, which is literally unthinkable in the respect schema.

This view of companionate marriage differs from the form it takes in other cultural settings where individualistic values are spreading (Hirsch and Wardlow 2006). The most important life goal for women in Santa Ana remains motherhood, and success is defined as making a good life with a respected husband and family (see Hirsch 2003, 12). To achieve these goals, a woman must marry, and in order to earn respect in the community, her marriage must conform to *some* aspects of the older schema—that is, her husband must publicly respect her and provide for their children. For young men, achieving adult status and community respect remain important life goals. While marriage and the establishment of one's own household is an important way to accomplish this, for many it is secondary to becoming independent and acquiring financial resources (Valdés 1996). No longer able to depend on subsistence agriculture or local employment, men view migration as a rite of passage that will afford them a successful future, leading eventually to the establishment of their own household (see Wilkerson, Yamawaki, and Downs 2009).

While many younger men I spoke with also desired a marriage based on trust (confianza) and wanted wives with whom they could be close, they still wanted to marry hardworking, decent women (*mujeres decentes*) who would be suitable mothers for their children. As one young man of 17 said during the 2014 focus group: "I can be with women who are beautiful and fun, but I want to marry a sheltered woman [*recogida*, also translated as "protected"] because she will be the mother of my children. She needs to be pure and also hardworking. When I am gone, I need to trust she will be faithful and take care of my children." Thus, migration to the United States and the anticipation of absence from their wife increases the importance of a woman being trustworthy for many of these young men.

The newer trust schema of marriage engenders different types of marital goals. Young women want to have their own home and live separately with their companion husband away from in-laws. They want their opinions to be taken seriously and to make joint decisions about their family and their future. Young men want to work in the United States in order to secure economic resources for the future. They want their wife to be a companion and to spend time with her, but they also want her to be a good mother and dutiful housewife. Neither sex focused much in the interviews on the need for equality in household duties, as we often see in US contexts. Rather, they assumed that a gendered division of labor was natural; the man would provide and the woman would run the house and care for the children. The difference in this new schema is that spouses would cooperate and work together, not separately, to ensure the prosperity and happiness of the family.

General Changes in Value Orientations

Many theorists contend that the general direction of social change globally is from agrarian, collectivist socioeconomic systems to larger-scale, more urban market economies with greater elaborations of social networks (Greenfield 2009;

Hart 2014; Moghadam 2004). The implication is that older value systems based on hierarchy and deference will gradually be replaced worldwide by individualist orientations emphasizing personal autonomy and egalitarianism. During the 1970s–1980s this type of transition appeared to be happening in rural Oaxaca.

Women who married in the late 1970s lived in accordance with the respect schema. But as economic conditions worsened with the decline of agricultural markets, men migrated to work in the United States, leaving their wife and children behind, isolated in the home of their in-laws. Disenchanted when the terms of the old system were not working for them and responding to newer ideas of companionate marriage, these women began to identify the source of their marital problems as patrilocal residence, which placed them under the watchful eyes of overbearing and unreasonable mothers-in-law (Hellman 2008, 47–51). They pushed to use their husband's remittances to build their own homes (Hirsch 2003, 67–68; Pauli 2008), a desire encapsulated in a saying popular in this era: *la casada casa quiere* (the bride wants a house). Women's desires were often persuasive to men, especially younger sons and those from poorer families, who viewed the construction of a new, modern house as a way to demonstrate success and earn status in the community. As couples began to build separate homes and as neolocal residence became more common, young wives gained greater personal freedom, but they also found themselves alone and isolated, trying to carry out men's agricultural work while also caring for the home and raising children. When remittances became sporadic or failed to arrive, moreover, women had to find other ways to earn income to make ends meet, which was difficult without skills or education.

At the same time, the prolonged absence of men opened new avenues of public participation for women. They began to fill seats on many town committees, voiced their opinions about needed improvements, and voted in civic elections for the first time in the late 1990s (Stephen 2007, 53). Many, such as Rosa's daughter Ofalia, the mother of Alma, began to envision different futures for their daughters. Ofalia summarized these views in an interview in 1994:

> My life has been so difficult. We married and began to build this house. Then my husband left for the north to make more money. My house is still not finished. If he has trouble finding work, he cannot send us money. I work our land to have corn to eat, but I also make and sell tortillas, take in washing, and sew for others. It is hard for us to survive some months. My parents can't help because my brothers are gone as well. I thought about

going north to join him, but it is too hard with the children. What is the solution? Only God knows. I don't want my daughters to live this way. I tell them to finish school so they won't be so dependent on a man.

The children coming of age in the 1990s and 2000s, however, had different experiences than their mothers. With almost 70 percent of the able-bodied men absent from the community, they were more likely than those of previous generations to be living with only one parent. Many felt a sense of loss and isolation that certainly fed into the increasing popularity of the new companionate model of marriage. One of my informants, Gaby, turned 15 in 2000. She spoke about her childhood:

I grew up without a father. My mother worked hard, but my siblings and I spent a lot of time alone. We had to work all the time, and some days we did not have enough to eat. My father would try to come home every year at Christmas. When he came, we would be so happy, but then he would leave again, and my mother would have another baby. My father did not even see my youngest brother until he was four years old! It was very hard. I felt very alone. I really missed my father. I always wanted to go find him and bring him back, but that wasn't possible.

In the life history interviews I conducted, many respondents recollected the trauma of growing up without their father as a key feature of childhood, recounting tales of the hardships that they and their mother had experienced. Like the children of migrants elsewhere, they often idealized their absent fathers, holding on to memories of isolated visits from them or the gifts sent from the United States. Not surprisingly, many of these girls explicitly stated they did not want a marriage like their mother had. Defining themselves as *mujeres modernas*, they pressured their potential husband to take them along to the United States. As one woman put it, "Porque casarme para estar sola? [Why would I marry to be alone?]" They talked of working with their husband to build a better life and of spending time together free from the watchful eyes of the community. A number of women did migrate, but they often found themselves more isolated, alone in a country where they had no legal status and could not speak the language. It was not uncommon for them to return to the village without their husband once they had children.

These examples indicate that while there was a general trend for the older respect schema to be replaced by a newer companionate model of marriage, the explicit goals and intentions of women differed by generation. This led to variations in the types of domestic arrangement made in the community. The attempts to navigate the changing socioeconomic circumstances and life conditions only intensified as the pace of change accelerated in the community.

Conflict, Dissonance, and Choice

Rapid and inconsistent patterns of socioeconomic change since the events of 9/11 have left young people in rural Mexico in a state of confusion. Economic modernization and a shift to capitalistic production slowed drastically with the passage of the North American Free Trade Agreement (NAFTA), and the foreclosure of opportunities stalled for many the fulfillment of more individualistic desires and goals. In other words, many young people were caught between an older way of life that was no longer working and a newer ideal that could not be realized, leading them to struggle with how best to respond and navigate these conditions.

Social psychologists in the 1950s and 1960s argued that people strive for cognitive consistency or balance (Abelson et al. 1968). The perception of inconsistency or contradiction generates tension in the perceiver, which causes dissonance, a negative drive state that people feel compelled to eliminate. Elliot Aronson (1968, 23) notes that individuals are most likely to experience distress when certain beliefs or ideas call for behaviors that are inconsistent with their self-concepts or when these conflict with beliefs held by members of their social reference group.

Claudia Strauss (2012, 99) outlines three possible outcomes of cognitive dissonance. The first is compartmentalization, where contradictory beliefs are maintained separately in the mind so that individuals voice them in different contexts or at different times and seem unaware of the potential conflicts among them. The second response is ambivalence. People are aware of and concerned about the conflicts stemming from divergent schemas but seem unable to resolve them in order to make decisions and take action (102). Bourguignon (2004) and Marrow (2013) further suggest that ambivalence for women (and, presumably, other powerless groups) can be unconscious and can manifest through embodied forms of expression like possession trance and psychosomatic illness. Third, Strauss (2012) proposes that some individuals are able to achieve integration between conflicting discourses. Mary Follett ([1924] 2018) notes that integration calls for a drastic reorganization of cognitive structures because the individual has to construct a new frame of reference and think through the full implications of contradictory beliefs and values, which is psychologically more difficult (Katz 1968). Naomi Quinn (1996) finds that when particular conflicts are repeatedly confronted, a culturally shared task solution may emerge. A fourth possibility may be that people avoid making a choice altogether by rejecting all the options or by opting out of the situation either explicitly through adopting a different lifestyle or implicitly by adopting an unconscious defense mechanism, like possession or psychosomatic illness, as a coping mechanism.

The ratification of NAFTA in 1994 and the subsequent elimination of agrarian price supports in Mexico made subsistence agriculture a precarious endeavor (Stephen 2007, 123–27), and rural poverty rates increased significantly. The US recession that began in 2007 made it hard for migrants to find regular jobs that paid as much as they had in previous years. In Santa Ana, remittance income declined for most families, and men were no longer able to return annually to visit, prompting fears that they would take up with American women and abandon their villages altogether.

The young women I spoke with in 2014 were better educated than previous generations, yet they had few opportunities to use their new skills locally. Men were still leaving for the United States, but now their return was uncertain, which caused the young women to fear becoming quedadas (women left behind) without the hope of marriage.[5] Caught between conflicting schemas, some girls compartmentalized the ideas of work and marriage, independence and companionship. Others fantasized about finding a man like the ones shown on telenovelas: a man who would treat them well (*por las buenas*) in a marriage characterized by companionship and intimacy. In reality, they felt pressure to secure a marriage partner before men migrated and in order to do so worked hard to achieve a stylish and modern appearance and to be more sexually open, moves that violated the respect schema of marriage and often exposed them to disapproval from family members and ridicule by others in the community. These developments led to myriad conflicts they were struggling to understand and resolve by employing all of the strategies outlined by Strauss (2012).

Alma's interview, quoted at the beginning of the chapter, raises the issue of how an educated young woman who espouses commitment to the trust schema of marital companionship ended up pregnant and unmarried, living patrilocally and dependent financially on her novio and her in-laws. She clearly states that she is not like the women of before and that she is not one to be pushed around.

She connects this view of her modern, independent self to her stated desire to find a husband who treats her well and wants to be with her, which she encapsulates in the fantasy scenario of how an ideal marriage would unfold. She then shifts gears to describe the external barriers preventing her from realizing these goals and acknowledges—but distances herself from—the implications of the respect schema when she says that "*some girls* [i.e., not her] are afraid if they don't find someone, they will be left-behinds [quedadas]." In other words, in the still-powerful respect schema, which is reinforced by community gossip, women have no choice but to marry the one whom destiny gives them, or they risk losing social adulthood.

Alma tries to navigate between her desire to have a companionate marriage to the man of her choice and her fear of losing altogether and never marrying. She decides to have sex with her boyfriend because in terms of the trust schema, it should be a joint decision that will bring them closer to commitment and marriage. When she ends up pregnant, however, she fears judgment from adherents to the respect schema, and in an effort to shore up her public reputation she chooses to move in with her in-laws as if she were a traditional wife. Her final lines signal her ambivalence about her beliefs and her choices: "maybe it will be okay"; "I have the hope that . . . we will marry." But the outcome for Alma is far from certain, and she more clearly referenced this ambivalence in another segment of the same interview. When I asked about her schooling and if she wanted to get a job, she replied:

> My mother [Ofalia, quoted previously] worked hard and sacrificed a lot so I could go to school. She wanted me to be able to support myself. I met Antonio in secondary school. He became my friend. We could talk about everything. I could have gone to the city to take another course, maybe accounting. But if I did go, then what would I do after? I knew no one there. What if I could not find a job? I have spent much of my life alone. I want to be a mother and have a family, to be together. I was confused about what to do.

In contrast with Alma's ambivalence, another young woman, Chela, showed evidence of some compartmentalization of beliefs. When I first interviewed her at age 16, she talked about her parents' desire for her to marry and stay in the community, living a traditional lifestyle. She linked her understanding of the respect schema to her admiration and love for her mother:

My mother did not really know my father when she married. They had seen each other on the corner, but when he asked his parents to talk to her parents, she was surprised. But the parents talked to her and told her he was a hardworking young man, and she thought she would like to marry him. They married, and my mother has lived here with my grandparents all her life. . . .

She has worked very hard to raise us and is very active in the church. Everyone likes her and says she is a good and virtuous woman. . . . My mother always had time for me and taught me how to take care of a home, cook, and work hard. And my father has said that I am just like my mother. I expect that I will marry and live here. I would be sad to go too far away from my parents, especially my mother. She would be lonely without me.

When I asked Chela what kind of man she thought she would marry, she emphasized the values inherent in the respect schema: "I hope I find a good man who is hardworking and will want to care for his family. That is the most important thing."

In subsequent interviews, she continued to voice her desire to live a traditional life and to marry within the community. Chela also noted she would depend on her parents' opinion in choosing a spouse. She never alluded to the trust schema values in describing the kind of spouse she wanted or how she envisioned her future married life. The only time she referenced the trust schema itself was in conversations with friends about the actions of characters on telenovelas or in discussions about how city women behaved. For example, she once commented to me that American women and Mexican urban women did not want to marry unless they could find a perfect love. She said, "These women are so crazy. They don't want to have families and find husbands who will provide for the children. They just want to have fun and go out dancing with these men who will never support them." Chela only referenced the values of the trust schema in this one context and never acknowledged them when discussing her life, family, or personal goals and aspirations. She appeared to keep them compartmentalized in her mind.

Another respondent, Cecelia, was 24 in 2014, and she had chosen a path different from those of Alma and Chela, handling contradiction in a more extreme way by rejecting both alternatives and removing herself from the community completely. Cecelia's father farmed and was one of the few men who did not migrate. Her mother maintained the household and raised animals for extra income. As the only daughter, Cecelia was close to her mother, who encouraged and supported her education. Cecelia completed secondary school in a nearby town and, with help from her mother, enrolled in a practical nursing course in the city. Her father opposed her education and insisted that she return to the village and marry. Cecelia refused and took a job in the city. She explained her decision: "Going to school in the city was hard for me. Coming from the village, I did not fit in. I had no friends, but I worked hard. I passed my course with good marks, and my cousin's husband helped me find a job. I make my own money now and plan to move into my own place soon. I am independent, and I can choose what I want to do. I have my own friends now." In this excerpt, Cecelia emphasizes her independence and autonomy in making these choices. She makes no mention of her father's disapproval or of village opinions derived from the respect schema. She also does not explicitly discuss marriage.

Later in the same interview, when I asked directly if she ever planned to marry or have children, she said: "I just turned 24. People here [in Santa Ana] say that I am being left behind [*me estoy quedando*]. My father says that no man will marry a girl who roams around the city and lives without supervision. My uncle worries too because many men in the city do not have good intentions. He says it is better to marry from the village where you know the family's character. The people here are very backward [*atrasado*]. I miss my mother, but it is better if I stay away." She voices her awareness of the respect schema, but she distances herself from it and acknowledges at the end that she avoids confronting contradiction and dissonance by staying away from the village. To attain autonomy, Cecelia feels that she must cut herself off from family and community, possibly foreclosing the option to marry and have children at all.

Only two of the women I interviewed in 2014 showed the beginnings of some type of cognitive integration between the conflicting schemas. Both were participants in a recently introduced microcredit lending program offered by an international foundation in partnership with an NGO. Women from three different towns formed a group, elected officers, chose a name, and then met regularly to award and collect loans and to attend required training sessions taught by outsiders on topics ranging from how to develop a business plan to building self-esteem. The goal of the program was to help rural women to build small enterprises to improve the lives of their families. The women used the funds to buy animals for breeding, undertake agricultural improvements, develop small food-vending ventures, and so on. All of the participants were married women with children. The two residents of Santa Ana whom I interviewed, Marisol and Teresa, talked openly about the conflicts their involvement with the NGO generated in their families and how they handled these. When I asked Marisol about this, she said:

> When I married and my husband left for the north, I had to live with my in-laws. I had two children there, and it was hard. We were trying to survive off our land, but the price of corn went too low. My husband could not always find work in the North [the United States], and there were months when we had many struggles to eat [and] pay for medicines and school. One day, a teacher at the school told me about the program. She knew I raised pigs when I could. She said that I could borrow money to buy the animals and their feed and then pay it back. When I told my in-laws, they were not supportive. They said, "How can you go traveling off on your own to meetings? What will people say? There will be strange men there. You need to be home with your children. Who will take care of them?"
>
> I called my husband. I reminded him that when we married, we agreed to talk through things and share our ideas. I told him about the loan program and that it would help us in our struggle to get ahead [*lucha de salir adelante*]. The life of our village has always been one of struggle. To get ahead, you have to work hard. I said he was doing his part. I wanted to help too, and this program was only for women. I told him my idea to buy more pigs and save the money so we could make sure our children could go to high school, and so we could get our own house someday. I said to him, "I am their mother. It is my first responsibility to care for them. I want to be a good mother by helping them this way. Give me your advice [*dame su consejo*]." He asked me what his parents thought, and I told him. He said I should take my son with me to the meetings and that way people would not gossip about me. I agreed with him, and so I joined the group. And my animals have done well, so we all live a little better now. Even my in-laws are in agreement that I am a good mother.

In this excerpt, Marisol describes wanting to engage in a behavior that she knows will be judged negatively by the gender norms of the respect model, especially since her husband is absent and she is living under the authority of her in-laws. In order to reconcile her conflicting goals, she creatively harnesses the life-is-a-struggle schema to the expectations of good mothering in the respect schema. She then invokes the trust schema to remind her husband that they have agreed to make joint decisions and work together for the good of the family. In keeping with this stance, she asks for his advice not his permission. He responds by suggesting a solution: she should take her son along to meetings to avoid gossip.

Unlike Marisol, Teresa was living with her husband and three children in their own home. He cultivated their small plot, but to make extra cash he also repaired automobiles at a garage in a nearby town, a skill he had learned in the United States. They were surviving but still needed to finish construction on their house and wanted to buy another plot of land. When Teresa learned of the project from Marisol, she brought it up to her husband. She too reminded him that life for villagers is a struggle, and she told him: "Since we married, we have worked hard together to build our house and take care of our family. You are the husband, and you provide our food and what we need every day. But everything is a struggle. We don't get anything by just sitting here. They don't give men the right to these loans, only women. I want to be a good mother to our children and help you with the finances so we can get the money to buy the land we need and improve our future." According to Teresa, her husband told her to join and said that it was good she was working to care for the family. He even stayed home to watch the kids sometimes when she had to go to a meeting, which he had not done previously.

Both of these women forged an integration of potentially conflicting views in a similar way. They did not directly challenge traditional gendered expectations nor did they employ empowerment discourses to argue that they should be given equal rights to work or the freedom to use their time as they saw fit. Instead, they expanded the definition of good mothering and the goals it entails. Holly Worthen (2012) documents a similar strategy among women involved in microcredit in Jalisco, Mexico, which suggests that a common cultural solution to resolving these conflicting goals may be emerging. While it might seem surprising that neither my respondents nor those of Worthen used empowerment schemas, given their exposure to them through NGO workshops, Quinn (1996, 416) points out that new cultural task solutions generally evolve out of older ones already at hand.[6] In this case, the tensions between the trust and respect schemas' expectations for women's roles were resolved by harnessing the existing model of life-as-struggle to ideas about how good mothers meet their family's needs.

The push for Marisol and Teresa to undertake the more difficult cognitive strategy of integration likely stems from their specific situation: they were presented with an opportunity that required a choice, which forced them to confront directly conflicting expectations and think about strategies to resolve them. As Worthen (2012, 374) points out, her respondents in a similar situation did not set out to change gender roles. Rather, once they joined the group and began to attend meetings, they became invested in defending their actions to others, which forced them to rationalize the conflicting expectations and ended up leading to changes in male and female roles.

Conclusion

In writing about the transformation of patriarchy, Kandiyoti (1988, 286) says, "New strategies and forms of consciousness do not simply emerge from the ruins of the old and smoothly produce a new consensus, but they are created through personal and political struggles which are often complex and contradictory." Examples of these contradictions abound in the data I have presented from rural Mexico. Women there, much like those discussed by Güvenç (this volume) in Ankara, Turkey, are struggling with rapidly changing circumstances and exposure to new ideas. The data demonstrate that the psychological motivations underpinning women's responses to varied beliefs and changing social conditions are complex and far from uniform. Schema theory posits that people assemble their understandings of the world both from their lived experiences and from exposure to different sets of beliefs and ideas that circulate as discourses through a community. Furthermore, not all cultural schemas are internalized to the same degree by different individuals.

In rural Oaxaca, changing socioeconomic conditions frame the parameters within which people adjust their marital and residential choices. These, in turn, affect the aspects of shared schemas that become meaningful and motivating at different moments in women's lives. The older generation of women in Oaxaca, for example, did not question their adherence to the respect schema of marriage, which derived from their shared experiences growing up in patrilocal families. Because there were no other options open to them, the accommodation to patriarchal practices seemed inevitable; it was how the world was. However, as migration became an option for men, infusing cash into the community, women began to resist the harshness of life as in-marrying daughters-in-law. Many were able to successfully play on men's desires, rooted in the respect schema, to be known as successful household heads and thus convinced their husbands to build separate houses and live neolocally. The residential changes women set in motion began to shape different lived experiences for their children.

The daughters of these women in particular were raised in nuclear households with more independence, and many were able to attend school, where they were exposed to outside ideas. These daughters perceived the new living arrangement and prolonged father absence as causes of their childhood suffering, and many explicitly said they wanted a different kind of marriage, a companionate one where they lived together with their husbands either in Mexico or in the United States. However, as political events made crossing the US border more difficult and dangerous, many of these young women remained behind in rural areas, unsure of how to navigate when their changing ideas conflicted with the realities of a life without many viable options.

Individuals differed in how they responded to this cognitive dissonance. Some remained confused and ambivalent and, much like Güvenç's Turkish respondents, resorted to the use of individual coping mechanisms. Others mentally compartmentalized the conflicting ideas in order to avoid distress. Only two women appear to have achieved a genuine integration of the competing schemas into a new framework by recasting their desire to participate in a microcredit group as a dutiful obligation in line with a third widely shared cultural schema: life-as-struggle. This feat of synthesis worked because it enabled family members to support these women's activities and not view them as challenging the existing social order. Much like Manago's (this volume) respondents who participated in the feminist drama group in Zinacantán, these compromises utilized existing cultural schemas and not the new language of rights and autonomy espoused by NGO leaders.

In every situation outlined in this chapter, women exhibited agency—that is, they actively attempted to understand the changing conditions of their social world and adjust their expectations and behaviors accordingly. It is possible to read into their responses elements of accommodation to patriarchal practices, but their mental views of these practices varied from unquestioned acceptance, to ambivalence, to outright rejection. Similarly, there were many examples of what observers would label resistance, even when that resistance did little to change the larger system or to overtly challenge patriarchal authority. This consideration of the array of beliefs and behaviors displayed by women over forty years in rural Mexico clearly demonstrates the complexity of the psychology behind the range of women's responses to patriarchy.

Notes

1. All translations are my own and have been checked by two research assistants from Oaxaca; pseudonyms for the name of the town and the participants have been used to protect confidentiality. Various phases of this project were approved by different Institutional Review Board applications at East Carolina University.

2. I borrow the terms to label these schemas (respeto/respect and confianza/trust) from those used by Hirsch (2003) in her pioneering and comprehensive work on changing conceptions of marriage in Mexico. My respondents used these same terms to capture some of the key aspects of their changing views of marital and gender relations. Nonetheless, some details of the schemas themselves and the elaboration of associated gender roles vary from aspects of Hirsch's descriptions, and I point out these discrepancies in the text.

3. See Quinn (2005a) for a fuller description of the methodology employed by cognitive anthropologists to elicit rich natural discourses suitable for schema analysis.

4. Ana Maria Alonso (1997) documents similar patterns in domestic violence cases brought to court in the 1850s in Chihuahua, Mexico. Women there argued to judges that their husbands were guilty of disrespecting them publicly and owed them "faithfulness, courtesy, trust and economic maintenance" (39).

5. The term *quedada* is used to refer to unmarried women who are thought to have missed the chance to marry and have a family (Napolitano 2002, 168). Married women whose husbands have stopped sending remittances or returning for visits are called *abandonadas* (abandoned women).

6. Similarly, Julia Broussard (2009) in an evaluation of an NGO designed to promote sustainable development among rural Chinese farm women found that the women reported that the education they received from the NGO caused them to alter their thinking and helped them to speak up and participate in decision-making. She said the NGO's schema was persuasive to the participating women because of traditional links in Chinese culture between education, thinking, relating, and speaking and because communist ideologies explicitly connect changes in backward or "feudal" thinking to gender equality. The environmental education component did *not* work because it was taught in a factual manner as scientific knowledge disconnected from the participants' schemas of thinking, speaking, and relating.

CHAPTER EIGHT

What Women's Experiences in Disadvantaged Families in Ankara, Turkey, Have to Tell about Patriarchy

GÜLDEN GÜVENÇ

Turkey is among those countries in the Middle East, North Africa, and South and East Asia that have what has been called a classic patriarchal system (Kandiyoti 1988, 278). Kandiyoti defines this system as one organized around the patrilocally extended household that gives senior men authority over all other residents. This authority is regularly reinforced by men's violence against women. Girls are married at a young age, join the husband's family of origin, and have to obey the male family members and the senior women, in particular their mother-in-law. The young married woman, the bride (*gelin*), is labeled as the "daughter of a stranger" (*el kızı*) and is separated from her own family. Brides are not allowed to work outside the home, but their status increases when they give birth, particularly to sons (who are expected to provide old age security), and later when they become another bride's mother-in-law. In classic patriarchy, the mother-in-law controls younger women's obedience to men. Thus, as women become mothers-in-law, they gain considerable authority in the household, and at times senior women can even come to have more power than their husbands, because as these senior men age, their household authority wanes (Kandiyoti 1988, 279).

In order to survive under patriarchal conditions, most young Turkish women today continue to adopt the traditional repertoires of intrafamily sacrifice and respecting elders; only a few challenge these approaches via resistance and struggles for power (Güvenç 2014, 81). However, the contemporary context for patriarchy differs radically by socioeconomic class. The particularities of patriarchy for different classes of women can only be understood and ultimately contested if researchers investigate women's familial conflicts and the personal dilemmas resulting from patriarchy firsthand. These issues are different for women in disadvantaged families and those from the middle and upper classes.

Middle- and upper-class women are more likely to struggle with the disjunction between patriarchal values and ideas imported from the West. Women from lower-class families are much more likely to still be living under the conditions of classic patriarchy. The case of the poor families who have migrated to cities, which I analyze in this chapter, provides a novel opportunity to investigate the conditions that foster patriarchal relationships when traditional extended household residential patterns are changing. Furthermore, two foundational conditions of classic patriarchy—the authority men traditionally derived from their full employment (in agriculture) and the support they traditionally gained from their extended patrilocal households—are likely to have eroded somewhat with impoverishment. Yet patriarchy persists. It persists in large part in the hearts and minds of the actors, including women. It is the psychology of the women living in patriarchal societies that I explore in this chapter. To do so, I draw on a study I conducted on how disadvantaged women in one urban squatter settlement talk about their responses to their husband's violence and other features of their familial relationships.

Other researchers have alluded to the psychological influence of patriarchal beliefs and practices, including the effects of religion and education, on women (Abu-Lughod 1985; Chong 2006; Khurshid 2015; Manago 2014; Marrow 2013), and they have called attention to women's apparent willing subordination to these patriarchal beliefs and practices (White 2013, 170). In the research reported in this chapter, I went a step further, closely examining the way women speak of the terms of this subordination and the possibilities for challenging it. My research questions were as follows:

1. How do urban disadvantaged women collaboratively (that is, in focus groups) make sense of their experiences regarding intrafamily stress, violence, anger, and miscommunication in a patriarchal context?
2. How and to what extent do they justify or naturalize in their talk the patriarchal relationships they experience?
3. What are the possibilities under the changing conditions they face for finding new ways to resist these patriarchal relationships?

In order to answer these questions, I aimed to identify, from their talk, the ways these women positioned themselves in their families, the strategies they used to do so, and the emotions they experienced in the process. My goal was to interpret the contradictions and dilemmas the women faced and to evaluate the potential for their construction of their own agency and hence new forms of subjectivity. This research thus sheds new light on the conditions needed for patriarchy to persist and how it might be dismantled.

In the following sections, I first summarize the broader social context of the disadvantaged women in Saraycık, an urban squatter settlement in Ankara, Turkey. Next, I briefly summarize the conceptual and methodological issues I had to resolve in my study. Finally, I describe the women's construction of emotions and coping strategies in daily talk, followed by a discussion of this discourse and some suggestions for future research.

The Social Context of Patriarchal Relations in Turkey

The development of modern technology and the mechanization of rural production in Turkey during the 1960s made agriculture more capital-intensive, resulting in the consolidation of landownership and the loss of smaller, family farms (Tekeli 1990, 145–46). In this process, although the use of advanced technology restricted both women's and men's participation in rural production, a division of labor developed. Some women continued to work in labor-intensive jobs, such as harvesting or manual tasks on tobacco or hazelnut farms, or in carpet weaving while most men left agricultural production altogether to pursue short-term seasonal jobs, like tourism, fishing, sponge diving, or working in the construction sector in cities. The result was an initial wave of male migration to urban centers in Turkey followed by the exodus of whole families from rural areas.

Families that migrated to urban areas started building squatter settlements on the peripheries of the cities where relatives had migrated previously. Thus, the extended family of classic patriarchy continued to serve as a means of social and economic solidarity in a new context. At the same time, the age and sex hierarchies that distinguished the rural patriarchal families seem to have been weakened after migration (Buğra and Keyder 2005, 26–27). This was, first, because patrilocal extended families might live in proximity but not together: for example, in the Saraycık case, family members lived in different flats in the same apartment complex. This living arrangement resulted in less intense daily oversight of younger women by their mothers-in-law. Second, many men were unable to find good jobs, and their unemployment, their marginal and low-paid temporary jobs (often seasonal ones), or other underemployment undercut their authority in the family. The lack of jobs led to interventionist policies by the Turkish government to provide a safety net for the newly landless and unemployed families. However, such policies excluded both women and men from production, relegating them to the care of their elderly parents/parents-in-law (Tekeli 1990, 148), on whom they continued to depend for material support. For example, in Saraycık, the elder generation typically owned the flats in which their sons and daughters-in-law lived, and the elders exercised considerable authority over their junior relatives, intervening regularly in their lives despite living separately. Many women so situated submitted to traditional patriarchal gender roles and relationships in exchange for the only economic security available to them, which Kandiyoti (1988, 282) has called the "patriarchal bargain."

Women and the Turkish State

In order to explicate fully the position of the disadvantaged women who are the focus of this chapter, I first briefly describe the overall situation of Turkish women vis-à-vis the Turkish state. Although women have been legally defined as equal to men in the public sphere (Tekeli 1990, 148), even modern urban middle- and upper-class women are not exempt from discrimination in the private sphere. In parallel with what has been called the nineteenth-century "cult of true womanhood" in North America and England, the primary duty of Turkish women is to become "enlightened mothers" (Sirman 2000, 252; Tekeli 1990, 148–49). This situation has led to a psychological split and hence a tension between the public and private images of educated women, which Toprak (1990) attributes to their legal emancipation without actual liberation. Consequently, many researchers in Turkey call attention to a lack of critical analysis and of a nuanced definition of modernity, which takes different indigenous forms in non-Western contexts and also reflects "local specificities" in the same society (Özbay 1990, 8–9; Sirman 2000, 250–55; Toprak 1990, 39–41).

Toprak (1990), for instance, points to the influence of Islam in Ottoman Turkey, at which time even well-to-do women were treated unequally. Islam was accepted by the Arabic tribes in the seventh century, and the Ottoman Turks were converted to Islam approximately in the tenth century. However, the Turkish republic, as the nation-state of the Turkish people, was not founded until the twentieth century. The situation of women described here was valid for almost all the Islamic women in the tribes of that time and continues to be the case in classic Islamic patriarchy. After the death of Muhammad, Islamic women lost their right of inheritance and their parental rights, and their general status came to be defined by arranged marriage without the option of divorce, by segregation and seclusion, and by subordination to men's authority (Mernissi 1991, 4, 120–24; Toprak 1990, 40). This subordination and this cluster of limitations, both legal and socioeconomic, legitimized patriarchy in the name of Islam. If a woman resisted a man's authority, she would be beaten. Women's primary duties were to be homemakers and mothers, and they could not go out of the house without the permission of their husband. Men were the rulers of the family.

It was this cultural regulation of women that Kemalist reforms in the Turkish nation were designed to change by transforming the society from an Islamic to a modern Western system. Secularization of the educational system, opportunities for career development and employment, equal rights in marriage and divorce, equal political rights, inheritance rights, and property ownership were accorded to both genders. With regard to child-rearing practices, "a shift from the model of total interdependence to the model of psychological independence" promoted individual independence and self-reliance, that is, autonomy (Kağıtçıbaşı and Ataca 2005, 335). However, education and employment were still limited to upper-class women. Even then, educated urban women found themselves torn between craving the new economic independence and keeping the traditional virtue expected of women, that is, sacrifice for the family (Sirman 2000, 254, 259). Legal measures and secularization were not sufficient conditions for the liberation of women. Sirman (2000, 263) summarizes the situation: "The modern Turkish woman is a subject with a specific agency, a socially competent individual who as a result of her education is able to cultivate her mind, but who also through love learns to sacrifice herself and desire for the care and guidance of others in the family and in the nation. It was perhaps this unity of self-assertion and compassion which appeared as a paradox to Turkish academics who attempted to explain women's position in modern Turkish society through the phrase 'emancipated but not liberated.'"

As depicted by White (2015), the male version of female sacrifice paints the man as the selfless hero ready to give his life for his nation, granting him the honorable death of a martyr. Thus, the central virtues of Kemalism and secularism are not that different from those of Islam and conservatism in Turkey, and they are reciprocal but unequal for men and women. Men's obedience is to the state and their sacrifice is in defense of the nation; women's obedience is to their husband and to family elders and their sacrifice is in defense of the family. White (2013, 101–94) describes how these principles not only penetrate public institutions and draw their boundaries, but also mediate the construction of men's multiple identities and subjectivities, which are fundamental to the reproduction of their solidarity networks in the nation-state.

Disadvantaged Turkish women in urban squatter settlements are heirs to this history of the various state attempts to legislate the status of all Turkish women, and yet their position differs from that of more advantaged women. The status of middle- and upper-class Turkish women may be considered the product of the modernity that penetrated the Ottoman Empire during its late phase and that flourished during the establishment of the nation-state. But this imported modernity has hardly reached or changed the lives of women in the lower socioeconomic strata. Instead, the disadvantaged women suffer from the particular conditions that result when historical patriarchy meets urban poverty. As Kandiyoti (1988) has explained, the patriarchal bargain is an entirely rational and understandable one for them to make.

Conceptual Definitions, Methodological Issues, and Reflexivity

My conceptualization of the material world in which the women of my study are immersed is based on my own observations and previous studies of poverty, illness, wars, ethnocentrism, exploitation, oppression, violence, and patriarchy. Women's position must be comprehended within this larger social context, that is, within the local history and local meanings of social and cultural relationships (Chong 2006, 719; Mathews 2005, 105–6; Seymour 2006, 304–5, 315). For instance, we should pay attention to the meanings and ideologies of emancipation and liberation embedded in the global discourses of the market economy, state policies, and legal, religious, educational, and media interpretations of these. The cultural meanings of all these socioeconomic institutions are at the core of contradictions and personal dilemmas (Chong 2006, 707, 710, 716) and cannot be omitted. While each formation has its own history, patriarchy resonates with what is going on in the global world that surrounds it, including the current discourses and practices of neoliberalism.

At the same time, the different moral stances women take, the individual decisions they make, and the autonomy some but not others manage to exercise under such conditions make it clear that to understand such matters, it is not enough to think in terms of their common economic and cultural circumstances and practices. The researcher must move beyond these commonalities to try to understand how individual women construct their subjectivities. In my way of thinking about it, subjectivity is grounded in two concepts: emotional regulation (strategies for coping with strong feelings) and agency (the capacity to achieve personal goals). Both aspects of subjectivity are critical to my analysis.

I begin with the assumption that local women make sense of their larger historical and socioeconomic context on their own terms, perhaps identifying and trying to develop emancipatory or liberatory practices despite—or even within—intersecting ethnic, class, familial, and gender relations (Sirman 2000, 263–65; Toprak 1990, 40). I argue that new forms of subjectivity, or even the beginnings of them, can be constituted out of the contradictions and individual dilemmas women face and that evidence for these subjectivities may emerge in their discourse (Hosking and Pluut 2010, 61–69; Quinn 1992, 121–23; Strauss and Quinn 1997, 8–10; Tirado and Gálvez 2008, 225–45; Wittig 1985, 802). At the same time, in almost no cases do the newer forms of subjectivity add up to effective resistance to patriarchy.

Although researchers who analyze discourse may take different stances toward the subjectivities and ideologies of study participants as these bear on their practices, all of us are concerned with both the subjectivity and the ideology of the researcher. Because doing research is an intervention in the daily lives of the participants, researchers must go beyond an understanding of the participants' perspectives and reflect on their own contribution to and, especially, their power in the research process. The privileged position of the researcher in producing knowledge is captured in the notion of reflexivity (Lutz and White 1986, 429–30; Potter and Wetherell 1987, 182–84). Researcher reflexivity involves the monitoring of the researcher's assumptions about the relationships between themselves and study participants, whose class, gender, sociopolitical, cultural, and linguistic perspectives are likely to differ from those of the researcher, which affects the shape of the research process (Hosking and Pluut 2010, 60–62; Lutz and White 1986, 415–20). With reflexivity, "knowing" becomes a participatory activity rather than a one-sided intervention of the researcher alone (Blackman et al. 2008, 14–16; Hosking and Pluut 2010, 60–62).

In line with a reflexive approach that grants an equivalent role to those conducting the study and to the participants in it, I found it necessary to modify my original research plan. Based on my initial proposal, women would have participated in a series of communication and assertiveness training sessions. But Saraycık women showed no interest in such sessions and failed to sign up for them. Instead, I was able to take advantage of their propensity for talking directly with one another about intrafamily issues. I adapted this local style of interaction for my research by designing focus groups to simulate the women's informal group exchanges. They willingly joined these focus groups, and I used this opportunity to ask open-ended questions bearing on my research, which they readily collaborated in answering. Thus, instead of attempting to train them, I ended up listening to the women's own accounts (Güvenç 2014, 80–81).

The Empirical Study

The women in my study talked about daily familial events and practices. Because of my desire to understand how they made sense of family life in Saraycık, I focused on how they described intrafamily relationships, their emotions surrounding these relationships, and the agency they exhibited in working out strategies for dealing with them. I conducted three focus groups with a total of thirty-four Muslim women, who were recruited from handicraft courses provided by the local government in conjunction with the nongovernmental organization Association to Promote Contemporary Life. Most women in this study were between 21 and 36 years old and were married. All had originally migrated from Central Anatolia and the Black Sea regions, had lived in Ankara for approximately ten to twenty years along with two to five other family members, and resided in the same building as their in-laws, although they and the in-laws lived in separate flats. Their mobility was usually limited to the confines of their district (Güvenç 2014, 79–80).

I asked six open-ended questions on stress, violence, anger, and communication, and I recorded and then transcribed the women's answers. The interview questions probed who was to blame for intrafamily conflict, the conditions leading to such negative experiences, the negative feelings that resulted from these experiences, and the coping strategies, if any, that women used to address them. In my subsequent analysis, I categorized the women's descriptions into three themes: relationships, emotions, and strategy building.

Women's Emotional Reactions to Familial Conflicts

The accounts of women related to familial issues revealed detailed descriptions of relationships they found problematic and the emotions that attended these. Women typically defined their problematic intrafamily experiences in emotional terms, such as the irritability, sadness, frustration, tension, or anger they felt,

Women's Experiences in Disadvantaged Families

and they attributed the causes of these experiences to relationship issues with children (beating, separation, illness), in-laws, or spouses (oppression, verbal or physical violence, and the like). They occasionally also referred to unfavorable social conditions, such as the lack of education or unemployment. At the same time, they blamed themselves for these relationship problems and described their psychological experiences in detail.

Women's emotional repertoires are illustrated by the following excerpt, in which they talk about their stresses:[1]

> Gülden: How do you define stress?
> Fatma: It is like sickness, one gets frustrated and sick.
> Hayriye: One has recurrent thoughts of sickness.
> Sevim: I become fearful and expect that something bad will happen.
> Gülden: Which events cause stress?
> Sevim: I live with my in-laws, and I feel awful when I am at home. I can't make up my mind whether to stay or leave.
> Gülden: How come?
> Sevim: My husband is very nervous. When he says something nasty, I respond back. If I don't do this, I feel extremely frustrated. But my father- and mother-in-law provoke him against me, and then he beats me.
> Defne: I think in our neighborhood we experience more stress because here we suffer a lot.
> Gülden: Can you describe your situation a bit more?
> Defne: My parents wed me to this man without asking my consent. Whenever I am cross with him, I beat my children. Then I get . . . terrible headaches.
> Sevim: I fight with my husband because he does not care for anyone at home. I get extremely angry. We have four children. Every evening as soon as he comes home, he finishes his dinner and falls asleep. He is not interested in what we do, how we feel. I get mad at him, but instead of quarreling with him, I beat my children.

These Saraycık women and others like them define intrafamily stress as a chain reaction that starts with the provocation of the in-laws and is followed by the husband's verbal or physical violence. Many women who experience this pressure confess that instead of fighting back, they beat their children. These women usually report being suffused with anger, self-accusation, frustration, fear, and anxiety, and they feel awful. Sometimes, the stress is expressed in bodily symptoms, such as headaches and illnesses. Under such pressure, the woman may find herself in a dilemma. For instance, Sevim feels frustrated and angry when she does not react against her husband's verbal aggression—but if she does respond, he beats her. The source of all four women's stress is clearly summarized by Defne when she asserts that women in their neighborhood suffer due to the insensitivity of their in-laws, husbands, or natal families. The following excerpt offers further examples of how women say they feel under such stress:

> Gülden: How do you feel when you are stressed?
> Ceyda: I do not want to live. I want to hit or beat children.
> Sinem: I cry, otherwise I cannot stand this situation. If someone condemns me, yells at me, I cannot respond, I only cry. But after the man [her husband] leaves, I regret [that] I could not answer back.
> Nazmiye: I also beat children, [and] I regret this afterward. I say I won't repeat it, but when I get mad, I cannot keep my promise.
> Jale: I get tired, I don't want to do anything. I perceive myself as a failure.
> Munise: At that moment, I can do nothing. I feel as if the world has turned upside down, I feel a burden on my shoulders. I say to my husband, "I wish to burn all my family [along] with the house." He responds, "Sure, do it, so that both of us [will] get burned and [we will] be free." I do not know what to do.

Almost all of the women say they are aggressive toward their children when they are stressed. They report weakness, helplessness, depression, and guilt at the end of these experiences, which they want intensely to overcome, but as another woman says, "I do not know how to do it."

Women who experience violence from their husbands may verbalize an urge to run away or commit suicide, while at the same time they worry about what might happen to their children if they leave. As already noted, children are the most likely external targets of women's anger in response to all sorts of domestic violence and threats. But when it cannot be externalized in this way, their anger may be directed inward in the form of thoughts of suicide. The following excerpt illustrates the suicidal feelings of three women who, once again, all report feelings of stress and frustration in addition to their self-destructive thoughts in response to the physical violence of their husbands.

Gülden: How do you feel when you face physical violence?

Bengi: I do not sleep that night. I wonder what I should do in order to fix things. However, I cannot do this. When things are out of my hands, I can't achieve what I want. I am sorry for myself sometimes [and] I want to commit suicide. I say if I disappear, things may cool down. I say maybe it is [because] of me that things get out of control. Things would be better if I [were] not around, and I think of suicide. There were times when I took two, three, four pills.

Ela: I also thought of suicide, but I don't anymore. If I experience violence, I become very unhappy and sad. I don't cry, but things get broken inside me. I miss the feeling of love, but my hatred and grudge[s] get bigger, and then I feel very sad. When my husband beats me, I can't treat him lovingly. At such times, I force myself to be like former times, but as I said I feel that something has been destroyed in me. Afterward, this feeling is over, of course, but at that moment [of violence], I feel great pain.

Aysu: To speak . . . the truth, at first I want to leave the house. I wonder if it would be better that way. If I kill myself, would it be better? Then, I start to worry about my children and can do nothing. I stop talking to my husband for weeks. I cry, I sulk. I share my feelings with no one. This is my character.

It is striking that although women may abuse and beat their children, motherhood still mitigates against suicide and presumably serves as an anchor for their feelings of self-worth.

Emotional Regulation and Other Coping Strategies

Very often, women seem to rationalize their husband's disrespect, insensitivity, or aggression, justifying it in terms of the men being caught between the provocation of their parents and the demands of their wife. This being the case, nothing can be done; their husband's violence is inevitable, and they must live with it. Thus, some women naturalize strategies of subordination: "Because you live together, you have to see it as normal. There is no solution. You see him all the time. There will always be fights, good days, bad days, peaceful days, restless days. One has to accept this." Women who see the world this way may confess that they sulk and cry at times out of frustration or beat their children, but they have other, more accepting responses to their husband's violence. Like Binnaz in the next excerpt, they may blame themselves and try to understand where they failed. Or, like other speakers, they may absent themselves or try to calm themselves down.

> Gülden: When you are faced with violence, how do you react and deal with it?
> Saniye: I usually repress my anger and cry.
> Binnaz: I take it as a matter of pride and try to understand why this happened, why we cannot talk about it. I criticize myself. I try to understand where I failed.
> Sena: When I experience violence, I think of nothing, I only bear a grudge. My husband forgets that he . . . hurt me, but when I remind him of this, he cannot come close to me. I go to my friends and do not see him till evening. If possible, I stay away.
> Gülden: When you undergo violence and react, does it work?
> Perihan: No, I become sad. Does it work? No, my children also start crying with me. I am helpless.
> Gülden: What should you do in order to overcome violence?
> Defne: Either my husband or I should leave the place so that there is no fight. If we start yelling at each other, violence increases.
> Gülden: What can be done to cope with aggression?
> Billur: If I can calm down, I can perceive things from a different perspective, but I am not [often] successful in doing this.
> Gülden: What do you do?
> Billur: One should not escalate the argument. One should have a positive outlook, but this is not possible. My children, for instance, become worse when I become violent toward them.

Here are a few other examples of acceptance and self-blame, drawn from elsewhere in the interviews:

> If one wants to control everything, manage everything, this won't work, because the other person has . . . pride, a capacity to do certain things. These should be accepted.

If I [could] express myself, I would get along better with my spouse. I create the problem and make everyone unhappy. Afterward I repent, but cannot find a solution.

What one says to oneself is very important.

Although a few women have strategies for responding to conflict situations (see below), many others are inclined to view themselves as helpless in the face of their husband's violence. Attempts to calm oneself down or to walk away from the situation can be seen as steps toward agency, but they are small ones indeed.

Very occasionally, men do treat their wives as autonomous individuals, but strikingly, these fortunate few women seem to be so immersed in patriarchal values that they have trouble accepting the opportunities for independence that their husband extends to them. For example: "My husband accepts my wishes, says that if I want to work, he says okay. He says that 'when someone is nasty toward you, don't be silent. Answer him or her back,' but I am not successful. Sometimes he gives me money to buy whatever I want, but I cannot do it."

In summary, although many women are aware of the nature of their marital conflicts and dilemmas and express the wish to have more of a say in family matters, most of them do not manage to do so. They often view these conflicts and dilemmas as unsolvable.

Attempts at Resolution

The next excerpts illustrate how some women, rather than taking responsibility for their anger toward their husband and in-laws, plainly attribute the source of the anger to these others, accusing them of instigating it.

Gülden: Suna, who becomes angry in the house? Is it you, your husband, or children?

Suna: My husband never listens to me. I become very angry and nervous. I become angry with the wives [elti] of my husband's brother [enişte]. They are proud of themselves and belittle others, so I feel anger. My husband is also very tense, and he is bothered [by] my attitudes. When I start talking, he refuses to answer me. He says that he does not want to argue with me. He wants me to be perfect, but I am not. He says that I talk a lot. He wants silence. My husband likes silence. I have no problems with my kids. I love them, and they do not have problems with me either. They never hurt me, but I have a lot of issues with my husband.

Suna blames her relatives for showing contempt toward her, and she blames her husband for not supporting her against them. Her descriptions of disappointment and disconnection, particularly from her husband, illustrate the rejection of her own psychological responsibility for miscommunication and other negative events and for the resulting emotions she feels toward her spouse and other family members.

An awareness of miscommunication and negative relationships is seen once again in the following excerpt, which suggests at least some women's resilience and their efforts to lead independent, separate lives in the face of their husband's and other people's repressive actions.

> Fatma: The intervention of others, for instance our relatives poking their nose into our family life at home, makes me very nervous. I want to deal with our own family problems myself. If I can't do this, then I want support from my husband. If he does not give me a hand, this is stressful for me, because I share my problems with him, but he does not help me. For instance, for years, for maybe ten years, we [have] lived together with my in-laws and other relatives. From time to time, I feel suffocated. I want to take my children and go away even though part of myself would be left behind. These [feelings] cause stress. When I talk to my husband, he says that everything will take care of itself in time. Maybe time passes too quickly for him, but it is too long for me.

Fatma clearly expresses her desire to change her life and to realize her own wishes. She rejects the intervention of her in-laws, pinpoints her feelings of suffocation, and expresses her impatience in terms of passing time. She expects support from her husband, but when she does not receive it, she imagines leaving home to start a new life with her children. However, the urge for flight again creates a dilemma for her; she feels as if "part of myself would be left behind." This dilemma prevents Fatma and other women from making independent decisions.

As these excerpts from the focus groups reflect, communication always carries a positive meaning in women's family life. "Good communication" conveys respect, sharing, openness, and support for positive relationships to solve problems. Individual women's "body and soul integration," as one woman put it, in response to satisfactory communication signals the identification of this kind of interaction with positive bodily sensations. On the other hand, physical violence or destructive criticism by a husband and unjust treatment by in-laws and other people point to miscommunication in relationships.

In contrast with these examples, the next one is exceptional. It shows a rare instance of how one woman was able to resolve at least some of her marital problems, overcoming miscommunication with her husband by means of a strategic ploy:

> Gülden: What can be done about problems related to miscommunication?
> Sevil: People in our community contribute a lot to miscommunication. There are some people with whom one is not comfortable, although there are those with whom you can get along. You cannot be on good terms with all your neighbors. Sometimes, people get jealous and start gossiping. This can take place in the family too. The in-laws may become jealous and influence the family members. My mother in-law says to my husband, "Your wife goes to the neighbor. Do you know why she goes there?" I do not care about what she says [because] I have a clear conscience. I can go anywhere if I want. I told my husband that if he did not trust me, he should not let me go out. For a while, he did not permit me to go out. Hale [another group member] here knows this. I even could not go out to shop. When he saw that he [was] responsible for everything, he gave up. He used to say that I stay at home all day long and do nothing. I answered him back that this was his thought and his decision. It was not my choice. Now, things have changed: he lets me go out.

Sevil's strategy exhibits not only open communication with her husband, but also patience, skillful maneuvering, and consistent use of a respectful tone of voice. At the same time, she makes plain to her husband that she has the potential for the same independence he enjoys in her use of language such as "if I want," "his decision," and "my choice." This style of talk offers a clue to how she has been able to construct and maintain her individual autonomy in her relationship with her husband and other family members. By turning patriarchal values against her husband, by challenging him to take control of everything at home, she makes him confront the actuality of her contribution to family life. Paradoxically, by acting submissively toward her husband instead of openly resisting him, she establishes control over his decisions and their relationship. Her example suggests one avenue for positive change in marital relationships. However, this strategy did not seem to be used and perhaps did not even occur to other women in this study.

Discussion

It has been argued that emotions are part of our sense-making equipment, functioning to help individuals identify how they feel and what they can do about these feelings (Edwards 1999, 273, 281). This explanation for emotions can be applied to the women in this study. As illustrated by many of the excerpts of their talk in the focus groups, they feel guilty and repent when they beat their children. They feel angry at the provocations of their in-laws, the neglect or outright violence of their husband, and unfair treatment by their relatives. They express various bodily feelings in association with stress, such as depression, headache, trembling, irritability, fatigue, drowsiness, or loss of appetite. They also verbalize feelings of fear, hatred, sadness, anger, anxiety, obstinacy, ineffectiveness, helplessness, failure, pain, lack of trust, and obsession when they experience miscommunication and anger against them.

The chain of events leading up to their anger often culminates in women turning around and beating or yelling at children. Sometimes, women are able to put aside their negative emotions by simply acceding to the demand that they play a subordinate role. This acquiescence may be accompanied by denying the existence of problems, accepting their fate, or blaming themselves, accompanied, nonetheless, by a lot of crying. Other more active strategies to which these women resort are running away or leaving the house to avoid the emotionally stressful situation. They may take drugs. They may stop talking to their spouse or the offending in-laws. They may compensate by finding solace in doing housework, knitting, sewing, or listening to music. They often use the coping strategy of emotion regulation, training themselves, for example, to stay calm in a potentially explosive situation. A more socially positive strategy that they sometimes use is sharing their problems and feelings with friends, as they did in the focus groups organized for this study.

Women also verbalize thoughts of defending themselves and resisting authority, but these thoughts are rarely if ever translated into action. Most women confess that their reactions are generally insufficient to change their oppressive relations with their in-laws and husband or to control their anger and aggression toward their children.

Because motherhood is the most valued identity of women in patriarchal cultures, it is endowed with much anxiety. Intent on becoming better mothers, many women cope by emotional regulation, such as restraining aggression toward their children. When they do project their anger onto children and beat them in spite of their best intentions, the women typically feel terrible for doing so. Motherhood makes these women's lives worth living and bolsters their self-esteem, but it is at the same time a source of pain and guilt for them. The contradictory nature of motherhood is sometimes the felt conflict that sharpens women's dilemmas and makes them consider whether they will continue to submit to their husband and in-laws or leave the problematic relationship. While ultimately they may not be in a position to leave, their contradictory feelings about motherhood must certainly lead to greater awareness of their own unfair treatment, possibly paving the way to future action for change.

Under the conditions described, where migrant families to urban areas experience male unemployment or underemployment and the attenuation of the extended patrilocal household, women continue to suffer greatly from patriarchal relationships. They explicitly criticize their in-laws' interventions and their husband's insensitivities (Güvenç 2014, 88–89). Contrary to the case of the Bedouin women described by Abu-Lughod (1985, 246–47), whose disguised literary protests were the only avenue they had to challenge patriarchy in the public arena, Saraycık women do not hesitate to express their sentiments toward their family members publicly. My findings in Saraycık with respect to women's willingness to accuse others signify flexibility and possible movement beyond the honor code. This suggests a capacity to negotiate with in-laws or a desire to build new strategies to make others understand their feelings and needs. In this respect, the lower-class women of this study may differ from the upper-class women under Turkish and other patriarchal regimes (e.g., the educated women in Pakistan described by Khurshid 2015, 108–11; and the women in South Korea described by Chong 2006, 703). Those more privileged women seem to have made a new kind of patriarchal bargain, settling for gains in their human rights (Sirman 2000, 253–54; White 2013, 169–70) in exchange for their willing assent to the expectation that they will sacrifice for the family. Upper-class, educated Turkish women also need to confront the limitations of their agency under patriarchy.

Conclusion and Suggestions for Future Work

My study on the understandings of one group of disadvantaged urban women about their own position reveals the sticky character of classic patriarchy, despite its destabilization under conditions of globalization, unemployment, and state policies reinforcing the exclusion of the disadvantaged from the economy (Buğra and Keyder 2005, 23–27). Yet these women do seem to be trying to figure out how to cope with their anger and other feelings, to build more adaptive mothering skills vis-à-vis their children, to resist patriarchal pressure from their in-laws, and to develop open communicative relationships with their husband.

If research psychologists aim to study how to actively contribute to women's empowerment in all these respects, they must start with the participants' own expressed conflicts and dilemmas about their daily problems and needs, instead of top-down research hypotheses and training programs. It is from an understanding of these issues that new forms of subjectivity and agency can emerge. In addition, the researcher must be aware that these contradictions and dilemmas, although embedded in a global context, have deep local cultural meanings. These various cultural meanings and the way that they articulate with global influences must be attended to.

Further, researchers should be reflexively involved with their research participants over the long term, promoting collaboration on the task of gaining insight into the struggles against patriarchal pressures and creating new ways for approaching these. This work might be usefully modeled on group therapy, which recognizes the unfinished nature of subjectivity at any given point and the need to construct alternative identities out of existing understandings. Last, small-scale, intensive, qualitative studies such as this one may be most appropriate in the early stages of such research, providing the best clues to participants' own understandings of their situations.

Note

1. All interviews were conducted in Turkish, and I translated them into English. The names of the participants are pseudonyms.

CHAPTER NINE

Theorizing Female Consent
Familism, Motherhood, and Middle-Class Feminine Subjectivity in Contemporary South Korea

KELLY H. CHONG

Several contributors in this book address women's accommodations to patriarchal values within changing familial contexts, and they document how particular socialization practices and psychodynamic processes in these families shape their motivations to do so. I widen the lens of analysis to examine the ways that state policies and neoliberal economic values have intersected to influence the structure and organization of the modern middle-class family in South Korea and to explore how these changes have, in turn, generated conflicting subjectivities for women who struggle to resolve them. Of particular interest is understanding why, in the South Korean situation of cultural and social flux, many middle-class women have chosen to resolve mental distress by embracing a conservative form of evangelical Christianity that paradoxically reinforces certain patriarchal aspects of Confucian values and practices in these changing family systems and mitigates against women's exercise of transformative agency even in the face of alternative options. In particular, I argue that while church participation serves various functions, the conversion experience itself represents a cultural compromise solution (Quinn 1996) for many middle-class women experiencing these common psychological conflicts. For them, the conversion process involves a sincere recommitment to the principles of the traditional patriarchal family by stressing the necessity of women's total obedience and endurance as fundamental principles for conjugal relations and prerequisites for family harmony and cohesion. Thus, I argue that Korean women's motivations for supporting the status quo are not simply a function of a lack of choices in life but are motivated by deeper, underlying positive conservative desires.

The realm of subjectivity—defined by Ortner (2005, 31) as ensembles of modes of perception, affect, thought, and desire that animate acting subjects as well as the cultural and social formations that shape, organize, and provoke those modes of affect and thought—provides a key link between the realms of structure and agency. This concept is particularly relevant for analyzing how women, through their inscription in specific social and material relations, discursive practices, and networks of power, come to be invested in certain subject positions.

I begin the chapter with an examination of how state policies and neoliberal values associated with rapid economic modernization have altered the structure and goals of the Korean middle-class family. I outline the impact of these changing values and family dynamics on the construction of different feminine subjectivities, examine the domestic conflicts and psychic fracturing experienced by middle-class women as they attempt to navigate new paths for themselves, and explore the role of religious conservatism as a cultural compromise solution to these conflicts. Finally, I consider the implications of these findings for theories of consent and agency.

I conducted ethnographic fieldwork between 1996 and 2006 in South Korea, including in-depth interviews and participant observation with sixty married women in two large Protestant evangelical churches, one Presbyterian and the other Methodist. My previous works (Chong 2006, 2008) examine the meanings and significance of evangelical participation for these women in their particular family and social contexts in order to shed light on the issue of women and religious traditionalism. This chapter draws on these data to focus particularly on the experiences of women between the ages of 35 and 55, who comprise the generation born between Korea's postliberation (from Japan in 1945) era and the 1960s. These women came of age between the 1960s and early 1980s, and their life experiences reflect the complexities and contradictions of South Korea's industrialization and modernization period.

State Policies, Economic Modernization, and the Changing Korean Family

An important premise underlying this chapter is that the family is a key institution that exposes the intersection of state and community values and restructures these into patterns of gender and age relationships and role expectations for its members. These expectations, in turn, influence the construction of individual subjectivities. The feminist scholar Valentine Moghadam (2004, 137) notes that the family is perhaps the only societal institution that is conceptualized as "essential" and "natural." Yet family structures and the roles members occupy change constantly in response to various social, economic, and cultural pressures. Moghadam (2004, 138) finds that the family question and its correlate, the woman question, tend to come to the forefront of state attention during periods of rapid social change, socioeconomic difficulty, or political crisis.

Dongno Kim (1990) documents two profound changes that accompanied the rapid industrialization of South Korea. The first was a massive shift from the extended to the nuclear family, and the second was a transformation in the social norms of families from what he describes as a community-oriented "traditional familism" to a "modern familism" that emphasizes the welfare of the nuclear family and the exclusive pursuit of its own interests. In comparison to the Western nuclear family, Kim argues that the modern Korean family as a unit is engaged in a more intensive pursuit of the attainment of its own economic success and social status at the expense of others or of the public good.[1] He draws on Banfield's (1958) concept of amoral familism, developed from research in southern Italy, to describe this competitive family form.[2] Critics of Banfield, such as Roy Miller (1974), have suggested that this type of familism is indicative not of a lack of morality but rather of a shifting notion of what constitutes moral action by family members. He contends that where families are the only viable economic unit between the level of the individual and the state and are buffeted by shifting and unstable social conditions, family members may tend to think of themselves as being at the mercy of conditions that they cannot control (Miller 1974, 518). In such contexts, moral action could be defined as prioritizing family survival even when it results in apparently antisocial or selfish acts from the community perspective (518). As a result, the family may become an even more powerful signifier, and there may be conservative trends to strengthen it in the society at large (Moghadam 2004, 140). Thus, rather than conceptualizing particular family forms as moral or amoral, it is more important to recognize that families construct and reconstruct themselves, the relations among members, and the ideas and values they transmit in response to shifting structural conditions.

In order to investigate the issue of Korean middle-class women's conservative agency and its relation to feminine subjectivity, we must first situate these women socially and psychologically within the intensely conflictive and destabilized cultural/social field characterizing contemporary South Korean society. Since the end of the Korean War (1950–1953), South Korea has been engaged in a full-fledged, state-led modernization program anchored by a single-minded, catch-up economic development project and accompanied by the adoption of various forms of Western modernity with the goal of lifting the country out of its economically backward status. Although premised on a fundamentally unequal economic and political relationship with the United States, the outcome of this intensive, late industrialization effort by South Korea is by now well known: the effort has catapulted the once poverty-stricken and war-ravaged country into the status of a world-class economic powerhouse. What has been less investigated, however, are the fascinating and complex cultural/social transformations that have accompanied this economic development process, referred to by Kyung-Sup Chang (1999) as "compressed modernity." These transformations have had significant implications for contemporary family and gender relations and the status of women.

South Korea is part of what Deniz Kandiyoti (1988) refers to as classic patriarchy, the clearest examples of which are found in the geographic areas that include North Africa, the Muslim Middle East (including Turkey, Pakistan, and Iran), and southern and eastern Asia (especially India and China). Since the beginning of the Yi dynasty (1392–1910), Korea has been remarkably successful in consolidating itself as one of the most paradigmatic neo-Confucian patriarchal societies. Neo-Confucianism, "a political ideology and an ethical and religious code developed and practiced in a patriarchal cultural context" (Chang 1997, 25–26), was appropriated by the new Korean state as a coherent basis of its social and political organization, and the inner workings and dynamics of what we have come to view as the traditional Korean family and gender system were built on it (Deuchler 1992). Reflecting the key hierarchical principles of neo-Confucianism, the most central of which are gender and age, the Korean patriarchal family was organized on a strict patrilineal and patrilocal lineage system whose solidarity was maintained and affirmed through the production of male heirs and which pivoted on a strict hierarchy and separation between men and women. This was viewed as a foundation of human morality and social order. Bolstered by a rule of strict exogamy, which deprived women of protection from natal families upon marriage, and other harsh, discriminatory legal measures that systematically deprived women of rights (including rights to inheritance, the remarriage of widows, and freedom of movement), this particular family configuration represented one of the most stringent forms of patriarchy. Defined solely by her identity as a dutiful daughter-in-law, obedient wife, and self-sacrificing mother and completely subordinate to her husband's family, especially her mother-in-law, a woman's only path to a semblance of status in the household lay in her capacity as a mother and specifically in her ability to produce sons and heirs.

The state-led transformations that began in the 1960s had momentous ramifications for women. Chang (1999) documents that within a single generation, South Korea transformed from a rural to an urban society. This move to industrialize accelerated the relocation of the population from rural to urban areas, and the urban population grew from 28 percent of the total in 1960 to 82.5 percent in the year 2015 (World Factbook 2018). Moreover, from 1920 to 1995, the proportion of extended families, associated with agrarian life, decreased by two-thirds while nuclear households in 1990 were 68.1 percent of total households (Chang 1999, 51–52). One of the key engines of these changes was the introduction of public education in the 1950s and subsequent advances in higher education. South Korea now has a literacy rate of almost 100 percent and has one of the highest proportions of college-educated citizens in the world: in 1990 an astounding 50.8 percent of men and 24.4 percent of women were enrolled in institutions of higher education (Brinton, Lee, and Parish 1995, 1106). Along with advancements in education, women's participation in the paid workforce, although mobilized initially as cheap labor for the expanding export sector in the 1960s, paved the road for new opportunities and life horizons for both middle- and working-class women. Finally, due to the immensely successful family planning program pursued by the state since the 1960s, South Korea has experienced a steep decline in fertility rates, which has led to a reduction in household size and the further increase in nuclear family households.[3]

While the Korean state pursued an aggressive project of nation building and modernization by mobilizing the talents and energies of its most precious resource, its people, it did so paradoxically by attempting to preserve the patriarchal gender and family order as the stabilizing organizational basis of society. The cornerstone of this plan was the construction of a highly gender-segregated, patriarchal industrial structure based on the male breadwinner model and designed to perpetuate the patriarchal family system by encouraging female domesticity, akin to what Heidi Hartmann (1981) refers to as the "partnership between patriarchy and capitalism." Along with the economic marginalization of women (for example, through wage inequality, discouraging or barring women from certain occupations, or placing barriers against career advancement), the interventionist South Korean state engaged in a conscious effort to preserve—while reshaping—the fundamental structure of the patriarchal family through cultural policies aimed at reifying normative subjectivities of women and men. These included systematic indoctrination and socialization through educational institutions (including state-initiated domesticating programs, such as classes on rational household management, child-rearing, fertility control, feminine etiquette, and hobbies), the media, and various governmental organizations, which worked to buttress the principles of patriarchal family and gender relations and to reshape the family in its contemporary form, mobilizing men as family providers and productive workers and women as biological reproducers and domestic workers for the project of modern nation building (Moon 2005).

These contradictory state policies attempted to maintain traditional patriarchal structures while putting into motion far-reaching forces of industrialization and modernization. In conjunction with more recent global neoliberal economic transformations, they created an intensely conflicted situation for contemporary middle-class Koreans. As Park (2013, 238) writes, middle-class Koreans are facing collective cultural ambivalence in the face of massive social upheaval, and such tensions are a source of great psychic distress, especially "when [the situation] is perceived by 'unaware' individuals as creating ambiguous social expectations regarding when to assert individual autonomy and when to display mutuality."

Sources of Conflicting Subjectivities Experienced by Women

The traditional Korean patriarchal family, premised on Confucian principles and on values of familism, generates a particular set of feminine desires and experiences concerning mothering and the family, which have continuing implications for women's gender consciousness under changing conditions. Korean feminist scholars, such as Haejoang Cho (1986), point out that one of the cornerstones of the Korean patriarchal family system is the extraordinary value it accords to women's domestic roles, especially motherhood, which provides a compelling structure of material and psychic rewards for women. Related to but going beyond what Western feminists refer to as "compulsory motherhood" (Rich 1980), the essence of this concept of motherhood is symbolized by the figure of the devoted, self-sacrificing mother. She is not only endowed with a high, if not mythic, status, but the welfare of mothers is bound up with the production of sons and heirs and the cultivation of their fealty, which further reinforces women's dedication to the role. According to Cho (1986, 292): "Legitimizing mother power might be the most successful way of accommodating women under the male-dominated social system. Compared with wife power, which can be [seen] mostly in Western countries, or sister power in Polynesian societies, mother power seems to be the most secure source of power for women under the patriarchal system. The enduring tie and strong attachment between mother and son can easily develop into the son's dependence upon his mother psychologically, culturally, and institutionally."[4]

Clearly, a source of the intense attachment to mothering found among Korean women is the tremendous degree of power accorded to mothers in this system, despite the fundamental belief in women's inferiority and the subordination of the female realm, which results ironically in women's contradictory image of themselves as being both powerful *and* powerless.[5] The Confucian family had a variety of mechanisms that ensured a reserve of power for women within the system, including a rigid gendered division of labor that provided women with a degree of independent power and authority in the domestic sphere as wives and mothers. This persists in the modern family form. Yet the cyclical nature of women's power, most of which is attained after the marriage of sons, when women become mothers-in-law, has become somewhat attenuated with the emergence of the nuclear family in South Korea.[6] Nonetheless, the continuing importance of Confucian ideas of filial piety and the expectations of mothers-in-law to have power and influence over sons and daughters-in-law can motivate women's accommodation to persistent patriarchal values. Consider the following narrative by a 43-year-old woman, which demonstrates the persistence of expectations for filial piety as well as the power mothers-in-law still have over their daughters-in-law:

> You see, the reason I was in such a bad mental shape was that I was very unhappy, stressed, and depressed at home. My married life hadn't been easy. My in-laws ran a cake-making business, which required a lot of work, a lot of which I ended up doing. And I had to do all the housework too. . . . My mother-in-law wasn't a bad person but the work was too hard. I felt like she was making me do everything and I was bad at refusing. I used to go home to my mother and cry all the time. . . . On top of it, it was unbearable because they didn't treat me with respect. You see, my husband's family is very conservative. Their attitude is, you don't have any right to speak—they totally ran over and ignored me. It was maddening and unbearable. So I was thinking, why do I have to live with this kind of disregard? . . . But if I didn't obey, I felt I was insulting my own mother and father, that my in-laws would think they hadn't raised me properly. So I couldn't rebel.

In accounting for the powerful mothering impulses among Korean middle-class women, one more significant factor must be considered: the psychodynamics of the mother's relationship with her son. According to Chodorow (1978), girls' psychological development differs from that of boys in part because a boy is led to dramatically sever his pre-Oedipal psychic bond with his mother in order to identify with his father and become a man, a break that is assumed to be actively encouraged and pushed by the mother. However, this supposed universal developmental process appears to take on different dynamics in the Korean context. Because a Korean mother's survival and fortune depend on her relationship to her sons, she may not encourage the kind of psychic break proposed in the Western psychological literature. Although Korean men certainly come to devalue women as the other in the process of their psychic development into adulthood, their evolution into manhood does not involve the kind of radical turning away from the mother that is seen in many other settings; rather, sons remain emotionally tied to their mother into adulthood, and mothers actively work to maintain these bonds. The traditional hostility between mothers-in-law and daughters-in-law stems partially from this continuing psychic attachment between mother and son and is one source of tension in the husband-wife dyad. In this kind of relational structure, women experience tremendous incentives to be mothers and develop powerful, inner psychic subjectivities as mothers—typically of a highly self-sacrificing and aggressively protective kind—which remain strong throughout their lives and are extremely difficult to psychologically repudiate. I would also argue that this type of psychic orientation is passed down to daughters and may be extremely motivating to them even when they have also embraced the desires that come along with education and modernization: to be more emancipated than their mothers.

The second central feature of familism that I believe gives force to women's conservative and mothering impulses is their desire to maintain family cohesion, which stems from the desire for the family itself, another essential psychological effect of this family-centered system. Korean society historically has invested tremendous energy in maintaining family cohesion, and women were traditionally given the primary responsibility for preserving this unity. They were viewed not only as faithful mothers and virtuous wives located at the center of their families but as the primary guardians of the household, responsible for meeting the physical and emotional needs of the members and for preserving the family's integrity and ensuring its survival. The emphasis on family cohesion became particularly significant during the socially tumultuous periods in Korean history, for example, the Japanese colonial period and the Korean War era, when women assumed even heavier responsibilities for holding their families together in the face of absent or deceased fathers. Indeed, Korean historical and literary narratives are filled with tropes of the self-sacrificing but aggressively strong mother who ensures the family's survival against all odds.

In regard to feminine subjectivity, one ramification of such a system is the engendering in women of an extraordinary desire for and sense of responsibility for maintaining family cohesion, including a commitment to ensuring their family's welfare and, more significantly, to preserving the family structure. This powerful sense of moral responsibility for others stems first from the intensely relational (as opposed to individualistic) and family-centered vision of Confucian social relations, which privileges obligations to others, especially family members, over individual fulfillment.[7] Unlike in the West, where the ideology of individualism has supported the development of a self-identity that powerfully competes with, if not dominates, a familial identity, the gender identities of Korean women tend to be inseparably tied to their family-oriented self-conceptions as mothers, wives, and daughters-in-law and to the expectations and responsibilities that are bound up with these roles.

This constellation of discourses about the family and relationships can work in significant ways to countervail emancipatory impulses. Some Western feminist researchers, such as Carol Gilligan (1982), have recognized the salience of other-directed moral responsibility as an important dimension of female consciousness. In Korean women, however, the moral responsibility toward the family, a sensibility that moves beyond mere other-directedness, appears to occupy a central place in their gender consciousness. Indeed, the force of this internalized moral sense is such that one of the most common emotions with which mothers in unstable domestic situations wrestle in regard to their children is guilt over what they perceive as their failure to fulfill their proper familial duties because of marital conflicts or their feelings of unhappiness in the marriage. For many of the conservative religious women I have encountered, it would not be an overstatement to suggest that their decision to embrace traditionalist gender/family principles as a means of resolving untenable domestic conflicts appears to be driven, even at the expense of their own personal happiness, by the need to alleviate the enormous burden of guilt at not having lived up to the demands of being proper mothers and wives.

Rapid modernization and increasing levels of education have helped introduce other sources for the formation of female subjectivity in South Korea, including a desire among many educated women for companionate marriage. This wish clashes with the traditional values of the familistic system, and women are the ones who must bear the burden of the contradiction. Many women experience frustration when, despite their expectations and hopes for a companionate relationship, they end up in a traditional marriage with a distant, authoritarian husband. In addition, conflicts with mothers-in-law are a major source of personal suffering, especially when juxtaposed against women's recent desires for more autonomy and respectful treatment. The following account from a 43-year-old housewife illustrates these tensions:

> From the very first, my married life was incredibly difficult. You see, when I first had a marriage interview with my husband, what struck me was that he seemed to be really sincere and honest. . . . I knew living with a mother-in-law would be hard but foolishly, I thought that if I was just all good, obedient, and faithful, and I could serve them well, everything would be okay. But it didn't turn out that way. From the beginning, my husband's family treated me very badly. From day one, my mother-in-law treated me horribly, finding all kinds of fault with me. . . . My mother-in-law has a horribly sharp tongue, that's her personality. . . . I have the opposite personality. I tend to keep things to myself because I am afraid to talk and afraid how it'll affect other people. . . . And my husband, he always took his parents' side from the beginning. You've got to understand, my husband is the most traditionally Confucian man. When we first got married, he said to me that his parents were like his limbs, irreplaceable and with him forever, but I was like clothing, disposable and interchangeable. My husband's way of thinking is that the wife is a dependent, inferior member of the family, so there is no need to respect a woman. He just did whatever he wanted. And his personality—it gets more difficult to deal with the longer I stay married to him. . . . But I am the only one who accommodates. . . . I still have so many scars from him, do you know what I mean?[8]

Adding to the distress felt by this generation of women are more recent transformations in the goals of the family in Korea, which accompany and are related to competitive familism. With the nuclear family taking on priority, for example, women experience greater demands on their time in the form of the reconfigured tasks of the modern housewife (Chong 2008; Kendall 2002). Moreover, the increasing sexualization of femininity, especially the twin demands to be both good mothers/wives and sexy partners, has further intensified pressures on women (Cho 2002). The following comment by a church pastor illustrates this particular pressure: "You know, the trouble with Korean women is that they don't know how to express affection and love properly. Once they get married, their attitude is, well, now I've given you everything, including my body, so what else do you want? So they become frumpy housewives, live in the kitchen, and nag their husbands. They don't know how to give affection, express love. They have to work on that more. See, men really enjoy that kind of stuff."

At the heart of competitive familism is a new set of activities that Hanna Papanek (1979) has called "status production" (e.g., the work of ensuring children's educational success or engaging in informal money-generating activities to supplement the family income). Lee (2013, 178) notes that the Korean emphasis on the importance of academic credentials as a sign of status has led to the emergence of "education mothers." Indeed, middle-class women, encouraged by the state to stay home and raise their children, are now depicted as essential figures for children's educational success and must be well educated in order to successfully advance their children's aspirations and build family status (Lee 2013, 179). Thus, modern middle-class wives in Korea have become "notorious for aggressively advancing their children and their husbands, with little concern for the larger community" (Cho 2002, 176). In this context, the institution of the family is no longer simply a vehicle for activating feminine desires oriented toward defending and preserving it, but instead propels women to aggressively advance the family unit against its competitors, buttressing the goals of competitive familism and further strengthening the nature of women's commitment to this key institution.

Women caught in unstable domestic situations experience conflicts generated by their internalized moral obligations to both preserve and aggressively advance the status of the family. When they are unable to do so because of problems with their spouse or frustrations relating to gender role limitations, they experience guilt about failing to be a proper mother and wife. These feelings of guilt and distress are evidence of women's inner psychic turmoil created by conflicting feminine subjectivities and the values and goals each engenders. The following narrative is from a woman who attempted to pursue higher education while married but ultimately failed:

> You know, all that studying was . . . worthless — I caused too much pain to my family. . . . It's not something somebody like me could or should

do. And it made me also realize that a mother needs to be with her kids through schooling. . . . I am so afraid that one day, my kids will turn to me and accuse me of not doing things that a mother should do. I don't want that to happen. I also realize that for all my troubles with my husband, it's better for my kids to be raised with their father. I also realize that for me, it's better to be with someone than not. If I didn't get married, I don't know what kind of a person I would now—very twisted and unhappy probably. I would probably be a really terrible person.

There is a long-standing view in psychology that labels the negative drive state produced by conflicting cognitions as dissonance (see Aronson 1968). Because the experience of dissonance is unpleasant, individuals strive to reduce or minimize it. Hinton (1996, 828) refers more specifically to psychosocial dissonance as a state that arises when an emotionally salient cultural model about the context-dependent self comes into conflict with another such model that violates the original self-concept. Because these contradictory self-concepts or subjectivities generate different desires and goals for action, people experience anxiety and are motivated to try to reduce the psychic distress they are experiencing. Aronson (1968, 5) suggests that people may avoid these conflicts by the use of denial or other psychological defense mechanisms, thereby moving them below awareness to an unconscious level. Strauss (1990) finds that such conflicts can be avoided when people mentally compartmentalize potentially contradictory schemas so the inconsistencies between them are never voiced in the same context or confronted explicitly. Other people, like the Maya women participating with the Western NGO described in Manago's chapter (this volume), may integrate the conflicting schemas into a new sense of self, although true integration, defined by Aronson (1968, 5) as a genuine resolution of conflict, calls for a more drastic reorganization of cognitive and attitudinal structures and is psychologically more difficult for individuals to achieve. Because of the difficulties involved in resolving cognitive dissonance, Quinn (1996) suggests that when people confront similar dilemmas on a recurring basis, they may forge common cultural solutions to them. Westen (2001, 41) refers to these "prepackaged" solutions to widespread societal conflicts as culturally patterned compromise formation. For the women in my study, conversion to Korean evangelical churches appears to be an example of a shared cultural compromise solution to the conflicts they faced when a new sense of feminine subjectivity conflicted with the gendered family roles and behaviors prescribed by an older one.

The Korean Evangelical Church and Cultural Compromise

Korean evangelicalism, first introduced by American missionaries at the turn of the twentieth century, has evolved in South Korea as an intensely patriarchal religion both theologically and culturally. Despite this, one of the distinguishing hallmarks of this religion has been the absolute centrality of women to its growth and maintenance; they are exceptional in their religious dedication and fervor. As illuminated by other research on women and religious traditionalism, an important finding of my study is that conservative beliefs and practices are appropriated by middle-class women as an important source of personal empowerment and deliverance from suffering. An equally central finding of my study is the extent to which these women's religious lives are characterized by a set of acute tensions between the dynamics of resistance and regulation, empowerment and discipline. For example, although women adopted evangelical beliefs and practices in order to cope with and even resist domestic patriarchy, many of them simultaneously became willing participants in an intensive institutional disciplinary process that in many cases resulted in their successful "redomestication" to the modern patriarchal family.

I argue that an evangelical church serves as a significant vehicle for emotional and psychological healing by promoting fervent spiritual practices that stress the complete surrendering of the self to divine control and profound self-revelation through cultivation of an intimate relationship with God. This process, which I refer to as "opening up," occurs not only individually but collectively in venues such as cell meetings (Chong 2008, 110–34). These weekly, home-based meetings are a combination of guided small-group Bible study and intensive fellowship and are highly effective institutionalized vehicles for fostering openness and the sharing of problems. In the churches I studied, the intimate sharing of personal lives through such small-group interactions provided collective opportunities for release, emotional venting, and mutual consolation, often functioning as the first step in the conversion process. One member described her experience: "When I went to a cell meeting for the first time, I experienced an indescribably peaceful feeling. What I realized there was that other people were not different from me in their lives, problems, and feelings. Until then, I thought my life was peculiar, but that was not the case. And I received consolation from that, before anything else."

For these evangelical women, participation in church life and activities also provided a means for improving their domestic coping. Despite the subordinate position of women within Korean Christianity, churches were critical to the lives of the women in my study as arenas of extradomestic, female-centered community. By coming together daily for a myriad of religious activities, the women forged a space of their own away from their families. Although most women believed that they were going to church in order to carry out their duties as Christians, these frequent gatherings often became central to them as a focal point of their social lives and as a crucial outlet that was acceptable in the eyes of their family. Many women actually described the church as a place of escape from home where they experienced a sense of autonomy and relief from domestic pressures. Consider the following comments of a woman for whom church participation had become a primary means to free herself from some domestic responsibilities and subvert her husband's authority:

> After I got cured of my ailments through God, I realized I simply didn't have any place to "rely on" besides God. . . . Even though I am so busy, I'm in three different choirs, I am in the intercessory prayer group, I never miss a cell meeting. . . . Yes, friends tell me I'm hanging too much onto God and religion. . . . They ask me, "What is the point of going to church so much?" But it's not that way for me! And my husband knows that too. . . . Before he got converted, he used to get very upset at my going to church but now, he knows that if I don't go to church like I do, I'd be a sick person!

Another way in which church participation plays an important role in helping women become better equipped to cope with their domestic challenges is by empowering them in various ways. First, women are offered a variety of second-tier lay leadership roles in the churches (serving as deacons, teachers, and cell group leaders) through which they are able to exercise their talents, show their leadership abilities, and receive recognition. Second, church participation and religiosity can function as tools of gender resistance and renegotiation in their marriages. Despite many women's accommodation, at times ambivalent, to the ideology of submission espoused by the churches, such accommodation can also be used as a strategy for domestic negotiation and for reforming the behavior of others, especially their husband. For example, many women believed that through their own perfect adherence to the rules of virtuous feminine behavior as taught by the church, they could inspire their husband to change from being domineering, dictatorial, or even abusive to becoming more respectful, loving, communicative, and openhearted. Ironically, strategies of perfect submission can also become a powerful weapon of resistance and defense by enabling women to develop a sense of moral superiority and possibly acquire greater domestic status and power. As one woman put it: "You know, if I didn't obey and just ran off like I wanted to, would my husband have the gratitude he now has for me, for what I . . . endured in the past?" Transforming the husband to become more domestic or family-oriented was another recurring theme. That change signified not only the husband's willingness to be more attentive to the home and children but also his taking on of more moral responsibility for domestic matters, which were formerly seen as solely the province of the wife. The ultimate victory occurred when a wife's efforts led to her husband's conversion.

Viewing submission simply as a strategy or as a hidden weapon in women's domestic and gender struggles is, however, inadequate in the Korean context. In spite of their attempts to appropriate evangelical beliefs and practices as instruments of gender negotiation—achieved with varying degrees of success—conversion for numerous women in my study also involved a sincere recommitment to the principles of the traditional patriarchal family. Indeed, one of the most surprising and ironic dimensions of evangelical women's religious engagement is the deep belief many develop in the evangelical-sanctioned ideologies of gender and the family, which lie at the root of their predicament and buttress the legitimacy of the traditional Confucian family system. This is accomplished particularly through a stress on the necessity of women's total obedience and endurance as the fundamental principle of conjugal relations and as a prerequisite for family harmony and cohesion. One cell leader described her church's belief this way: "I really believe sincerely that for any woman, obedience is something she has to deal with and accept. Without the wife obeying the husband, God will not use that home. We think the husband has to treat the wife well for the wife to obey, but that's not the case. A wife has to obey first, unconditionally. . . . A wife obeying, raising her husband continuously and making him the leader, that is the most essential aspect of marriage, the most important part [that] everything else will follow."

Thus for some middle-class women in Korea, participation in an evangelical church after conversion appears to be a culturally available compromise formation or solution to the conflicts emerging from the contradictory feminine subjectivities engendered by rapid social change. It works both because the teachings of the church draw on traditional Confucian values and shared ethics of familism already salient to these women and because participants undergo a conversion experience that is emotionally arousing and socially reinforced.

Once these women convert, moreover, they accept and appear to internalize a more conservative model of family and gender roles that reinforces some aspects of Korean patriarchy.

Westen (2001, 41) notes that many times, a culture does not offer people satisfying compromise solutions, and individuals have to create their own, which can range from the highly adaptive to the highly maladaptive. Mathews's (this volume) research on Oaxacan women provides an example. Rural women in that part of Mexico, much like my South Korean informants, experience extreme emotional distress stemming from conflicts between traditional notions of family and gender roles and recent discourses emphasizing individual autonomy and egalitarianism. Because they live under unpredictable, constantly changing social conditions characterized by a lack of economic options locally and high rates of male absence due to migration, these women remain ambivalent, caught between shifting senses of self and unsure of what life choices to pursue. While Mathews's respondents attempt to resolve these conflicts in different ways, as of yet no cultural compromise solution appears available to them. Similarly, the lower-class Turkish women reported on by Güvenç (this volume) are also experiencing rapid changes in family form coupled with unstable economic conditions. Their emotional distress results from high levels of domestic violence instigated by the inability of husbands and in-laws to uphold male supremacy and patriarchal household forms. These women often cope with their high levels of ambivalence and frustration by beating their own children, a maladaptive response. Güvenç documents their struggles to find new ways of expressing their emotions, but it appears that they have not yet developed any workable compromises or found any readily available shared solutions to these interpersonal dilemmas.

Conclusion: The Problem of Consent and Agency

I have examined the basis for the intransigent issue of women's ongoing consent to patriarchal relations and situations of gender inequality in the modern world by focusing on the case of contemporary, middle-class, evangelical women in South Korea. A key premise of this chapter is that subjectivity provides an important link between structure and agency, enabling a critical examination of the intersecting forces exerted on individuals by state policies, global economic changes, and transformations in family structure. These changing structural conditions, moreover, provide the context in which families frame the roles and behaviors judged appropriate for their members and socialize them into associated desires and motivations. Underlying the changes in family structure in South Korea are certain implacable desires, including women's ongoing wish to be part of families and to be mothers. I have argued that it is within the Korean family, with its technologies of normalization, that such desires are powerfully constituted and regulated, not just through overt oppression but through "defining the parameters and content of choice, fixing how we come to want what we want" (Henriques et al. 1984, 219), generating what Henriques and colleagues refer to as the "intransigence of desires." For many middle-class Korean women, the adoption of a conservative, evangelical model of family and gender helps alleviate psychic distress and motivates them by supporting their ongoing desire to perform as proper wives and mothers. We might therefore conclude that women have accommodated or actively consented to patriarchal ideas that oppress them.

The question of consent, that is, why women assent to and participate in maintaining their subordination, is a troublesome one from the normative Western feminist perspective, which operates from the basic liberal principle that the ultimate aim or desire of women everywhere is to be emancipated from the structures of patriarchy that constrain them from realizing their potential as autonomous, self-determining beings. Some feminist scholars have engaged this troubling issue of women's accommodation to repressive ideologies by highlighting the dimensions of the resistance implied in the actions of the subordinated (Kondo 1990; Ong 1987; Scott 1985). Drawing inspiration from theoretical approaches that can broadly be characterized as poststructural and influenced particularly by such thinkers as Foucault ([1978] 1990) and Gramsci (1992) and by what Sherry Ortner (1984) has labeled practice theory, this line of theorizing emphasizes the importance of human beings as strategizing agents acting in their interests against oppression, but it also works with "notions of power as decentered and of culture as a site of both the inscription of power and resistance to power" (Rubin 1996, 238). These works highlight the ways in which subjugated individuals or groups exercise agency and engage power through various forms of resistance, particularly non-overt or everyday forms, and in the process move us beyond the conventional binary of domination and consent.

One area in which these theoretical perspectives have been fruitfully employed is the exploding scholarship on women and religious traditionalisms, which addresses the counterintuitive phenomenon of contemporary women's (re)turn across the globe to evangelicalism, fundamentalism, Orthodox Judaism, and traditionalist Islam. To account for what can be perceived as a knotty paradox of women's consent to oppression, many of these studies have made effective use of resistance-oriented frameworks: women's apparent compliance to traditionalist gender relations should not be seen simply as a capitulation to patriarchy, but can be viewed as an instrumental effort to negotiate domestic and marital relations, pursue their own interests, or even subvert patriarchal relations and find feminine empowerment (Bartkowski 2001; Brasher 1998; Brusco 1995; Gallagher and Smith 1999; Griffith 1997; Stacey 1998).

Other scholars, drawing heavily on poststructuralist theories of subject formation, have taken the creative approach of bypassing the issue of resistance and consent altogether through an effort to theorize alternative, non-Western forms of religious subjectivity and agency through which such conservative actions can presumably be understood (Avishai 2008; Jacobson 2006). Mahmood (2001), for example, focuses on Islamic women's cultivation of docility as a moral virtue and a form of female agency, rather than as capitulation or consent to patriarchy.

Although these lines of interpretation have elevated to a more sophisticated register our understandings about women's subordination within and outside religious traditions, such approaches have also diverted our attention from an equally important dimension of contemporary women's engagement with patriarchies: the unavoidable fact of women's resistance to change and their ongoing adherence to patriarchal beliefs and practices. I contend that if we are to take seriously women's agency (which I define, modifying the usage in Giddens [1984], as the capacity to think, feel, desire, make choices, and act creatively against a given social background), it is not only the topic of resistance and protest to which we should pay attention. We must also examine the motivations behind women's acquiescence to patriarchal structures, that is, why women would *choose*, in the face of alternative options, paths of action that lead to their subordination under existing gender arrangements. I have attempted to do this in this chapter by using the concept of subjectivity to link structure with agency through the medium of the institutions of state and family. My intent is not to categorically denigrate the institution of the family nor to call for its eradication in South Korea and elsewhere. But an analysis that links state policies and changing family structures to the emergent subjectivities and goals of women is a crucial step that must be taken before feminists can formulate ways to interrupt and change the stubborn cycle that reproduces gender inequalities across generations. The promotion of more egalitarian family arrangements in

South Korea and other parts of the world requires not only changes in social structure, but a redistribution of material resources in terms of more egalitarian workplace policies, transformations in cultural and cognitive images, and concerted efforts to uncover the myriad and formidable barriers that exist in the less easily observed arenas of human life, including the deeply held motivations and desires nurtured in the family.[9]

Situations of intense cultural transformation, such as that facing women in contemporary South Korea, are challenging for all involved, but they also represent opportunities to usher in changes for the better. As other chapters in this volume demonstrate, women may forge new social bargains or work for transformations in family structures and role expectations. Furthermore, rather than serving as a source of confusion and pain, the psychic conflicts resulting from the experience of contradictory subjectivities can provide women with opportunities to eventually create new, integrated subjectivities combining the old and the new.

Notes

1. According to Kim (1990), one hallmark of this system is the severe disjunction between family interests and social/public interests. Kim explains that modern, competitive familism developed in South Korea because the rapid industrialization through the 1960s and 1970s furnished social conditions favorable to it, namely, the need for already self-interested families to aggressively maximize their economic interests in an environment of economic scarcity that also contained the possibility for upward mobility. This competitive behavioral pattern was further encouraged by the underdevelopment of the social welfare system.

2. Although the family has been the object of flourishing investigations in gender studies, the issue of familism has not received the attention it deserves in sociological literatures. One exception to this perhaps is the literature on Chicana/o families where attention has been paid to the Chicana/o form of familism to uncover the differences between Chicana/o families and European American middle-class families (see Baca Zinn 1982; Segura and Pierce 1993; Mirande 1977; Williams 1990). I would argue that Chicana/o familism also differs from the Korean familism I describe in this chapter.

3. Starting with about six children per family in 1960, the fertility rate plummeted to 1.6 in 1990, an impressive 73 percent decline, making South Korea a "below-replacement" society. As of 2005, the fertility rate was 1.08.

4. For similar findings regarding the psychodynamics of the mother-son relationship in the Arab cultural context, see, for example, Hatem (1987) and Joseph (1993b).

5. As Martina Deuchler (1992, 4) puts it: "The Confucian image of women was thus a double one; she had to be modest and submissive, but also strong and responsible. On the level of Confucian idealism, the image was considered virtuous; on the level of daily life, it often meant bondage."

6. This is because many women no longer have the same opportunity to become a powerful mother-in-law who presides over multigenerational extended households. Moreover, many parents-in-law are developing a wish to maintain some degree of independence from their children in old age. It is crucial, however, to remember that modern Korean families still function in many ways like the traditional family despite the structural changes. This is attested, for example, by the continuing importance of filial piety, including the expectation that children must take care of their parents, and obligations to extended kin (see Chang 1997; Kim 1990, 414).

7. See Kim (1996). For theorizations of relational subjectivity/identity in the Middle East, see Joseph (1993b) and Gallagher (2007).

8. While the older generation of married women (in their forties and fifties) struggles primarily with negotiating improved marital and domestic relations, the younger generation of married women (in their thirties) wrestles in addition with the conflicts between the more individualistic desires for self-realization or self-fulfillment and the pull of traditional femininity and family obligations.

9. Compare my analysis with the interesting perspective of Barbara Risman (1998), who explores the problem of female consent in the context of modern American families and gender relations. In the American context, she explains, although cognitive images have changed, we must focus on changing interactional pressures and institutional designs that compel women to conform to existing gender norms despite the absence of individual desires to do so.

CHAPTER TEN

Property, Patriarchy, and the Chinese State

LETA HONG FINCHER

When I interviewed university graduate Wang Li in 2011,[1] she was a young Communist Party member employed with generous benefits at China's Public Security Bureau in Beijing. She had recently taken her life savings of 60,000 renminbi (RMB; almost US$10,000 at the time) and given it to her boyfriend to help buy an apartment in his name in preparation for their marriage. The couple originally wanted to rent, but their parents said they must purchase a home before marrying. Although Wang is an only child, her parents did not contribute money toward the home purchase because they believed it was the responsibility of the man's family to provide the home. The boyfriend's parents had saved 200,000 RMB for the down payment, and they insisted that the home be registered solely in their son's name. Wang felt that this was unfair since she was contributing her life savings to the purchase, so she argued with her boyfriend for six months, from October 2010 through the following March, over the home registration: "I won't hide it from you. My boyfriend and I started to quarrel.... I only spoke with two good friends about our fighting, but I was really thinking of breaking up with him. I felt he didn't trust me. He had this attitude toward my family that I didn't understand, and for a while we were very cold to each other."

Wang was so angry with her boyfriend that she almost called off the wedding. But even Wang's mother urged her to make up with her boyfriend because it was not worth breaking up the impending marriage over the issue of property registration, and she said that Wang should simply agree to register only her boyfriend's name on the property deed. Wang continued to waver about the marriage until one day her boyfriend's mother called her in tears, saying that Wang's professional success threatened the security of the upcoming marriage, so it was very important to register the home in her son's name. Wang told me:

> His family thinks I'm more capable than him. Even though I'm younger, the companies I worked for are better than his [Wang's income was higher

than that of her boyfriend]. So his mother thinks her son needs some kind of guarantee. She thinks I'm more likely to leave him than he is to leave me. His mother started crying on the phone and I thought, forget it. . . . After all, she's my elder [*zhangbei*]. Since she started crying, I knew that this issue was also really hurting her. So I thought, forget about it, whatever works is fine.

Wang agreed to register the home in her boyfriend's name, and in November 2011 they married. She was only 25 years old at the time she agreed to marry. She could have simply broken up with her boyfriend, which she had wanted to do, and would still have had time to find another potential marriage partner with whom she was happier. Why did she relent? One major reason is the persistence of the family deference system, which (as illustrated throughout this book) is not unique to China. Wang's belief in filial piety, in her duty to her elders, all of whom pressured her to marry and to register the marital home in the man's name, outweighed Wang's desire to have economic independence. Even her own mother told her that it was not important to have her name registered on the marital property.

Another reason Wang agreed to marry was that she and her elders viewed her as being on the cusp of becoming a *shengnü* (leftover woman), a term widely used to describe an unmarried woman older than around age 27. Since Wang was 25 years old, she did not view herself as having the luxury of waiting to find a more suitable husband. Even though many women in Beijing marry in their late twenties or later, Wang said that in her parents' hometown of Changchun in northeastern China, "most women marry at around 24 or 25."

I repeatedly asked Wang throughout our two-and-a-half-hour interview if she regretted giving up her effort to register her name on the marital property deed along with her husband's name, but she showed no sign of regret: "I really think it doesn't matter now. If someday we don't have feelings for each other, the marital property won't matter to me. I have the ability to find another house on my own. Some young women complain [if their name is not on the property deed] because their own guarantee is gone, [and] they feel insecure. But this money is not important to me. If all this goes to him only, it's okay."

Wang's story and the stories of many other women and men I interviewed illustrate how the buying structure of China's real estate boom has created stark new gender inequalities in wealth.[2] I argue that because of the persistence of patriarchal norms in contemporary Chinese society, women have largely missed out on a dramatic accumulation of real estate wealth in China, valued at more than $17 trillion in 2010, according to the Hong Kong and Shanghai Banking Corporation (Zhang, Shahani, and Chan 2010). Two patriarchal norms are particularly relevant in the pressuring of women to forfeit property ownership in China. First, the man has usually been viewed as the head of the household and the official homeowner, even though most women today contribute financially to the purchase of the home. Second, parents have tended to help their sons buy homes but not their daughters, and family deference systems have usually compelled the daughters to accede to the wishes of their parents and future in-laws in determining whose names are registered on the marital property deed. There are exceptions to these home-buying patterns, with a minority of homes registered jointly in the names of both the husband and wife, and some homes registered solely in a woman's name. However, the survey data available indicate that the vast majority of residential property is registered in men's names. In this chapter I examine why so many women acquiesce to their own subjugation with regard to marital property rights.

Some scholars have referred to trends, such as a general "empowerment of urban daughters" under China's one-child policy, especially with regard to education (e.g., Fong 2002), or a "decline in patriarchal power" (Yan 2003). I argue that despite the gains made by women in education, expectations about women's empowerment in China have proven to be overly optimistic.

On an empirical level, I identify two major obstacles to gender equality that have emerged in the twenty-first century. First, the skyrocketing home prices as a result of China's real estate boom have contributed to new gender inequalities in wealth that did not exist prior to the privatization of housing. Second, a state-run media campaign to stigmatize urban, educated single women has intensified the pressure on young women to marry, prompting many to give up much economic power in the marriage out of fear that they will not find another husband. My findings suggest that many of the advantages young women gain through education and early career success evaporate as soon as they marry and try to buy a home.

On a theoretical level, my findings support Cecilia Ridgeway's (2011) argument that gender inequality in the modern era is a product of competing forces and that inequality reproduces itself in new forms, including through social and economic transformations that work to level gender differences in power.

I discuss how in the case of China, the authoritarian state has also played an important role in perpetuating gender inequalities in spite of attempts by individual women to resist traditional gender norms.[3]

Patriarchy in Postsocialist China

Around 1980, the Chinese government implemented a one-child policy, which over time combined with the preference for boys to result in an extremely skewed sex ratio, with boys vastly outnumbering girls (Greenhalgh and Winckler 2005). Studies show that the one-child policy benefited urban daughters, particularly in educational achievement, because they did not have to compete with brothers for parental investment (Fong 2002). Yet although women have made gains in areas such as education, China's postsocialist transition to a market economy has entrenched gender inequalities in other ways. China has experienced some resurgence of traditional gender norms, such as the essentialization of gender roles (Evans 2002) and a widening gender income gap (Li and Li 2008).

China's privatization of housing has also had profound implications for gender inequalities. In 1998, the government terminated socialized housing to set up a market-based system of homeownership, and since the mid-2000s, house prices have increased sharply. Many studies find that most urban homes in China are "severely unaffordable" according to price-to-income ratios (e.g., Man, Zheng, and Ren 2011). A survey of the four first-tier cities of Beijing, Shanghai, Guangzhou, and Shenzhen conducted by Horizon China (2012) found that the average home cost more than fifteen times the buyer's annual income, while more than a third of buyers said their home cost more than twenty times their annual income. Yet by most accounts, China has one of the highest homeownership rates in the world.

As divorce rates in China have risen, decisions about "who gets the house" have been increasingly fraught (Davis 2010, 2). China's Supreme People's Court thus issued a new interpretation of the country's Marriage Law (Supreme People's Court of the People's Republic of China 2011). Now, unless legally contested, marital property essentially belongs to the person who bought it and whose name is on the deed. According to the available data, that person is most likely to be a man. An official Chinese government survey of 105,573 people in 2010 states that 67.1 percent of men own or co-own property compared with 37.9 percent of women (All-China Women's Federation and National Bureau of Statistics of China 2011). The survey by Horizon China (2012) of first-tier cities shows that

80.3 percent of marital property deeds include the man's name, while only 30 percent of marital property deeds include the woman's name, indicating that the percentage of marital homes solely owned by women is very small. Another official publication from 2008 found that 87.83 percent of homes were owned by men (He 2008, 449). Figures from all of these surveys group co-ownership and sole ownership together, obscuring the extent to which property is owned only by men.

My findings suggest that just as patriarchal norms often dispossess rural women from their land, urban educated women in China are also pressured to cede ownership of their most valuable asset, the marital home, to men. I argue that pressure on urban women in their mid-twenties to marry often causes them to make excessive compromises when they purchase a marital home, in part out of fear that they will not be able to find another husband if they assert their will.

In China, because of a lack of viable investment alternatives, residential real estate is the most important asset for most households. The severe unaffordability of homes in China means that it is virtually impossible for one young person alone to make the down payment on a home in a first-tier city, and it is difficult even in a second-tier or third-tier city. The buying structure of China's residential real estate market requires the pooling of family assets to purchase an urban home. No matter how high their income, most young people cannot buy an urban home in a top-tier city if their parents or other family members are unable or unwilling to help them.

Despite the state media narrative that the tremendous pressure to buy an urban home falls solely on the shoulders of men, my findings demonstrate that women, too, experience tremendous pressure to buy a home upon marriage. But whereas the men by and large wind up owning valuable real estate wealth (as long as they have parents, girlfriends, wives, or other relatives to help them with its purchase), the pressure on women to buy a home often ends up with the women helping to finance a home, but forfeiting their ownership of the real estate wealth. Moreover, I find that even high-income, highly educated women fall into the same gendered home-buying patterns indicated in the large, quantitative studies. The Horizon China (2012) study of China's top housing markets states that more than 70 percent of women contribute significantly to the purchase of the marital home. Most of the educated, home-buying women in my sample contributed heavily to the home purchase, even when it was registered solely in the man's name. The gendered buying structure of China's residential real estate market has created a stark new form of gender inequality in wealth, which counteracts the equalizing effects of women's improved education and early career opportunities.

Methods

This chapter is based largely on in-depth interviews with 60 people (36 women and 24 men). I conducted interviews with 39 people in Beijing, 18 in Shanghai, and 3 in Xi'an between November 2010 and August 2013, with some people interviewed several times. Almost all interviews were recorded and lasted from 90 minutes to more than 3 hours. I took notes during all interviews, which were conducted in Chinese (Mandarin), and I translated the quotes included here into English. To ensure the anonymity of the participants, most interviews took place in cafés, where I paid the bill. Most of the interviewees were from a broader convenience sample of 283 people from cities across China who sent messages to me on the popular social media site, Sina Weibo. I set up my Weibo account in August 2011 after the new interpretation of China's Marriage Law was announced. I included my name and affiliation on my Weibo profile and invited anyone interested in taking part in my research on gender and home buying to send a private message through Weibo or send an email to an account I set up for this study. In addition, I analyzed the content of multiple state media reports, newspaper columns, and sources on the Internet regarding home buying and the phenomenon of leftover women (shengnü).

China is experiencing rapid urbanization. People from rural origins moving to cities have caused a historic shift in the country's population from majority rural to majority urban. About half of my interviewees are only children, while the other half have siblings and moved to Beijing or Shanghai from a place with fewer family-planning restrictions. I included people with siblings and only children in my study in order to obtain information on parents' differential treatment of daughters and sons. Almost two-thirds of Chinese couples are not bound by one-child policy restrictions, and urban couples can circumvent the restrictions in various ways (such as paying a fine) (Wang et al. 2013). I conducted three interviews in Xi'an to gain some insight into whether gendered home-buying dynamics are different in a second-tier city, where real estate is not as prohibitively expensive. Most of my interviewees have a college-level education or above, an average or high income, are in their mid-twenties through early thirties (the prime age for marriage), and are first-time urban home buyers.

Thirty-one of the interviewees had already bought a home, while most others were hoping to buy one.

My sample was not representative. I used my research to illuminate the evidence from large quantitative surveys showing that most residential real estate is owned by men (All-China Women's Federation and National Bureau of Statistics of China 2011; He 2008; Horizon China 2012). This helped me to analyze the processes by which women who express egalitarian beliefs about gender often end up acting against their own economic interests and forfeiting ownership of valuable homes when they marry.

All of my respondents across China have been affected by government restrictions on buying property. In Beijing as of this writing, government restrictions on buying property are more rigid than in Shanghai. For example, under regulations announced in February 2011 (Beijing Government 2011), Beijing residents without a household registration in the city (*hukou*) are not permitted to buy residential property until they have worked in Beijing for five years and can produce official pay receipts. Beijing residents with a hukou who already own one home are only permitted to buy one more new home. Shanghai regulations permit residents without a hukou to purchase one home after proving that they have worked in the city for just one year. Shanghai residents with a hukou are allowed to buy a maximum of two homes. By including data from several different cities in China, I show that the role of gender in China underlies other variations affecting home-buying patterns, such as location, education, household registration, income, and whether one is an only child.

Findings

My research reveals a gendered pattern: parents of sons tend to make financial sacrifices to buy their son a home, while parents of daughters often decline to help buy a home, even if they have the means to do so (when I refer to "help buying a home," I mean giving either a cash gift or a no-interest loan with no time limit for repayment). I did not find a single case where parents with a son and a daughter helped their daughter buy a home with no conditions but did not help their son, if he planned to marry. By contrast, I found twenty cases where parents helped buy a home for their son but not for their marriage-age daughter. Many women said their parents did not contribute money toward a home for them because they believe the man's family should provide the marital home.

I conducted in-depth interviews with six women in Beijing and Shanghai who do not have brothers (five of whom are only children) whose parents declined to help them buy a home but gave substantial sums of money to a male relative to buy a home.

Most of the male-owned marital homes (the primary residence purchased for a heterosexual couple) in my sample were heavily financed by the wife or girlfriend. That is, either the woman contributed at least tens of thousands of RMB to the down payment, or she paid a significant portion of the mortgage, or both. For example, when Shanghai resident Hong Lei and her boyfriend began discussing marriage in 2005, her boyfriend's parents made a down payment on a home worth 930,000 RMB, which was registered in the man's name. Hong's boyfriend set up an automatic deduction from his bank account so his monthly salary would go toward paying the mortgage, while the two of them lived on Hong's salary. They married less than a year after the home purchase. When the concrete contours of the new home (*maopifang*) had been constructed, Hong used her 120,000 RMB in savings to pay for renovations (*zhuangxiu*), furniture, and appliances to make the new home livable. She also set up an automatic deduction from her monthly salary to contribute to the mortgage payments. Hong, a 32-year-old fund manager with a 4-year-old daughter, estimated that the home had appreciated by more than 300 percent to 3 million RMB, but she still did not wish to ask her husband to add her name to the deed. "I don't care too much about real estate," said Hong in 2012. "Besides, his parents paid the deposit on the home, and it would not be fair to add my name."

One woman helped her male cousin buy a home rather than buying one for herself. Guo Yuan, a 28-year-old sales manager in Shanghai and an only child, had saved tens of thousands of RMB, which she had hoped to use for a deposit on an apartment in her name. Instead, her parents persuaded her to help the family by contributing to the home purchase of her male cousin (*biaoge*) in Jiangxi province. "My biaoge is already 34 and has been unable to find a wife," Guo said in 2012. "My parents thought that if we helped him buy a home, he might be able to get married."

Soon after, Guo decided that she needed to marry immediately, because at age 28 she had crossed the threshold for becoming a shengnü. She accepted a proposal from a man she had met three months earlier, and even though she loved her job, she turned down a lucrative promotion, which would have required more travel, because she felt that it was difficult for a man to accept a woman with a powerful job. Asked why she had felt the need to marry so quickly, she said, "We are members of society after all. It's very hard to prevent everyone around you from affecting you, unless you are very, very strong in your heart." When we met, Guo was shopping for a home with her fiancé, who had not agreed to add Guo's name to the deed even though she planned to contribute to the down payment.

The consequences can be dire if the woman's name is not on the deed. At the time of our interview in 2012, Wu Mei was a high-income, 31-year-old lawyer in Beijing who had divorced her abusive husband in 2011 after five years of marriage. Her top university scores had secured her admission to law school in Australia. Shortly after she returned to Beijing at age 25, she had married an acquaintance deemed suitable by her family. In 2007, Wu and her parents contributed around 200,000 RMB toward an apartment worth 1 million RMB, which was registered in her husband's name. After the couple moved into the home, the abuse began. "I cried every day on my drive home from work," said Wu. "I just wanted to escape." Her high salary enabled her to rent an apartment while she tried to get her husband to agree to a divorce. Wu, a litigator, is knowledgeable about China's legal system, and she told me that a divorce lawsuit would have been lengthy and traumatic, with no guarantee of success. She finally bought her freedom from the abusive marriage by paying her husband another 100,000 RMB. He retains sole ownership of the home, which had more than tripled in value by 2012. Wu does not want to marry again until she has bought a home in her own name. "If I had had a home of my own when we were married, he never would have threatened me like that," she said.

Wu's case is particularly interesting from a theoretical perspective, because it illustrates the fact that even when the woman's income is extremely high, the husband's bargaining power in the relationship is significantly enhanced by his sole ownership of the marital property. As a corporate attorney, Wu earned around 1 million RMB a year, a salary that placed her in the top 1 percent income bracket in China. Wu's income far exceeded that of her husband, yet she believed that because their home was registered solely in her husband's name he felt free to abuse her because she had no other home to go to.

Wu's income did buy her a degree of power compared with other women, however. Wu said in 2012 that several of her close female friends had confided that they, too, were deeply unhappy in their marriages and wished they could leave their husbands: "One night, four of us [female friends] were all eating dinner and crying at the same time. . . . My friends think about divorcing, but my income is much higher, my living is guaranteed. . . . They don't have the courage to divorce and lose everything like I did. They can't afford it, so they don't do it [get divorced]."

My findings support the literature suggesting that if one partner is economically dependent on the other, the dependent one has less power in the marriage (Chang 2010). As Mariko Lin Chang (2010) illustrates in her research on the persistence of the gender wealth gap, when women have less wealth than men do in a marriage, women are more vulnerable to their partner's demands. When women have their own source of wealth, their bargaining power in the marriage increases.

Leftover Women and Intense Pressure to Marry

Most women in my study expressed anxiety about becoming a shengnü if they are not married by their late twenties, and many said they married quickly specifically to avoid being designated a leftover woman. The intense pressure to marry comes from parents, friends, and society. But it also comes from the state media, which have propagated the notion of leftover women, a term defined by the All-China Women's Federation as "single women above the age of 27" (Xinhua 2011), which was adopted in 2007 as part of the official lexicon of China's Ministry of Education (Ministry of Education of the People's Republic of China 2007). The term circulated through multiple official news reports from 2007 through 2015. My findings suggest that one of the key reasons that so many women marrying after 2006 have been willing to give up ownership of the marital home is that they are afraid of becoming a leftover woman and jeopardizing their chances of ever finding a husband (Fincher 2014).

Greenhalgh and Winckler (2005) in their extensive research on China's population-planning policy write that the state has moved away from the "hard" enforcement of coercive family planning, such as forced abortions, to "soft" techniques, such as education and media reports. Chinese subjects, influenced through state media reports, can then govern themselves in accordance with the priorities of the state. One of the state's population-planning objectives is eugenics "to ensure the 'quality' of coming generations" (Greenhalgh 2010, 781).

In 2010, the Marriage and Family Research Association affiliated with the All-China Women's Federation carried out a nationwide survey of more than 30,000 people in 31 provinces in conjunction with the Committee of Matchmaking Service Industries and the Baihe dating website. The widely circulated official write-up of the survey on Chinese attitudes toward love and marriage uses the subheading "See What Category of 'Leftover' You Belong To" (Zhi 2010). It identifies the first category as single women aged 25–27 years, who are called leftover fighters (*sheng dou shi*), a play on the title of a popular martial arts film. The article says these women "still have the courage to fight for a partner." It then describes several other categories, and the final one is women 35 and older, who are called the "great sage equal of heaven" (*qi tian da sheng*), a play on the Monkey King legend. This category of woman "has a luxury apartment, private car, and a company, so why did she become a 'leftover' woman?" Results from the survey have been recycled frequently in the Chinese media and on the Internet, including a Xinhua news report, "China's 'Leftover Women' Unite This Singles Day." The report states, "More than 90 percent of men surveyed said women should marry before 27 to avoid becoming unwanted" (Xinhua 2011).

The All-China Women's Federation has played a key role in stigmatizing educated single women since 2007, when *leftover women* became a term used by the government. The women's federation publishes articles on its official website with headlines such as "How Many Leftover Women Really Deserve Our Sympathy?" (China News Agency 2011). This column, which ran in March 2011 just after International Women's Day, said: "Pretty girls don't need a lot of education to marry into a rich and powerful family, but girls with an average or ugly appearance will find it difficult. These kinds of girls hope to further their education in order to increase their competitiveness. The tragedy is, they don't realize that as women age, they are worth less and less, so by the time they get their M.A. or Ph.D., they are already old, like yellowed pearls" (China News Agency 2011).

The year 2007, when the Chinese state officially adopted the term *leftover women*, was also the year that China's State Council issued the "Decision on Fully Enhancing the Population and Family Planning Program and Comprehensively Addressing Population Issues" to address "unprecedented population pressures" (Xinhua 2007). These pressures include the sex imbalance, which "causes a threat to social stability," and the "low quality of the general population, which makes it hard to meet the requirements of fierce competition for national strength." The State Council named "upgrading population quality [*suzhi*]" as one of its key goals and appointed the women's federation as one of the primary implementers of its population-planning policy along with other agencies, such as those concerned with propaganda, public security, and civil affairs (Xinhua 2007).

Calling young, single women "leftover" is particularly ironic when China actually faces a shortage of marriage-age women. The country's sex ratio imbalance—caused by the preference for boys and the widespread abortion of female fetuses—has created a demographic crisis. There are tens of millions of surplus or leftover men (*shengnan*), who will be unable to find a bride (Hudson and Den Boer 2004). From my analysis, state media reports on leftover women mostly share the same goal: convince single, educated women to stop being so ambitious, lower their sights, and marry one of the millions of men around them.

My interviews indicate that the media campaign to stigmatize single, professional women has had a powerful effect on many women in their twenties and early thirties. For example, a 26-year-old Beijing resident and only daughter, Li Fang, explicitly said in 2011 that she had been eager to marry because of her age: "If I hadn't gotten married now, I would still have to date for at least one or two years. Then I would already have passed the best childbearing age, and I would be a leftover woman." Li said that she was already in the age category of "leftover fighter" (sheng dou shi; Zhi 2010). She did not feel she had any claim to ownership of the marital home, which is registered solely in her husband's name: "I don't have the right to expropriate [*boduo*] property from someone else's family, someone else's parents."

Li did not share a bank account with her husband and did not know how much money was in his account. She was fired from her job as a human resources manager because the company did not want her to take two weeks of unpaid leave for her honeymoon, and she did not wish to forgo the honeymoon. Yet she did not discuss finances with her husband because the topic "would hurt [his] feelings [*shang ganqing*]," and her husband never raised the issue of how her unemployment affected their spending habits. Li formerly had a monthly income of 4,000 RMB, and she said her husband made around 10,000 RMB a month. Rather than ask her husband for money after losing her income, however, Li said she was drawing down her own savings to pay for groceries, transportation, and clothing. When I asked how long she thought her savings would last, she said she was not worried. She had around 200,000 RMB in her own bank account, which she said would last until she found another job.

It is easy to foresee problems in Li's future after she has a child, which she wishes to do. For example, Zhang Yuan and her husband took out a mortgage on a Beijing home in 2005 for 250,000 RMB. Even though Zhang shared the down payment and mortgage payments with her husband, she told me in 2011 that she agreed to register the home under his name alone because she "trusted him." When their son was born in 2007, Zhang quit her job as a graphic designer to become a stay-at-home mother. After her son went to preschool in 2010, Zhang, 37 years old, has tried to restart her career and has had many job interviews, to no avail. "I am getting worried about my future because it is so difficult for a woman of my age to find a job," she said. Meanwhile, the home registered solely in her husband's name had appreciated by almost 800 percent and was worth around 2 million RMB in 2013.

Discussion

My study suggests that conclusions in the early 2000s about China regarding the "empowerment of urban daughters" (Fong 2002) and the "decline of patriarchal power" (Yan 2003) were overly optimistic. New forms of gender inequality in postsocialist China have emerged even as old forms of gender inequality in areas such as education have abated. As Ridgeway (2011, 28) points out, "People rewrite gender inequality into new social and economic arrangements as these are created, preserving that inequality in modified form in [the] face of socio-economic changes that work to undermine it." Many of the advantages that daughters in postsocialist China gain through education and early career success disappear once they marry and try to buy a home.

Even when they contribute heavily to the purchase of the home, many moderate- to high-income, college-educated women allow the home to be registered solely in the man's name. I also have found that unequal ownership of property appears to increase the husband's bargaining power in the relationship, even if the wife is making a high income, since the value of the home as an appreciating fixed asset far exceeds one person's annual income.

Many urban Chinese women with a university education have launched promising careers, which give them a sense of fulfillment and raise their expectations for further advancement. Women in their twenties and early thirties express a strong desire to own a home of their own and to be economically independent, but they encounter a "resistive, backlash reaction" (Ridgeway 2011, 81) because of their parents' and other elders' gender stereotypes. The entrenched tradition of filial piety and family deference compels young women to acquiesce to the wishes of their elders when marrying and buying a marital home. Further obstacles to women's goal of buying their own home are posed by the buying structure of the real estate market, which makes it almost impossible for one person to afford the down payment on an urban home in a top market. Intense pressure to marry in their mid- to late twenties has been exacerbated since 2007 by the state media campaign about leftover women.

Ridgeway (2011, 198) attributes persistent gender inequality in the United States largely to people's cultural beliefs, which "lag" behind changing social and economic structures. In China, the cultural beliefs of many parents lag severely behind the rapidly changing social and economic structures, but the gender norms of women in their twenties have evolved much faster in an egalitarian direction. This is demonstrated by the many women who express a desire to buy a home in their own name, only to see their ambitions thwarted. In addition, I argue that authoritarian Chinese state policies have played a significant role in reinscribing gender inequalities, actively dragging cultural beliefs about gender backward and counteracting the equalizing effects of improved educational attainment and increased personal ambitions among women. The media campaign about leftover women functions effectively as the state's backlash against educated women's desire to delay marriage in order to advance their careers. Were it not for the powerful, stigmatizing effect of the new discourse about leftover women, I believe that young women would not give in so easily to pressure to register the marital home solely in the man's name and would hold out for more egalitarian home-buying and marital arrangements.

I have identified some key reasons that valuable residential real estate is concentrated in the hands of men and why many young, educated women feel they have little bargaining power when it comes to asserting their rights to marital property. First, the severe unaffordability of homes in China means that it is virtually impossible for one person to make the down payment on a home. The buying structure of residential real estate in China depends on the pooling of assets to purchase a home. The norm of male homeownership dictates that the assets in the family largely flow toward men. The parents and other elders who contribute money to a down payment also have outsized power over whose name is registered on the property deed. Since relatives tend to contribute more money toward buying a home for a man, even when a woman getting married contributes money to the down payment, her portion tends to be less than the amount contributed by the man's family. The man's family then tends to win the negotiation over whose name to put on the deed.

Second, even if a woman's family spends more money on the home purchase than the man's family does, homeownership is a defining feature of masculinity and the patriarchal norm of the man as the head of the household is deeply entrenched. If the woman has paid more for the home than the man has, or if her income is higher than his, she may have to compensate for injuring the man's masculinity by allowing him to have sole ownership of the marital property. This is reinforced by the fact that the man's parents tend to insist on this point, while the woman's parents tend to be more concerned about their daughter's marriageability.

Third, family deference systems persist in modern China, just as in many other countries examined in this volume. Young Chinese men and women continue to feel a deep sense of filial piety and obligation to the family. Even if a woman has succeeded in having her name added to the deed of a marital home, the man's loyalty tends to lie with his parents and other relatives, who may have contributed more money toward the down payment. Further, a woman's sense of obligation to her family may compel her to pass up the opportunity of buying a home of her own in favor of helping a male relative financially. Even if she feels no loyalty to the male relative, her sense of filial piety may compel her to give money to her parents, who will then give it to the male relative. If the couple is not yet married when the home is purchased (a common phenomenon), a woman's own parents may advise her not to fight for her name to be registered on the marital property deed, for fear of driving away the male marriage partner.

Fourth, the Chinese state and society place extreme pressure on educated women to marry. Through the state media, the government has disseminated the *shengnü* term for unmarried women over the age of 27, and it is now ubiquitous in popular culture. Many educated women in their mid-twenties to early thirties are so afraid of becoming a shengnü that they make excessive compromises; they fear becoming too old to find a husband. Many women are unwilling to break off an engagement if the man does not add their name to the deed. Married women often fear that asking their husband to add their name to the deed might jeopardize the relationship. Even if a young woman dismisses the sexist messages of the state media, her own parents are still strongly influenced by the media and exert pressure on her to marry. If the parents of a woman are not anxious about their single daughter, they tend to come under pressure from other relatives or colleagues, who ask, "Why haven't you married off your daughter yet?"

Fifth, money is fungible. If a woman does not contribute directly to a down payment on a house, she is generally expected to pay for the home renovations, furniture, or a car, but the woman's money is not seen to *count* as much as the man's. One common gendered division of home payments is for the woman's income to go toward paying household expenses, while the man's money may go entirely toward building equity in an appreciating fixed asset registered in his name. If a woman is a stay-at-home mother or wife and does not work for money, she is often not seen as contributing financially to the household.

Sixth, government regulations aimed at controlling speculation in the property market often make it extremely cumbersome for a couple to buy property jointly. For example, if the couple registers both names on the first marital property, they must pay a much larger down payment on a second home. Even if a woman has a strong desire to register the marital property in her name alongside the man's, she accepts that it would be more *practical* to register the property in one person's name only, and that name tends to be the man's.

The complicated, multilayered interactions of different economic, social, and government regulatory pressures tend to pose many obstacles for a woman trying to assert her desire for financial equality in her relationship. She generally will give in rather than insist on registering her name on the property deed.

Notes

1. All names of interviewees are pseudonyms. I conducted the interviews in Chinese and translated the quotes into English.
2. I am indebted to Rebecca Karl for the concept of a "buying structure."
3. I am grateful to Fred Block for this insight.

CHAPTER ELEVEN

Reflections on Kidnap and Rape Culture
A Cross-Cultural Comparison of Patriarchy

CYNTHIA WERNER

Two central questions addressed in this volume are why women in many cultural settings often seem to accept or accommodate patriarchal beliefs and practices that are harmful to them and why women often seem to be complicit in their own exploitation. The chapters by Manago and Khurshid link the values children acquire in extended patrilocal households to broader concepts of family honor. Daughters are expected to maintain that honor by behaving modestly and obediently, being sexually circumspect, and accepting the choices made by parents for their marriages. Daughters who fail to do these things bring shame to the family, and therefore young women's behaviors are monitored by family members, who may chastise and punish them for infractions or reward compliance with more behavioral latitude. In rural agrarian settings, the community also plays a role in reinforcing compliance with values of honor and shame by using gossip about women's bad behaviors to cast aspersions on the families that should be controlling them and on the women themselves.

In this chapter, I bring into the discussion another important factor influencing women's accommodations to patriarchy. In some contexts, women's choices and behaviors are also regulated by specific patriarchal value systems that transcend individual families and cut across ethnic, religious, and national beliefs. Specifically, I draw parallels between two seemingly unrelated corners of the world and compare rape culture, particularly as found on US college campuses, with kidnap culture, as practiced in parts of Central Asia. Although the cultural settings might be quite different, the comparison between these two cases provides a useful exercise for understanding the dynamics of patriarchy as a system that constrains women's choices, erases their sense of active agency, and harms them psychologically and physically. In order to understand the choices that women make and the psychological impacts of these practices, it is important to consider the social and cultural contexts of these decisions. I argue that these contexts extend beyond the household to include the broader community. Further, I argue that the perpetuation of a patriarchal value system within each type of community helps explain why so few women on US college campuses decide to report sexual assault and why so few kidnapped brides in Central Asia decide to reject the marriage. In both settings, surprisingly similar dynamics come into play. Members of the broader community say and do things that, intentionally or unintentionally, reinforce the idea that these acts of violence against women are normal and acceptable. Similarly, when officials (at either the state or the university level) deny social, legal, and moral support to victims, they help reinforce rape culture and kidnap culture.

The Victims of Patriarchy

I begin by providing two vignettes that introduce the social practices of kidnap culture and rape culture and their psychological impacts. The first illustrates a case of nonconsensual bride kidnapping in southern Kazakhstan, where I have done field research (Werner 2004, 2009), while the second portrays the sexual assault of a young US college student.

———

In the late 1990s, a 19-year-old woman named Aizhan Bakytzhanov was abducted against her will by a fellow student named Marat Tursunbekov while traveling from her rural hometown to the small city of Turkestan, Kazakhstan, where she was attending the university.[1] *Aizhan had been dating another young man but wanted to complete her university degree before getting married. Marat was a close acquaintance from high school. On the day of the abduction, Marat and three friends waited for Aizhan to exit the train station and then deceived her by casually offering her and her aunt a ride home. The two women trusted him and therefore accepted the offer to save the hassle of taking a taxi. Marat first dropped off Aizhan's aunt, and then turned around and started to drive to his parents' home in the village. When Aizhan realized that he was kidnapping her, she started to struggle and begged him to take her home. His friends responded by grabbing her arms and holding her in place. Along the way, the men stopped the car to drink shots of vodka. Aizhan tried to escape by running across the wide-open steppe, thinking that if she could avoid going to his house, then maybe she could get out of* the situation without anybody knowing. After a short chase, the four men grabbed her and forced her back into the car. Eventually, they arrived at Marat's house, where Aizhan was happily greeted by Marat's mother and members of his extended family, who had gathered to celebrate the marriage. The women of the family took Aizhan to a back room and repeatedly encouraged her to put on a white bridal scarf, symbolizing her status as a bride. They also asked her to write a letter to her parents, stating that she had chosen to marry Marat. Aizhan refused to wear the scarf or write the letter.

Several hours later, Marat's family sent a small delegation of relatives to Aizhan's house to explain her whereabouts and to offer an "apology" payment (as a substitute for the bridewealth payment). Breaking customary practice, his family sent the delegation without a letter from the reluctant bride. Before they arrived, Aizhan's parents had heard from friends that their daughter had been kidnapped. Although it is extremely rare for women to go to the police, it is a crime to abduct a woman without her consent. Aizhan's father was the village police chief, and he was angry that somebody had dared to kidnap his daughter against her will! He therefore rejected the cash apology payment that Marat's relatives sheepishly tried to give him. He and his wife set off to retrieve their daughter, hopeful that the situation could be resolved. They knew that this move would dishonor the family, but they were willing to accept the ensuing shame out of love for their daughter.

When they got to Marat's house, they immediately understood why his family had acted so brashly. Marat's paternal uncle, a man who had mentored and assisted Aizhan's father during his studies, was sitting on the front porch. The uncle had been invited from Almaty to celebrate his nephew's marriage. As Aizhan's father approached his former mentor, the older man greeted him warmly and said that he thought Aizhan would make a fine daughter-in-law. The uncle was either unaware of the circumstances or unbothered by the fact that the bride was reluctant to marry his nephew. In a sad turn of events, Aizhan's father decided that out of respect for his former mentor, he could not rescue his daughter from her undesired fate. Instead of taking her home, he and his wife asked to speak to her. Aizhan came out of the house and begged her parents to take her home. Her father explained the situation and told her that it would be too shameful for her to return home. After her parents left, Marat's family held a short ceremony at home to celebrate the marriage. Although Aizhan ended up staying, she remained unhappy and divorced Marat seven years later. They had two sons together.

On August 31, 2010, Lizzy Seeberg, a 19-year-old college freshman at St. Mary's College in Notre Dame, Indiana, was sexually assaulted by a Notre Dame University football player in his dorm room after two acquaintances left them alone. Lizzy had recently told her parish youth group that she was a virgin who planned to "save herself for marriage." On the night that she was sexually assaulted, she told her therapist and a good friend. The next day, she went to the hospital and consulted with a victims support group on campus before courageously reporting the incident to the campus police. She was motivated by the belief that her action might prevent the same young man from assaulting another young woman. A few days after she reported the crime, a friend of the attacker sent her a disturbing text message stating that it was a "bad idea" to mess with Notre Dame football. He later sent a second warning: "Don't do anything you would regret." This upset Lizzy and made her feel like a traitor. Notre Dame was not just any school to her. She had grown up with relatives who attended both Notre Dame and St. Mary's, and they were all big fans of Notre Dame football. From her perspective, the investigators seemed to be taking their time with the case, and she couldn't understand why the young man who had sexually assaulted her was still able to go to class and attend football practice. These things weighed heavily on her mind.

On September 10, nine days after giving her statement, Lizzy Seeberg took her own life by intentionally overdosing on an antidepressant. On September 15, the football player (who was never publicly named) was interviewed by campus police for the first time about the night that he allegedly assaulted her. He denied her version of events, explaining that she came up with her story after he rejected her sexual advances. On February 11, 2011, a university disciplinary hearing concluded that the young man did not violate the university's sexual misconduct policy. Lizzy's version of her experience was found to be inconsistent with other accounts of the events leading up to the alleged assault.

A number of problematic details, however, led the media to question whether Notre Dame had taken Lizzy's case seriously. After Lizzy reported the incident to campus police, university officials did not contact the county police or the special victims unit for sexual assault cases. A former Notre Dame security officer acknowledged that the delay in interviewing the accused football player can be explained by university procedures, which make it difficult for the police to contact athletes without going through the athletic department first. Throughout the investigation, the university refused to publicly acknowledge Lizzy's allegations, to explain how the university was investigating the case, or to take any action against the football player. Notre Dame protected the name of the accused assailant and allowed him to play in every game of the season. Finally, during the hearing, the student's lawyer, a Notre Dame alumnus, publicly declared that Lizzy's story was a "complete, phony lie."

As these events unfolded, it became clear that Lizzy's case was not an isolated incident at Notre Dame. When another woman was raped by a different Notre Dame football player in February 2011, she also received intimidating emails from other members of the team. She refused to go to the police because, in her mind, that action had only made things worse for Lizzy Seeberg. Taken together, these incidents led many alumni and students to question whether the university was so concerned about protecting its image (including the reputation of the football team) that it was unwilling to take steps to address the problem of sexual assault on campus (Henneberger 2012; Kingkade 2013).

In each of these vignettes, women do have agency, yet their choices take place in a context where they are negatively judged for decisions that fail to accept and maintain the patriarchal value system. Aizhan had the choice of accepting marriage to the man who kidnapped her (and giving up her freedom to choose her own spouse) or declining the marriage (and harming her own and her family's reputation and honor). Given these options, she chose to accept the marriage. Lizzy had the choice of quietly tolerating the sexual assault (and giving up her right to demand her own sexual freedom) or accusing her assailant (and risking her personal safety and her school's reputation). Lizzy carefully weighed these options and then ultimately found another way out: by taking her own life. Both of these cases speak to the power of the patriarchal value system in regulating the behavior of young women.

In the 1970s, Western feminists (writing about Western settings) argued that rape was more common than typically understood due to low rates of reporting (Brownmiller 1975; Connell and Wilson 1974). Brownmiller's landmark book, *Against Our Will: Men, Women and Rape* (1975), transformed the way people viewed rape by challenging the popular perception that women who were raped had most likely done something wrong and therefore *deserved* it. Instead, she emphasized that rape should be viewed as an act of violence and a means by which men maintain power over women. Anthropologist Peggy Sanday (1981) argued that the propensity for rape varies cross-culturally and that rape-prone societies share certain characteristics, such as ideologies of male dominance and the acceptance of interpersonal violence. Feminists defined the United States as a "rape culture" or "rape-supportive culture" in which the media and popular culture help to normalize and tolerate the existence of rape by supporting "the objectification of, and violent and sexual abuse of, women through movies, television, advertising, and 'girlie' magazines" (Burt 1980, 219).

In April 2011, the US Department of Education sent out a "Dear Colleague" letter to universities, specifying that sexual assault cases fall within the domain of Title IX of the Education Amendments, a federal policy designed to prevent sex discrimination at institutions of higher education. Since then, the issue of rape culture has garnered a lot of national media attention (Cohan 2015; Dick 2015; Krakauer 2015). Sexual assault victims who feel that their universities are mishandling their cases are increasingly filing complaints with the Office for Civil Rights (OCR), alleging that the university has violated its commitment to Title IX.[2] The Title IX movement has brought greater awareness to the prevalence of rape culture in the United States.

The Title IX movement has been bolstered by the #MeToo movement yet challenged by other events. The #MeToo movement, which was started in 2006 by Tarana Burke, went viral on Twitter in October 2017 when actress Alyssa Milano tweeted the phrase "Me Too" and encouraged others to do so if they had experienced sexual harassment or sexual assault. In addition to emboldening more and more women (and men) to talk about their personal experiences, #MeToo has outed dozens of powerful men who have sexually harassed and assaulted women.

While these social movements have succeeded in bringing increased awareness to the issue of sexual assault (both on and off US campuses), there has been a series of controversial events that have limited the extent to which they have succeeded in transforming patriarchal values in society. In October 2016, when a YouTube video was released in which Republican presidential candidate Donald Trump described how he sexually assaulted women, some members of society excused his behavior as "locker room talk," and Trump won the election. Similarly, in September 2018, when Christine Blasey Ford came forward to accuse Trump's Supreme Court nominee, Brett Kavanaugh, of sexually assaulting her at a high school party, members of the public and US senators chose to believe that she was lying about the past or that she was accusing the wrong person. In his testimony, Kavanaugh denied any memory of the event, and he was confirmed as a Supreme Court justice. Then, in November 2018, President Trump's secretary of education, Betsy DeVos, released new guidelines for Title IX procedures on US campuses that offer more protection for those accused of sexual assault and sexual harassment. All of these events suggest that social change in the United States has been a slow, nonlinear process.

In a comparative framework, Western notions of rape culture provide useful insights for understanding the issue of bride abduction (bride kidnapping) in Central Asia. Bride abduction is one of several paths to marriage among the Kazakhs and Kyrgyz, two distinct yet similar Turkic-speaking, Muslim ethnic groups in Central Asia. Among both the Kazakhs and Kyrgyz, the family and gender system emphasizes patrilineal descent, clan-based exogamy, patrilocal marriage, and the subservient status of young daughters-in-law. Traditionally, girls were socialized to respect their elders and to behave in a way that would not bring shame (*uyat*) to the family. Marriages were arranged when the bride and groom were young children. Upon marriage, the groom's family paid bride-wealth in the form of livestock to the bride's family. Bride abduction existed in the pre-Soviet period, but it was an unusual occurrence that sometimes transpired after matchmaking efforts fell apart. During Soviet rule (1920–1991), the state, seeking to emancipate women, expanded educational opportunities for women, created conditions to get women into the workplace, and banned feudal patriarchal customs, such as child betrothal and polygyny. Although the state did not completely eliminate the patriarchal value system, it did succeed in transforming women's lives in many ways, including their paths to marriage. By the late Soviet period, the majority of Kazakh and Kyrgyz women completed high school, and it was uncommon for a woman to get married before doing so.

New paths to marriage emerged in the Soviet years and continue to exist in the present. On one hand, there are modern marriages, where the young couple meet on their own and decide to get married. These marriages are inspired by Soviet and Western values. On the other hand, there are traditional arranged marriages, where family elders continue to play a role in the selection of the marriage partner and participate in a series of matchmaking events. In a modern twist on the traditional marriage, a young couple might initiate the process by asking their parents to go through the rituals of arranging the marriage. Since the fall of the Soviet Union in 1991, these traditional marriages have become less common throughout Kyrgyzstan and parts of Kazakhstan, and there has been a rise of kidnap marriages. When kidnap marriages initially became popular in the Soviet period, many kidnapping cases were consensual: the bride appeared to be conforming to the patriarchal value system by accepting the marriage, yet she was often eloping with her preferred partner. In the post-Soviet period, there has been an increase in the frequency of nonconsensual kidnappings in both

Kyrgyzstan and Kazakhstan. Regardless of the path to marriage, young brides (*kelin*) are still expected to show respect to their parents and deference to their in-laws, though the level of submissiveness varies significantly from one family to the next (Werner 2004, 2009).

I first learned about bride kidnapping while conducting fieldwork in a village in southern Kazakhstan in the mid-1990s. Within a one-year period, my host family's daughter was kidnapped by her boyfriend as a strategy to get around her parents' objection to the marriage, and my neighbor's daughter was abducted against her will. Both cases demonstrate the forces of patriarchy that exist in Kazakh society, which affect the psychological well-being of young Kazakh women. In the first case, my host family's daughter became extremely anxious upon discovering that her parents were taking steps to arrange a marriage with their friend's son. She wanted to marry her boyfriend, and she was able to avoid the arranged marriage by going along with a kidnapping script, acting as if things were out of her control when her boyfriend abducted her. In the second case, the neighbor's daughter was emotionally distraught after being abducted by a secret admirer whom she had never met. After she was kidnapped, she had a short amount of time to decide whether she would consent to the marriage, and this important decision had to be made with limited knowledge of what it might be like to be this man's wife and to live with his family. This "choice" was made under extreme duress: as she pleaded through tears to be returned home, the prospective groom's female relatives pressured her to accept the marriage by repeatedly telling her that her life would be more difficult if she refused due to the stigma of being a girl who returned home. Although her own parents were heartbroken about the situation, they agreed after the kidnapping that she should accept the marriage due to the social consequences of refusing.

Both of these cases reveal the ways in which women's agency is constrained by a patriarchal value system. Even in the situation where my host's daughter chose to resist patriarchal ideals by avoiding an arranged marriage, she did so in a way that helps perpetuate the value system that makes it normal and acceptable for men to kidnap women. As I spent more time in the community, I continued to hear about other cases of bride abduction, and I learned more about the cultural patterns and rules that informed this local practice, which varied from consensual cases, roughly equivalent to Western elopement, to nonconsensual cases (Werner 2004, 2009).

Borrowing ideas from the literature on rape culture, I suggest that several aspects of Central Asian society help support a kidnap culture. Similar to the

US setting, where rape myths contribute to a rape-supportive culture, there are kidnap myths that create an environment where bride abduction is socially acceptable. Although some locals find the practice to be objectionable, the widespread belief that a kidnapped bride should stay, combined with narratives (in Kyrgyzstan) about how this marriage practice ties into national identity (Werner 2009) contribute to a kidnap-supportive culture. Kidnap myths affect how bride abduction cases are viewed by the public and by officials. Although there have been a growing number of studies on bride kidnapping in Central Asia (Amsler and Kleinbach 1999; Borbieva 2012; Handrahan 2004; Kleinbach 2003; Kleinbach, Ablezova, and Aitieva 2005; Kleinbach and Salimjanova 2007; Lom 2004; Mack 2015; Werner 2004, 2009), this chapter represents the first attempt to use the concept of kidnap culture and to compare kidnap culture in Central Asia with rape culture in the United States.

Parallels between Nonconsensual Bride Abduction and Sexual Assault

A number of striking parallels between the practice of nonconsensual bride abduction in Central Asia and the problem of sexual assault on US campuses become apparent when the two are compared to one another (table 11.1). Although it is difficult to get reliable statistics, both practices are widespread in their respective settings. Survey research has consistently confirmed that approximately one out of four college women in the United States are sexually assaulted by the time they graduate (Cantor et al. 2015; Fisher, Cullen, and Turner 2000; Koss, Gidycz, and Wisniewski 1987; Krebs et al. 2007). Several studies suggest that at least that many young women are abducted against their will by potential suitors in some regions of Central Asia (Handrahan 2004; Kleinbach, Ablezova, and Aitieva 2005; Shields 2006; Werner 2004). According to Shields (2006, 89), approximately 30 percent of all marriages in Kyrgyzstan occur through nonconsensual kidnapping, though the rates are as high as 80 percent in some areas. Anecdotal and survey evidence suggests that the frequency of nonconsensual kidnapping is not as high in Kazakhstan. Anecdotal evidence suggests that the practice occurs throughout the country but is more common in the south. In my own survey in southern Kazakhstan's *oblast* (province), approximately 11 percent of all marriages that were formed in the 1990s were due to nonconsensual kidnapping (Werner 2004).

In both settings, younger women are more vulnerable than women who are just a few years older. In rural regions of Central Asia, women often get married

Table II.I. Parallels between Bride Abduction and Sexual Assault

Similar features	Bride abduction in Central Asia	Sexual assault on US campuses
High rate of frequency	Regional surveys find that rates of nonconsensual kidnapping are quite high, yet they vary across time and space. One study suggests that 30% of all marriages in Kyrgyzstan can be attributed to nonconsensual bride kidnapping. Another study finds that in the 1990s 11% of marriages in one region of Kazakhstan were formed through nonconsensual bride kidnapping.	National surveys find that approximately 25% of female undergraduates are sexually assaulted in college.
Age is a factor	Younger adult women are at the greatest risk.	First- and second-year students are at the greatest risk.
Acquaintances vs. strangers	Women are more likely to be abducted by an acquaintance than by a stranger.	Women are more likely to be raped by an acquaintance than by a stranger.
Use of force	Men sometimes use physical force to abduct women.	Men often use physical force to rape women.
Use of deception	Women are often deceived in some way during the act of abduction.	Women are often deceived in some way prior to a rape.
Illegality	Nonconsensual bride abduction is illegal.	Sexual assault and rape are illegal.
Low rate of reporting	It is extremely rare for this crime to be reported to the police.	The majority of victims do not report the sexual assault to the police or campus authorities.

Similar features	Bride abduction in Central Asia	Sexual assault on US campuses
Popular narratives and myths	Kidnap myths reinforce ideas about proper behavior and make it seem acceptable for men to kidnap women.	Rape myths reinforce ideas about proper behavior and make it seem socially permissible for men to rape and sexually assault women.
Interpretations of consent	An absence of explicit consent is interpreted in different ways.	An absence of explicit consent is interpreted in different ways.
View of rapists and kidnappers	Young men who kidnap women are often viewed as "nice guys."	College students who commit rape are often viewed as "nice guys."
Use of coercion	Women are psychologically coerced to accept the marriage.	Women are psychologically coerced to stay silent.
Fear of threats and reprisals	Women who resist kidnappings are threatened and stigmatized.	Women who file rape allegations are threatened and stigmatized.

before they turn 20, and the age of 25 is generally believed to be the upper limit for a woman to get married. In my own sample, women were typically kidnapped between the ages of 17 and 20. Some women in Kyrgyzstan are kidnapped when they are still minors, some as young as 14 (Shields 2006). In the United States, women who are first-year and second-year college students are more vulnerable than women who are juniors and seniors (Cantor et al. 2015; Krebs et al. 2007).

The film *The Hunting Ground* (Dick 2015) features several women who were targeted by rapists during their first few weeks on campus before they had established social networks away from home. These women often first encountered their rapist at a party where alcohol was being served. Men who rape try to find women who will be easy targets, such as women who are consuming a lot of alcohol or those who attend a party alone. Once women have established social networks on campus, they are less likely to attend a party alone, and they are more likely to have friends watching out for them at social events. Despite popular images of rapists as complete strangers who drag women into dark alleys, more often than not female college students are raped by acquaintances, friends, and boyfriends. Zinzow and Thompson (2011) find that 92 percent of rapes on college campuses are committed by somebody whom the victim knows, including the victim's romantic partner.

Similarly, in Central Asia, the majority of women who are abducted against their will are kidnapped by acquaintances, including impatient boyfriends and rejected suitors (Shields 2006). Sixty-five percent of the women in Handrahan's (2004) study and 88 percent of the women in Kleinbach and colleagues' (2005) study were kidnapped by acquaintances. Motivations for kidnapping vary. In some regions, kidnapping has become the norm, and young men (and their families) feel that this is a preferred way to get married; it is more efficient and economical than an arranged marriage (Mack 2015). In some cases, there is also an assumption that the woman or her parents might refuse if the groom were to pursue another path to marriage. In other situations, young women who are kidnapped by their boyfriends are often not ready to get married due to the stress of leaving their parents' home, concern about becoming a daughter-in-law, and the expectation to bear children as soon as possible. Once kidnapped, however, a young woman is likely to accept the marriage in order to avoid the stigma of being a "girl who returned home."

In both contexts, men often use physical force to commit these acts of violence against women. A report by Krebs and colleagues (2007) reveals that 25.3 percent of sexually assaulted undergraduate women are attacked with physical force, though a significantly larger percentage of sexual assaults on campus (58.4 percent) take place when a woman is incapacitated or unable to provide consent. Men also use force to kidnap women in Central Asia; in most instances, the perpetrator relies on the assistance of several male friends to intimidate the woman and ensure that she does not escape, as described above in Aizhan's case. Depictions of kidnapping frequently describe how women are grabbed and dragged, and sometimes their heads are covered (Shields 2006, 106).

Besides physical force, men use deception to kidnap and rape women. Bride kidnappings often begin when a woman, like Aizhan, is offered a ride by an acquaintance. It is common for the groom's male and female relatives to help plan the kidnapping (Mack 2015). Male friends are usually enlisted to help with the kidnapping itself, and in some cases female friends of the groom help to convince the young woman to do something that leads to her own kidnapping (Shields 2006). In other cases, female friends are unwittingly part of the plot;

they might be dropped off before the bride is taken to the groom's house, or they might be taken along for the ride. Once the woman realizes what is happening, physical force and coercion are used to ensure that she does not escape and that she accepts the marriage. One woman, for example, told me that her husband's friends (who assisted with the kidnapping) threatened to rape her if she did not accept the marriage.

Deception is also used in cases of sexual assault. For example, a male college student might initially appear to be a nice guy, offering to take a woman home after a party. Then, after he has the woman alone in the car, he stops somewhere to rape her (Armstrong, Hamilton, and Sweeney 2006).

These general characteristics demonstrate the precarious position of young women in patriarchal societies. In both settings, men take advantage of a patriarchal value system that allows them to get away with these practices. Although sexual assault and nonconsensual kidnapping are regarded as serious crimes punishable by law in the United States and Central Asia, these statutes are rarely enforced. Convictions and sentencing vary in the United States depending on state law and the severity of the crime. In Kyrgyzstan, the punishment for kidnapping is a fine equivalent to 100–200 times the minimum monthly wage or up to five years in prison (Shields 2006, 119).

In both contexts, the number of cases reported in survey research far exceeds the number of cases that are reported to the police (Cantor et al. 2015; Shields 2006). On US campuses, women usually have the option of contacting law enforcement (to initiate a criminal investigation) or campus authorities (to initiate a disciplinary review), or doing both. In one survey, less than 28 percent of the victims of sexual assault reported to either law enforcement or campus authorities (Cantor et al. 2015, iv). Women might try to resist the rape, but afterward they are unlikely to report the crime to the police or campus authorities, and reported cases rarely end in convictions.

While levels of reporting are low on college campuses, it is even rarer for the victims of bride abduction to contact the police. During the course of my fieldwork in Kazakhstan, I did not hear of a single instance where a woman contacted the police after being abducted. The local judge confirmed that there were no cases on record in the village, and he told me that the reason there are no cases is that all kidnappings in the village are "consensual" and therefore legal. His response contradicted the stories that I gathered from women who had been kidnapped, but the village judge is not the only one who holds this view. Studies show that law enforcement officials in Central Asia, in general, do not regard nonconsensual kidnapping as a serious issue (Shields 2006, 121–23). Even in cases where family members encourage a woman to return home, it is unlikely that the abduction will be reported to the police, in part because the family does not want to bring attention to the event. There is also a general perception that reporting the abduction will not lead to prosecution of the kidnapper and might have negative consequences for the woman and her family (Werner 2004). In one study, only 3 out of 860 kidnapped women in Kyrgyzstan filed a report with the police; none of them found justice (Shields 2006).

Why do women who are victimized by these crimes tend to accommodate patriarchal rules? Furthermore, why do other women (especially in Central Asia) take on roles that help men get away with these crimes? In the following section, I demonstrate that women's responses to these practices are constrained by attitudes, beliefs, and actions in the broader society that intentionally or unintentionally suggest that these practices are normal and acceptable. I explore the power of beliefs commonly referred to as *rape myths* and extend this idea to Central Asia by introducing the concept of *kidnap myths*. These myths represent the core of the patriarchal value system, and they come into play when women are put in a position where they have to decide whether to accommodate patriarchy.

The Power of the Patriarchal Value System

Rape myths (false beliefs about rape, sexual assault, and interpersonal violence) help reproduce a social environment that makes rape socially permissible despite its illegal status. Rape myths create a "climate hostile to rape victims" (Burt 1980, 217). The following statements are examples of common rape myths: "only bad girls get raped"; "women ask for it"; "women falsely accuse men of rape when they've been sexually rejected"; and "women want or enjoy rape" (Armstrong, Hamilton, and Sweeney 2006; Burt 1980; Harding 2015; Sanday 1996). A summary of several common rape myths can be compared to a summary of kidnap myths (table 11.2).

One of the defining characteristics of rape culture is the existence of patriarchal social constructs that suggest that women are expected to be sexual gatekeepers (see Khurshid and Manago, both this volume). While it is okay for men to be sexually active studs, women are judged for behaviors that include excessive drinking and sexually permissive actions. Social views about sexual behavior (e.g., definitions of what constitutes "slutty" behavior) change over

Table II.2. Rape Myths versus Kidnap Myths

Rape myths	Kidnap myths
Only bad girls are raped.	Only bad girls return home, and girls who return home will have a bad fate.
Women lie about being raped.	Women pretend to be upset when they are kidnapped.
It wasn't really rape; it was consensual sex.	The kidnapping was consensual.
She wanted it.	Women will eventually be happy with the marriage.
Men are sexually aggressive by nature.	Kidnapping is a national tradition (in Kyrgyzstan).
He couldn't have done it; he's a nice guy.	He's a nice guy; he'll be a good husband.

time, yet there continue to be fundamental gender differences in how society views the sexuality of men and women (e.g., the concept of a slut remains). One of the rape myths is that "good" girls do not get themselves into situations where rape is possible, and "bad" girls or slutty girls are just asking for it. Yet there is social pressure for college women to participate in college parties, and it is socially acceptable for men to be sexually aggressive and to talk about their sexual conquests. When women are designated as sexual gatekeepers and men are viewed as sexual aggressors, men are relieved from the responsibility of obtaining authentic consent (Armstrong, Hamilton, and Sweeney 2006). From this perspective, intoxicated women are perceived to be asking for it, and some men have nonconsensual sex with an unconscious woman without viewing it as rape. In a Stanford University rape case in 2016, Brock Turner's father suggested that his son's greatest mistake was getting drunk, not raping an unconscious woman (Hunt 2016).

These social constructs contribute to a system where victim blaming is common and victims experience high levels of shame. In addition to the rape myth that certain victims want it or deserve it, men are protected by a rape myth that suggests that women make false accusations when they are jilted, when they regret having sex, or when they want to ruin a boy's life. The rape myth about false accusations is reinforced by high-profile cases, such as a 2006 Duke University case where people came to believe that the woman made a false accusation. Initially, members of the lacrosse team were cast as monsters for gang raping a woman, but they were exonerated when the boys' lawyers convinced the public that the woman had made false accusations in the past and that she was interested in a cash settlement. Just as the initial allegations tarnished the reputation of Duke, the subsequent findings seemed to restore the reputation of the accused men as well as the "honor" of Duke University (Cohan 2015).

A related rape myth, "it wasn't really rape," is linked to the issue of consent. In the absence of explicit agreement to sexual activity, the public makes judgments about what exactly constitutes consent (Sanday 1996). All parties may acknowledge that sexual contact occurred but disagree about whether it was consensual in situations where consent was not explicit. Popular understandings of rape do not always line up with legal definitions. Opinions vary among members of society, and this then influences how individual cases are evaluated in public opinion and in legal cases. In the United States, jurors are likely to acquit when a woman is raped after engaging in some consensual sexual activity, such as kissing, even if physical force is used. For example, in one high-profile case, a woman was raped in her own home while watching a movie with a friend whom she had dated previously. They had been making out, but he forced her to have sex. Although she told him to stop, the jury didn't find her *no* to be convincing enough because she didn't struggle, she didn't call out to her friend in the next room, she asked the assailant if he was using a condom, and she gave the perpetrator a ride home afterward (Krakauer 2015).

A final myth is the idea that men who rape are actually nice guys who wouldn't do something as awful as rape. This myth is especially salient in cases where the rape is committed by popular and attractive high school and college students. This was one of the key issues in the Duke University case mentioned above, where the lacrosse players were generally believed to be upstanding members of the community. Such men do not personify the popular image of a rapist. This rape myth was also a dominant trope in the Supreme Court confirmation hearings for Brett Kavanaugh. Kavanaugh and his supporters repeatedly asserted that he was just a nice guy who enjoyed parties and beer. Another example of this myth is a Steubenville, Ohio, rape case involving two white high school football players who raped an intoxicated teenage girl and shared pornographic photos of her on Facebook. Rather than focusing on the victim's experience, CNN anchor Poppy Harlow expressed sympathy for the boys, who were found guilty on all charges (Shapiro 2013).

Women's decisions to come forward after a sexual assault are influenced by these rape myths. The idea of reporting is psychologically distressing in a society where rape myths persist, and women are unsure how the broader community will respond if they report the crime. Some victims do not want family members to know what happened, or they do not want to deal with the stress of answering questions about their experience that might challenge their reputation and credibility. This is especially true in cases where women blame themselves or worry about violations of campus policies on alcohol use (Cantor et al. 2015; Krebs et al. 2007). Sometimes, the experiences of others inform a woman's decision to come forward or not. For example, after Lizzy Seeberg's case went public, a woman who was sexually assaulted by another Notre Dame football player chose not to go to the police out of fear of a negative public response (Henneberger 2012).

Kidnap culture is also supported by a number of myths that make the practice socially acceptable and normal. One of the most powerful kidnap myths is that only bad girls return home. This is quite different from the US context, where bad girls put themselves in positions where they deserve to be raped. Similar to the US context, however, this myth is linked to the notion that women should be sexual gatekeepers. In Central Asia, an unmarried woman's reputation as a presumed virgin is linked to her family's honor. This shows up in local languages where the word for girl (*qyz*) doubles as the word for virgin. The family's honor is at stake when a girl is kidnapped because her status as a virgin can now be questioned by the larger community. In this cultural setting, the only way to restore the family honor is for the woman to accept the marriage. Local proverbs and superstitions support this view, suggesting that a young woman cannot turn back once she has crossed the threshold of the groom's house (Werner 2004). A woman who agrees to stay is accepting her fate, while a woman who returns home is damaging her family's honor: she is a failed gatekeeper. This kidnap myth explains why the girl who returns home (*qaityp kelgen qyz*) is a stigmatized social category. Related to the belief that bad girls choose to return home is the belief that girls who return home will suffer a bad fate.

Another kidnap myth is the belief that women are only pretending to be upset when they are kidnapped. The idea here is that a young woman will act as if she is distraught and unhappy when she arrives at the groom's house because it would be culturally inappropriate to appear too eager to leave her own family behind and to become sexually active. The situation is complicated by the fact that some kidnappings are consensual, and brides who are kidnapped consensually might go through the motions of acting more upset than they actually are when they arrive at the groom's house. Central Asians have words to distinguish between nonconsensual (*kelisimsyz alyp qashu*) and consensual (*kelisimmen alyp qashu*) kidnapping (Werner 2004). If a woman is dating the abductor and she writes a letter shortly after she arrives at his house, members of the community are likely to describe the abduction as a consensual kidnapping; however, if a woman is abducted by a stranger and actively resists the kidnapping, people are more likely to describe the abduction as a nonconsensual kidnapping. Similar to the US context, the issue of consent can be murky in public opinion. It can be difficult for members of the broader community to distinguish between situations where women are truly upset and situations where women are acting upset. This possibility allows members of the broader community to believe that any particular case of kidnapping really was consensual.

A related kidnap myth is the idea that *all* kidnappings are consensual. I first encountered this myth in Kazakhstan when asking the village judge whether there were any legal cases regarding kidnap marriage. His perspective was that there are not any cases because the brides do ultimately put on the bridal scarf, write the letter, and stay at the groom's house. In addition, most likely, there were no legal cases on record because women (and their families) do not feel comfortable reporting these incidents to the police. I have also encountered this kidnap myth on a few occasions while discussing my research with cosmopolitan Kazakhs, who find it hard to believe that this still happens in their modern country. (This kidnap myth appears to have more salience in Kazakhstan due to the regional concentration of this practice and the demographic diversity of the population.)

Often, members of the community are not terribly concerned about the status of a kidnapping because of another common kidnap myth, the idea that a kidnapped bride will eventually be happy with the marriage, even if she is distraught initially. During one interview with several young men who had abducted women, I was told that they do not worry if a woman starts to cry because "she will be happy after one week" (Werner 2004, 86). As another study confirms, there is generally a lot of social pressure to disregard the emotional trauma that a woman might experience during a kidnapping (Handrahan 2004).

In the regions of Central Asia where kidnapping is common, there is also a general belief that kidnapping is an acceptable way to get married. This belief is perhaps most strongly held in Kyrgyzstan, where the practice has been reinvented in the post-Soviet period as a national tradition (Kleinbach and Salimjanova 2007; Mack 2015). In this context, the act of kidnapping is a display simultaneously of a man's masculinity and of his ethnonational identity (Handrahan 2004). By extension, a Kyrgyz woman who returns home is not only rejecting the man and his family, she is also viewed as a traitor to her ethnonational identity.

One final kidnap myth is the idea that men who abduct women, like men who sexually assault women, are nice guys. Although men who kidnap women are committing a crime, they are rarely portrayed as criminals. Members of the general public continue to regard these men, as well as their male accomplices, as nice guys. After a woman is kidnapped, the groom's female relatives are the ones who try to convince the bride that the groom will make a wonderful husband.

The patriarchal value system, exemplified in these rape myths and kidnap myths, is mobilized after a rape or kidnap takes place. The men who commit these crimes rely heavily on these values as they try to coerce a woman to accept what happened in order to avoid embarrassing herself and her family or her university. These acts of coercion are inextricably linked to shame, a powerful source of motivation in patriarchal societies. Moreover, it is common for other members of society to play a role in the process of coercion.

After a kidnapped bride has been taken to the groom's house, for example, the groom's female relatives use intense psychological pressure to convince her to accept the marriage. Although one might expect these women to have sympathy for the kidnapped bride, their primary interest is to protect the reputation of their family, which would be damaged if the young woman returned home. In addition to pressuring her to accept the white bridal scarf and to write a letter to her parents stating that she willingly agrees to the marriage, the older women threaten to curse the kidnapped bride's life with unhappiness if she refuses. Her own parents and other relatives might also pressure her to stay due to a common belief that bad things happen to women who turn back after they have crossed the groom's threshold.

Two features of the early socialization process play a powerful role in the bride's decision-making process. First, it can be difficult for women who are socialized to respect their elders to resist pressure from the groom's female relatives. As one young woman said, "They sat with me, trying to convince me. They said, 'He's a good boy, he doesn't smoke, doesn't drink, won't beat you, he is very gentle. If you go now you don't know who you'll eventually marry.' . . . They pressured me to do this [write the letter]. I didn't want to do it, but in the end, I did" (Shields 2006, 105). Second, it is difficult for women who are socialized to maintain the family's honor to do anything that might bring shame to their family. When a young woman is kidnapped, elders on both sides essentially remind her that rejecting the marriage will bring shame to both families.

Similarly, after a woman has been raped, the perpetrator coerces her into staying silent. The rapist has obvious motives, but in many cases, other individuals also act on behalf of the offender and try to convince the woman to avoid reporting the crime to the police or campus authorities. In the film *The Hunting Ground*, Erica Kinsman describes how members of the community called her a "slut" and a "liar" after she filed a rape allegation against fellow University of Florida student Jameis Winston. In other words, she was shamed as somebody who was not an ideal sexual gatekeeper. Rather than assuming that she was telling the truth about the incident, people questioned her character and her credibility (Dick 2015). Sometimes, the people who question a woman's credibility are the very people who are in positions intended to help the victims of sexual assault, such as police officers or prosecutors. In some cases, police officers or campus authorities may ask questions that imply that they do not believe the accuser, and prosecutors discourage women from pressing charges unless the evidence is impeccable (Krakauer 2015).

Conclusion

There are many different ways that women are affected by patriarchy. I have focused here on young women who find themselves the victims of patriarchal practices in two different settings: the United States and Central Asia. Despite cultural differences between these two sites, there are striking similarities in the way that young women are impacted by patriarchy. In the United States, one out of four college women is likely to become the victim of sexual assault before she graduates (Cantor et al. 2015; Fisher, Cullen, and Turner 2000; Koss, Gidycz, and Wisniewski 1987; Krebs et al. 2007). Meanwhile, in some regions of Central Asia, the odds of a young woman being kidnapped against her will by a man who wants to marry her are similarly high (Handrahan 2004; Kleinbach, Ablezova, and Aitieva 2005; Shields 2006; Werner 2004). In both situations, women cannot prevent these acts from happening, but they do have options in how they respond. Theoretically, it is possible for a woman who is raped to report the crime, and it is possible for a woman who is kidnapped to reject the marriage. However, in practice, most women opt to accommodate patriarchy by remaining silent (in the case of rape) and by accepting the marriage (in the case of bride kidnapping). The majority of college women who are sexually assaulted do not report the crime to the police or to campus authorities. Similarly, the majority of young Central Asian women who are kidnapped end up accepting the marriage rather than returning home to their families.

This comparison brings greater visibility to the patriarchal value system. Despite the differences between these two societies, women's lives are similarly affected by the perpetuation and reproduction of patriarchal values and beliefs that constrain women's agency. Moreover, the men who commit these acts can rely on this value system to protect them from strong repercussions for kidnapping or sexually assaulting women. Men who rape women know that they are likely to get away with it because their victim will be afraid that if she goes to the police, her credibility will be questioned and her reputation and behavior will be scrutinized. She may also fear future reprisals from her rapist. Similarly, men who kidnap women know that they are likely to get away with it because the bride will be convinced that he is a nice guy and that this type of marriage is a national tradition. They will also accept out of fear of the stigma of being a girl who returned home.

These patriarchal practices are not limited to the perpetrator and the victim. Indeed, the reason that the patriarchal value system is so powerful is that the ideas and beliefs exemplified in rape myths and kidnap myths are shared by a large segment of society. Kandiyoti's (1988) seminal work suggests that the household serves as the source of women's accommodation. My chapter, however, demonstrates that the community also influences women's conformity to patriarchy. This is evidenced by the things that community members say and do after a woman has been sexually assaulted or kidnapped. Although there are significant cultural differences regarding how a sexual gatekeeper should behave in each society, young unmarried women in both societies are still likely to be judged for being sexually permissive in ways for which men would not be judged. But women who conform to gender expectations are unlikely to come under public scrutiny.

Sexual assault and bride kidnapping bring a woman's status as a sexual gatekeeper into question. After a woman has been sexually assaulted or kidnapped, members of the community (and the household) play a role in influencing how a woman responds. As I have demonstrated, victims of sexual assault may be verbally threatened by friends of the assailant, and victims of kidnapping might be verbally pressured by family members of the groom to accept the marriage. In both settings, public scrutiny is likely to intensify if the woman attempts to resist patriarchy by reporting a rape or rejecting a suitor. A woman who chooses to report a sexual assault to campus authorities or to the police is likely to face public questions about her behavior before she was assaulted (e.g., "did she deserve it?") and questions about consent (e.g., "did it really happen?"). In Central Asia, a woman who rejects a marriage is likely to deal with public scrutiny regarding her character and marriageability.

Although in this chapter I have shown the power of patriarchal value systems in two different settings, I am optimistic and believe that the value systems are capable of change. State actors and campus administrators can and should play a role in attempting to change the cultures that normalize rape and nonconsensual kidnapping. In this regard, the comparison between kidnap culture and rape culture has the potential to be instructive.

I believe that the United States can still be described as a rape-supportive culture, yet I think there is some evidence to suggest that the culture has been changing in a positive direction since 2011. The federal government and campus administrators are playing a role in shaping these changes. Lizzy Seeberg's case is one of several prominent cases that have exposed the ways in which colleges and universities have contributed to a patriarchal system where male students have been able to get away with sexually assaulting female students. Seeberg's case prompted the US Department of Education's Office for Civil Rights to conduct a seven-month investigation to determine whether Notre Dame's handling of sexual assault cases was in violation of Title IX policies. Notre Dame voluntarily entered a settlement agreement with the OCR and established a plan to improve its procedures for preventing and addressing sexual assault. From 2013 to the present, sexual assault victims have banded together through the grassroots campaign Know Your IX. As a result, more than a hundred universities are now being investigated by the OCR (Dick 2015). In response to new federal guidelines and Title IX investigations, many campuses are changing the way they handle sexual assault cases: developing victim-centered approaches and introducing new educational programs that focus on bystander awareness and "yes means yes" approaches to consent (Welch 2014; Winerip 2014). Not only do these changes create the possibility of reducing the frequency of sexual assault, they may also provide psychological support for sexual assault victims. It is too early to say whether these developments have weakened rape culture in the United States, but it is likely that the policy changes recommended by the Trump administration have slowed down the momentum.

In Central Asia, despite some activism on behalf of kidnap victims, there are signs that suggest that kidnap culture has become more entrenched since the

1990s, especially in Kyrgyzstan (Werner 2009). In post-Soviet Central Asia, the rise of nonconsensual kidnapping is linked to a revival of ethnonational identities. In Kyrgyzstan, where the rate of nonconsensual bride abduction seems to be higher, this practice has increasingly been reimagined as a national tradition (Kleinbach and Salimjanova 2007; Werner 2009). Consequently, local women and activists who challenge the practice are viewed as traitors to their ethnicity. Although a number of small NGOs are concerned with women's rights in Kazakhstan and Kyrgyzstan, the central government is not doing much to address kidnap culture (Shields 2006; Werner 2009). Many government officials simply do not regard bride abduction as a problem. The authors of a Human Rights Watch report note that police officers "treated it as a laughing matter, giggling when the topic was brought up" and offering to "kidnap Human Rights Watch's researchers while they were in town" (Shields 2006, 126). These developments suggest that kidnap culture remains entrenched in Central Asia, and the psychological impacts of kidnapping are likely to be compounded by the fact that there is minimal social and moral support for women who are abducted against their will.

Notes

1. Pseudonyms are used for all accounts of bride kidnapping. An account of this case was published previously (Werner 2004).
2. Although men can also be the victims of sexual assault (Kassie 2015), this chapter is limited to cases of rape and sexual assault against women on US campuses.

CHAPTER TWELVE

Conclusion
Charting a Way Forward

HOLLY F. MATHEWS AND ADRIANA M. MANAGO

The authors in this volume have endeavored to shed light on some of the psychological underpinnings of patriarchy by analyzing the perspectives of women residing in what we have referred to as the patriarchal belt and its colonies, borrowing from Deniz Kandiyoti's (1988) formulations. A central question driving our analyses is why women uphold or resist certain patriarchal customs even as their foundations shift with globalization, increased formal schooling, and myriad economic changes associated with declines in subsistence agriculture. The very question of women's accommodation could be critiqued on the grounds that we are presupposing that women have options for resistance. In other words, one could conclude that women accommodate to men's power because they have no other choice. Yet as we discussed in the introduction to this volume, Saba Mahmood (2005) and others have warned that we must be careful to separate notions of agency from concepts of the liberal autonomous subject that are particular to Western cultural world views. Participating in cultural practices does not necessarily equate with reduced agency; in fact, agency is required for inhabiting cultural norms. Unlike Mahmood, who locates agency on the cultural-discursive level, developmentalist Gisela Trommsdorff (2012, 19) locates agency in psychological processes and asserts that children learn over the course of development to intentionally act to self-regulate by "organizing inner mental processes and behavior in line with cultural values, social expectations, internalized standards, and one's self-construal." Socialization is an active psychological process of synthesizing and coordinating. Humans construct ways of understanding themselves and the world in order to organize and direct their behaviors and to satisfy fundamental human needs for connection and self-preservation in a given social environment.

The varied and complex psychological processes and external constraints illuminated by the contributors to this volume are not the only ones involved in women's responses to patriarchal beliefs and practices. Indeed, we contend that there is no one overall explanation for the persistence of patriarchy; rather, its adaptability and fragmentation require careful and localized empirical investigation to account for its remarkable persistence and to formulate multifactorial explanations for women's psychological responses to it. These chapters begin that process and map out a range of practices from child socialization and family communication patterns to the construction of the relational self and the forging of intrapsychic autonomy, and from the internalization of competing discourses and the formation of cultural compromise solutions to the use of gossip, stigma, and violence. Each of these operates, sometimes in conjunction with others, to influence the range of women's responses to patriarchal beliefs and practices. This list is not exhaustive, but it represents a starting point on a project that we hope others will take up and expand on.

One limitation of this volume is that we do not directly address men's understandings of patriarchy. This is not because we do not think such a project is important—indeed, we believe it to be a vital next step—but because our initial efforts drew on the types of data that we as female researchers working in other cultures had greatest access to and interest in collecting. These data, however, present only a partial picture. Many of our contributors provide tantalizing glimpses into the worlds of men, which need further investigation and analysis. For example, why do the fathers of Susana and Salma defy community sentiments and push for the education of their daughters, while immigrant husbands in Ankara beat their wives? We need more information on how men understand patriarchy and why some aspects of it are persuasive whereas others seem less compelling and more open to change. Scholars such as Matthew Gutmann (1997, 2006) in Mexico and Steve Derné in India (1995, 2000) have begun this process of examining how men's conceptions of masculinity are shaped in relationships with women and families. We hope that a second conference and subsequent volume bring together a different team of researchers to further these efforts. Any account of institutions, interpersonal dynamics, and identities that reproduce patriarchy is incomplete without both women's and men's voices.

Although the authors in the current volume did not interview men, an important concept represented across all disciplines is hegemonic masculinity, which Connell and Messerschmidt (2005, 832) summarize as ideals of manhood that are premised on women's subordination to men and that require all men to position themselves hierarchically relative to each other. Ideals of manhood, they argue, are locally specific, dynamic, and contested, and they shift in response to exigencies in the environment. Although the concept has been criticized for its ambiguity, it is useful for highlighting how men's intersectional identities in terms of social categories, such as age, race, class, and sexuality, influence their particular experiences of domination or oppression. Hegemonic masculinities depend on the subjugation of the feminine for their existence, but tactics of female subordination vary, as the chapters in this volume demonstrate.

In examining the gender politics involved in socially constructing hegemonic masculinities, Kandiyoti (1994) considers the subjectivities of Middle Eastern male authors and other men. Kandiyoti draws attention to how men's experience of their masculinity changes over the course of the lifespan in gender-segregated family institutions in this region. Her analysis highlights an important turning point in adolescence, when young men transition from childhood experiences of superiority and power over female family members to experiences of subordination in the world of adult men. Although Kandiyoti does not take a psychoanalytic perspective in her research, this shift in interpersonal power dynamics is likely to be experienced by the men as a crisis in identity development, motivating them to repair the fractures in their sense of self (Erikson 1968). Identity resolutions are, by definition, unique to individuals, but perhaps they also represent cultural task solutions, as described by Quinn (2006, 374). For example, as Kandiyoti's analysis suggests, some men identify with equality feminism, perhaps because of their own experiences of subordination during adolescence. Men's meaning making in their identity development during the transition to adulthood is likely to be very informative in understanding why, for example, some fathers are motivated to change the parameters of the patriarchal bargain with daughters.

Similarly, Ernestine McHugh (2004, 584) notes that girls in rural Nepal grow up as valued members of their natal families, but as they enter adolescence and see their neighbors and sisters given away in marriage to relative strangers, their sense of belonging to home and family becomes more tentative. They begin to realize, she writes, that their place in the family is temporary and to fear the coming transition to a position of outsiderhood and subordination as new brides. We might expect these girls also to experience identity crises and, in a paradoxical effort to repair fractures in their psyche, seek to strengthen ties to the natal family by reaffirming the right of the father to arrange marriages. Such impulses may help to explain why Khurshid (this volume) reports that despite being educated, her rural Pakistani respondents renewed their commitment to obeying their father in the realm of interpersonal relations, reaffirming the authority of fathers to arrange marriages.

Such examples might seem to suggest that we are blaming women for their own subordination by focusing on the reasons for their accommodations to patriarchy or, alternatively, that the contributors have been unwittingly guided by a Western liberal agenda that pushes for autonomy, choice, and empowerment even when women themselves do not seem to value these goals. Our answer to this charge is that as feminist researchers we are committed to portraying the situations women face globally as accurately as possible, even as we acknowledge the ever-present problem of bias in ethnographic research. As social scientists, moreover, we are sensitive to the importance of cultural relativity and affirm that our first priority is to take women's own accounts of their experiences and values seriously, so that we can attend carefully to the options they wish to pursue and the methods they suggest for doing so.

The fact remains that for women in many parts of the world, including the United States and Europe, patriarchal practices are still prevalent and pernicious in the ways that we have recounted. As feminists, we are committed to the possibilities for change, yet our findings clearly indicate that there are no simple solutions or across-the-board programs that we can recommend. Instead, several contributors refer to the important work being done by a variety of Western aid groups, governmental agencies, and private NGOs in many of their research communities. Khurshid's data, for example, came from her larger case study of a women-centered transnational development organization headquartered in the United States with offices in Pakistan. This impressive group organized more than 200 girls' schools serving 16,000 students in low-income areas of Pakistan and recruited and trained more than 600 women from these communities to work as teachers. Khurshid notes that the organization operated with a more liberal, Western view of education and envisioned the participatory nature of teacher-training workshops as a way to encourage women to form and voice opinions in their families and communities with an implicit goal of fostering their empowerment. While the organization did at times succeed in integrating its programs with local cultural values, on other occasions it opposed practices that stood in the way of gender empowerment. The women teachers generally embraced local values, but they sometimes disagreed with community elders, especially with regard to women's right to education. This complexity, according to Khurshid, reveals the local as a contested site, involving the interplay of multiple actors with different motivations and agendas, a complexity that outside experts often fail to grasp when attempting to implement programmatic changes based on their own agendas.

In the conclusion to her chapter, Güvenç reflects on the research process undertaken with a local NGO that had decided to provide impoverished migrant women with assertiveness training so they could become empowered outside the home. Güvenç changed her initial plans when the Saraycık women did not sign up for the training and said they preferred instead to talk about family problems and their emotional distress. In response, Güvenç negotiated a different research process, asking the women open-ended questions and listening carefully to their thoughts and ideas, instead of attempting to direct or train them with prepared programs (see Güvenç 2014). After completing these listening sessions, she went a step further and asked the women what she and the NGO could do to support them. In other examples discussed by Manago and Mathews in this volume, women participating in NGO workshops and microcredit lending programs selectively incorporated the discourse of rights and choice into their preexisting family values. Thus, they were able to make changes in their lives that improved their economic conditions, although they still struggled to maintain harmonious family relationships and positive standing in the community. Most often, NGO leaders were not aware of how women were internalizing or using the values behind the curricula being taught, but the women themselves made creative use of the materials to think through their own life situations in new ways.

These examples indicate that programs for change, as Chong notes in the conclusion to her chapter, must go beyond the alteration of the structural conditions that oppress women. They must also attend to the motivations behind women's acquiescence to patriarchal strictures and to the subtle influences of family and community. As Güvenç's case study demonstrates, NGOs and other development agencies often initiate programs for change before they have listened carefully to the ideas of the people they plan to help. Program leaders who are flexible, willing to adapt to the complexity of local contexts, and able to cede control to the participants are more likely to be successful.

If we return to Kandiyoti's (1987, 324) question about the relationship of emancipation to liberation, which was raised in the introduction to this volume, a central paradox emerges. One of this book's reviewers highlighted the paradox by asking us what we envision as the solution for women who embrace emancipatory goals and values but who also remain rooted in and loyal to family and community systems that reinforce patriarchal precepts. We think part of the answer lies in women and men developing new kinds of family systems that emphasize the importance of relationality over hierarchy. Carol Gilligan (2011, 19, 22) points out that patriarchy, by elevating some men over others and all men over women, is an order of domination that separates rather than unites, thereby creating rifts in the psyche, dividing everyone from parts of themselves. The solution, she argues, is not to liberate women; rather, it is to free everyone by adopting a feminist ethic of care that resists the divisions that maintain the patriarchal order.

We can turn to the anthropological literature for examples of societies that embrace different models of relationality. Kathleen Barlow (2004, 525), for example, writes that the Murik people of Papua New Guinea have a version of motherhood that serves as a template for many other types of relationships and as a source of power. The core attributes of Murik mothering include nurturing, protection, teaching, and generosity. Barlow (2004, 526) writes, "The pervasive model of the person in Murik culture is a maternal one and maternal qualities are valued and so identified in everyone, including adult men." Moreover, the caretaking capacities most strongly exhibited by mothers of young children are deployed to create strong economic and political networks. This view of mothering also changes the trajectory of child development, especially of boys, who do not become men by rejecting feminine qualities and behaviors. Barlow (2004, 527) concludes that Murik relationality raises the possibility of a psychology of mothering that is not predicated on loss, absence, or lack. Its central feature is that Murik mothers encourage children's ability to relate to others by facilitating both attachment and agency. The Murik example enables us to conceive of mothering as an activity that is not exclusive to a single maternal figure or even to women (531) and in so doing suggests a new way of conceptualizing families: organized by seniority but not by patriarchy.

Peggy Sanday (2002, 3) spent two decades researching the Minangkabau of West Sumatra. They describe their society as organized by the principle of *adat matriarchaat*, which combines intergenerational maternal kin links with control of land and the co-residence of related females; their maternal symbols and customs are closely allied to respect for nature. This principle is a basis for Minangkabau identity, which, Sanday says, emphasizes consensus, coexistence, and compromise. As a result, she writes, the genders are interlinked rather than ranked: "Mutual agreement is the ultimate sovereign in Minangkabau life, taking precedence over the power of men or women as a group" (Sanday 2002, 174). Perhaps not surprisingly, domestic violence and rape are nonexistent, regarded by the people as evil and abhorrent. More remarkable, Sanday (2002, 19–20) notes, is how the principle of adat matriarchaat has adapted to the spread of patrilineal Islam, reaching an accommodation in which Islam is regarded by community members as a state of mind and a basic cultural presence, which is translated into Minangkabau ways of relating to others rather than being seen as a set of strict rules and dogmas to govern everyday practices.

These examples show that nothing is inevitable about the emergence of patriarchy, nor does the spread of patriarchal practices associated with particular cultural and religious systems have to result in hierarchy and women's oppression. There are alternative ways of conceiving of the social order, and principles of relationality can be foregrounded. But, we might ask, how is this to be accomplished where no matrilineal principle already exists? What are the opportunities for creating new forms of relationality in contradistinction to patriarchy?

We see hints of these possibilities in this volume. A key finding in many of our chapters is that women reaffirm the importance of motherhood and family even in the face of social pressures that threaten to tear them apart and ideologies that privilege self-interest over collective goals. In our research across the world, women report again and again that they find strength in family connections. Marrow's study (this volume) of North Indian family psychodynamics shows how the self-concepts of junior female family members are formed by their emotional relationships to senior women and the love and nurturance these relationships provide. Families, moreover, provide protection and security in an unstable world. As Suad Joseph (2012, 18) writes, "Of the women with whom I have worked in Lebanon for over four decades . . . none have said to me that they want to be freed from their families." Indeed, women and men the world over are struggling to maintain family structures even as they forge adaptations to the new realities of political turmoil, transborder migration, and globalizing cultural forces.

Manago (this volume) has found that middle-aged Maya women who participated in a feminist theater troupe gradually absorbed some feminist ideas, becoming more self-reliant and assertive, and they also remained committed to family values, which are central to their identities. However, they began to reform these family values by emphasizing gender egalitarianism. In rural Bangladesh, women living amid worsening economic conditions could no longer depend on the patrilocal extended families of their husbands for support and took up wage work in the garment industry (Ahmed and Bould 2004, 1339). Freed from direct patriarchal control, many of these women chose to use their wages to help their own parents and natal families and to provide for the education of their children, particularly their daughters. In the process, these women reported that they envisioned transformations in the roles of daughters in the family because daughters could now support their aging parents. In both settings, women have begun to transform families away from patriarchal patterns even without a preexisting matrilineal principle.

We all remain hopeful that change is possible because we have observed it firsthand. Seymour dramatically concludes her chapter by recounting a conversation with the son of one of the daughters from her original study of child socialization in North India. He spoke passionately about issues of gender inequality and suggested that to produce substantive change in India, women, who do most of the caretaking of children, must begin to socialize boys differently. They should, he said, teach boys from early childhood that they are *not* superior to women and that they should not tolerate beliefs and practices that encourage gender inequities. This, as Seymour points out, is an idealistic but subversive idea. The Maya women members of the feminist theater troupe have already begun the process of putting such a program for socializing male children into action: "I raised my son with this value ever since he was a little boy; he can cook, he can wash, he can iron, he can do the housework and he is not commanding his wife to do it, my son" (Manago and Greenfield 2011, 15).

However, the construction of new kinds of families will only be possible if the barriers to such efforts—created by patriarchal ideals and practices at the institutional level—are removed. We cannot begin to refashion families and societies until we understand and oppose the conditions that perpetuate hierarchy and oppression. Fincher's chapter, for example, documents the unprecedented gains made by urban Chinese women in education and employment. Yet women's parents and the larger culture still pressure them to marry and, in accordance with patriarchal values, register the marital property only in their husband's name. When women accede to these pressures, they pay a price, losing out, as Fincher documents, on the expansion of value in the real estate market and on other assets that could help them divorce when a marriage does not work out. Her case study points to the very real danger of the pervasive neoliberal logic that encourages women to view inequality as an individual and not a systemic problem. It is hard to envision solutions if you think that your situation is unique or that your problems are your own fault.

Only by calling attention to underlying assumptions can we raise them to the level of consciousness, and only when collectives reaffirm individual perceptions does change become possible. Werner's chapter highlights the pervasiveness of rape myths across different cultural contexts and shows how these act to normalize and excuse crimes like sexual harassment and sexual assault. Indeed, the striking parallels between the treatment of Anita Hill in 1991, when she testified to having been sexually harassed by US Supreme Court nominee Clarence Thomas, and that of Christine Blasey Ford in 2018, when she testified to having been sexually assaulted by Supreme Court nominee Brett Kavanaugh, suggest that sexual violence continues to persist unchecked even at the most powerful levels of the US justice system. Yet there are reasons to be optimistic about the potential role of social media in consciousness raising and social change. For example, the Phenomenal Woman Action Campaign organized 1,600 men to take out a full-page *New York Times* advertisement in support of Blasey Ford, a nod to the ad signed by 1,600 African American women in support of Hill in 1991. The #MeToo movement was started by Tarana Burke in 2006 and went viral on social media in 2017. It has led thousands of women in the United States to come forward publicly and share their experiences of sexual harassment and assault, spurring investigations and indictments of many perpetrators.

#MeToo is now global. Amanda Erickson (2018) writes that a Pakistani woman, Sabica Khan, shared on Facebook about being assaulted during a pilgrimage to Mecca, which helped launch a movement called #MosqueMeToo. Hundreds of women across the Arab world have shared their own stories of being harassed and assaulted in places of worship. Repnikova and Zhou (2018) report on a storm of social media protests against sexual predation and assault in China, which has led to accusations of sexual misconduct against more than twenty intellectuals, media personalities, and activists and to the public shaming and dismissal of several university professors.

Equally important are emerging forms of collective protest, which have already led to important legal and social changes. In the wake of the inauguration in January 2017 of US president Donald Trump, women's marches were held in hundreds of locations across the country, inspiring women to file as candidates for political office. In 2018, record numbers of women were elected to the US Congress and to state legislative offices. Earlier, women were active participants in the Arab Spring beginning with the protests in Tunisia in 2011, and by 2017 their efforts had led to the passage of a historic law making all forms of violence against women punishable. In 2012, the brutal gang rape and murder of New Delhi student Jyoti Singh spurred ongoing protests by tens of thousands of Indian women and men, which led to many widespread legal changes. In 2016, thousands of women across Latin America, infuriated by the senseless killing of a 16-year-old girl in Argentina, also protested violence against women. And Saudi women showed great courage in 2017 as they walked silently in protest until the government finally granted them the right to drive. These examples demonstrate how women and men are standing together to oppose all forms of sexual assault and harassment, and they lead us to conclude that collective hope remains our best catalyst for action.

We end by quoting Rebecca Solnit in *Hope in the Dark* (2016, xiv): "Hope locates itself in the premises that we don't know what will happen and that in the spaciousness of uncertainty is room to act. When you recognize uncertainty, you recognize that you may be able to influence the outcomes—you alone or you in concert with a few dozen or several million others. Hope is an embrace of the unknown and knowable, an alternative to the certainty of both optimists and pessimists."

REFERENCES

Abelson, Robert P., Elliot Aronson, William J. McGuire, Theodore M. Newcomb, Milton J. Rosenberg, and Percy H. Tannenbaum, eds. 1968. *Theory of Cognitive Consistency: A Sourcebook.* Chicago: Rand McNally.

Abu-Lughod, Lila. 1985. "Honor and Sentiments of Loss in a Bedouin Society." *American Ethnologist* 12 (2): 245–61.

———. 1990. "The Romance of Resistance: Tracing Transformations of Power through Bedouin Women." *American Ethnologist* 17 (1): 41–55.

———. 2009. "Dialects of Women's Empowerment: The International Circuitry of the Arab Human Development Report 2005." *International Journal of Middle East Studies* 41 (1): 83–103.

Acker, Joan, 1989. "The Problem with Patriarchy." *Sociology* 23 (2): 235–40.

Adely, Fida J. 2009. "Educating Women for Development." *International Journal of Middle East Studies* 41 (1): 105–22.

Ahmed, Sania Sultan, and Sally Bould. 2004. "One Able Daughter Is Worth 10 Illiterate Sons: Reframing the Patriarchal Family." *Journal of Marriage and the Family* 66 (5): 1332–41.

Alesina, Alberto F., Paola Giuliano, and Nathan Nunn. 2013. "On the Origins of Gender Roles: Women and the Plough." *Quarterly Journal of Economics* 128 (2): 469–530.

All-China Women's Federation, and National Bureau of Statistics of China. 2011. "Report on Major Results of the Third Wave Survey on the Social Status of Women in China." *China*, October 21 [in Chinese]. http://www.china.com.cn/zhibo/zhuanti/ch-xinwen/2011-10/21/content_23687810.htm.

Alonso, Ana Maria. 1995. "Rationalizing Patriarchy: Gender, Domestic Violence and Law in Mexico." *Identities* 2 (1–2): 29–47.

Amsler, Sarah, and Russell Kleinbach. 1999. "Bride Kidnapping in the Kyrgyz Republic." *International Journal of Central Asian Studies* 4 (4): 185–216.

Appadurai, Arjun. 1990. "Topographies of the Self: Praise and Emotion in Hindu India." In *Language and the Politics of Emotion*, edited by Catherine A. Lutz and Lila Abu-Lughod, 92–112. New York: Cambridge University Press.

Arab Families Working Group. 2008. *Framing: Rethinking Arab Family Projects.* Vol. 1. Davis: University of California Press.

Armstrong, Elizabeth A., Laura Hamilton, and Brian Sweeney. 2006. "Sexual Assault on Campus: A Multilevel, Integrative Approach to Party Rape." *Social Problems* 53 (4): 483–99.

Aronson, Elliot. 1968. "Dissonance Theory: Progress and Problems." In *Theory of Cognitive Consistency: A Sourcebook*, edited by Robert P. Abelson, Elliot Aronson, William J. McGuire, Theodore M. Newcomb, Milton J. Rosenberg, and Percy H. Tannenbaum, 5–27. Chicago: Rand McNally.

Atalay, Zeynep. 2017. "Partners in Patriarchy: Faith-Based Organizations and Neoliberalism in Turkey." *Critical Sociology*, August 22. https://doi.org/10.1177/0896920517711488.

Avishai, Orit. 2008. "'Doing Religion' in a Secular World: Women, Conservative Religions, and the Question of Agency." *Gender and Society* 22 (4): 409–33.

Baca Zinn, Maxine. 1982. "Familism among Chicanos: A Theoretical Review." *Humboldt Journal of Social Relations* 10 (1): 224–38.

Baklinski, Thaddeus. 2011. "India's Gender Imbalance 'Worst in Recorded History.'" *LifeSite News*, April 15. https://www.lifesitenews.com/news/indias-gender-imbalance-worst-in-recorded-history.

Bandura, Albert. 2001. "Cognitive Theory: An Agentic Perspective." *Annual Reviews in Psychology* 52: 1–26.

Banfield, Edward C. 1958. *The Moral Basis of a Backward Society*. New York: Free Press.

Bargh, John A. 2008. "Free Will Is Un-natural." In *Are We Free? Psychology and Free Will*, edited by John Baer, James C. Kaufman, and Roy F. Baumeister, 128–54. New York: Oxford University Press.

Barlow, Kathleen. 2004. "Critiquing the 'Good Enough' Mother: A Perspective Based on the Murik of Papua New Guinea." *Ethos* 32 (4): 514–37.

Barth, Fredrik. 1954. "Father's Brother's Daughter Marriage in Kurdistan." *Southwestern Journal of Anthropology* 10 (2): 164–71.

Bartkowski, John P. 2001. *Remaking the Godly Marriage: Gender Negotiation in Evangelical Churches*. New Brunswick, NJ: Rutgers University Press.

Bartkowski, John P., and Jen'nan Ghazal Read. 2003. "Veiled Submission: Submission, Power, and Identity among Evangelical and Muslim Women in the United States." *Qualitative Sociology* 26 (1): 71–92.

Beijing Government. 2011. "Beijing Carries Out State Council Property Controls, 15 Regulations." *Xinhuanet*, February 16 [in Chinese]. http://news.xinhuanet.com/house/2011-02/16/c_121088355.htm.

Bennett, Judith M. 2006. *Patriarchy and the Challenging of Feminism*. Philadelphia: University of Pennsylvania Press.

Blackman, Lisa, John Cromby, Derek Hook, Dimitris Papadopoulos, and Valerie Walkerdine. 2008. "Creating Subjectivities." *Subjectivity* 22 (1): 1–27. doi:10.1057/sub.2008.8.

Boehm, Christopher. 2012. *Moral Origins: The Evolution of Virtue, Altruism, and Shame.* New York: Basic.

Bolles, A. Lyn. 2016. "The Curious Relationship of Feminist Anthropology and Women's Studies." In *Mapping Feminist Anthropology in the Twenty-First Century,* edited by Ellen Lewin and Leni M. Silverstein, 84–104. New Brunswick, NJ: Rutgers University Press

Borbieva, Noor. 2012. "Kidnapping Women: Discourses of Emotion and Social Change in the Kyrgyz Republic." *Anthropological Quarterly* 85 (1): 141–69.

Boserup, Ester. 1970. *Women's Role in Economic Development.* London: Allen and Unwin.

Bourguignon, Erika. 2004. "Suffering and Healing, Subordination and Power: Women and Possession Trance." *Ethos* 32 (4): 557–74.

Bowles, Samuel, and Herbert Gintis. 2011. *A Cooperative Species.* Princeton, NJ: Princeton University Press.

Bowman, James. 2007. *Honor: A History.* New York: Encounter.

Brasher, Brenda E. 1998. *Godly Women: Fundamentalism and Female Power.* New Brunswick, NJ: Rutgers University Press.

Brinton, Mary C., Yean-Ju Lee, and William L. Parish. 1995. "Married Women's Employment in Rapidly Industrializing Societies: Examples from East Asia." *American Journal of Sociology* 100 (5): 1099–1130.

Broude, Gwen J. 1981. "The Cultural Management of Sexuality." In *Handbook of Cross-Cultural Human Development,* edited by Ruth H. Munroe, Robert L. Munroe, and Beatrice B. Whiting, 633–73. New York: Garland STPM Press.

Broussard, Julia T. 2009. "Using Cultural Discourse Analysis to Research Gender and Environmental Understandings in China." *Ethos* 37 (3): 362–89.

Brown, Judith K. 1970. "A Note on the Division of Labor by Sex." *American Anthropologist* 72 (5): 1073–78.

Brownmiller, Susan. 1975. *Against Our Will: Men, Women and Rape.* New York: Simon and Schuster.

Brusco, Elizabeth E. 1995. *The Reformation of Machismo: Evangelical Gender and Conversion in Colombia.* Austin: University of Texas Press.

Buğra, Ayşe, and Çağlar Keyder. 2005. "Poverty and Social Policy in Contemporary Turkey." Paper presented at the Boğaziçi University Social Policy Forum, January. http://www.spf.boun.edu.tr/docs/WP-Bugra-Keyder.pdf.

Burt, Martha R. 1980. "Cultural Myths and Supports for Rape." *Journal of Personality and Social Psychology* 38 (2): 217–30.

Buss, David M., and David Schmitt. 1993. "Sexual Strategies Theory: An Evolutionary Perspective on Human Mating." *Psychological Review* 100 (2): 204–32.

Butler, Judith. 1997. *The Psychic Life of Power: Theories in Subjection*. Palo Alto, CA: Stanford University Press.

Caldwell, John C. 1982. *Theory of Fertility Decline*. New York: Academic.

Cantor, David, Bonnie Fisher, Susan Chibnall, Reanne Townsent, Hyunshik Lee, Carol Bruce, and Gail Thomas. 2015. *Report on the AAU Campus Climate Survey on Sexual Assault and Sexual Misconduct*. Rockville, MD: Westat.

Chang, Kyung-Sup. 1997. "The Neo-Confucian Right and Family Politics in South Korea: The Nuclear Family as an Ideological Construct." *Economy and Society* 26 (1): 22–42.

———. 1999. "Compressed Modernity and Its Discontents: South Korean Society in Transition." *Economy and Society* 28 (1): 30–55.

———. 2010. *South Korea under Compressed Modernity: Familial Political Economy in Transition*. New York: Routledge.

Chang, Mariko Lin. 2010. *Shortchanged: Why Women Have Less Wealth and What Can Be Done about It*. Oxford: Oxford University Press.

Chapin, Bambi L. 2014. *Childhood in a Sri Lankan Village: Shaping Hierarchy and Desire*. New Brunswick, NJ: Rutgers University Press.

China News Agency. 2011. "How Many Leftover Women Really Deserve Our Sympathy?" All-China Women's Federation website, March 8 (original location). Deleted from website December 2012. http://blog.ifeng.com/article/10313293.html.

Chisamya, Grace, Joan DeJaeghere, Nancy Kendall, and Marufa Aziz Khan. 2012. "Gender and Education for All: Progress and Problems in Achieving Gender Equity." *International Journal of Educational Development* 32 (6): 743–55. doi:10.1016/j.ijedudev.2011.10.004.

Cho, Haejoang. 1986. "Male Dominance and Mother Power: The Two Sides of Confucian Patriarchy in Korea." In *The Psycho-Cultural Dynamics of the Confucian Family: Past and Present*, edited by Walter H. Slote, 277–98. Seoul: International Cultural Society of Korea.

———. 2002. "Living with Conflicting Subjectivities: Mother, Motherly Wife, and Sexy Woman in the Transition of Colonial-Modern to Postmodern Korea." In *Under Construction: The Gendering of Modernity, Class, and Consumption in the Republic of Korea*, edited by Laurel Kendall, 165–95. Honolulu: University of Hawai'i Press.

Chodorow, Nancy. 1978. *The Reproduction of Mothering: Psychoanalysis and the Sociology of Gender*. Berkeley: University of California Press.

Chong, Kelly H. 2006. "Negotiating Patriarchy: South Korean Evangelical Women and the Politics of Gender." *Gender and Society* 20 (6): 697–724.

———. 2008. *Deliverance and Submission: Evangelical Women and the Negotiation of Patriarchy in South Korea.* Cambridge, MA: Harvard University Press.

Christ, Carol P. 2016. "A New Definition of Patriarchy: Control of Women's Sexuality, Private Property, and War." *Feminist Theology* 24 (3): 214–25.

Christensen, Carl W. 1963. "Religious Conversion." *Archives of General Psychiatry* 9 (3): 207–16.

Cohan, William D. 2015. *The Price of Silence: The Duke Lacrosse Scandal, the Power of the Elite, and the Corruption of Our Great Universities.* New York: Scribner.

Cohen, Lawrence. 1998. *No Aging in India: Alzheimer's, the Bad Family, and Other Modern Things.* Berkeley: University of California Press.

Connell, Noreen, and Cassandra Wilson, eds. 1974. *Rape: The First Sourcebook for Women.* New York: New American Library.

Connell, Robert W., and James W. Messerschmidt. 2005. "Hegemonic Masculinity: Rethinking the Concept." *Gender and Society* 19 (6): 829–59.

Crenshaw, Kimberlé. 1991. "Mapping the Margins: Intersectionality, Identity Politics and Violence against Women of Color." *Stanford Law Review* 42: 1241–99.

Crittenden, Alyssa N., and Frank W. Marlowe. 2013. "Cooperative Breeding and Attachment among the Aka Foragers." In *Attachment Reconsidered: Cultural Perspectives on a Western Theory*, edited by Naomi Quinn and Jeanette Mageo, 67–83. New York: Palgrave Macmillan.

D'Andrade, Roy G. 1992. "Schemas and Motivation." In *Human Motives and Cultural Models*, edited by Claudia Strauss and Roy G. D'Andrade, 23–44. Cambridge: Cambridge University Press.

Daniel, E. Valentine. 1984. *Fluid Signs: Being a Person the Tamil Way.* Berkeley: University of California Press.

Davis, Deborah. 2010. "Who Gets the House? Renegotiating Property Rights in Post-Socialist Urban China." *Modern China* 36 (5): 1–30.

Dehaene, Stanislas, Felipe Pegado, Lucia W. Braga, Paulo Ventura, Gilberto Nunes Filho, and Antoinette Jobert. 2010. "How Learning to Read Changes the Cortical Networks for Vision and Language." *Science* 330 (6009): 1359–64.

Derné, Steve. 1995. *Culture in Action: Family Life, Emotion, and Male Dominance in Banaras, India.* Albany: State University of New York Press.

———. 2000. "Culture, Family Structure, and Psyche in Hindu India: The 'Fit' and the 'Inconsistencies.'" *International Journal of Group Tensions* 29 (3–4): 323–48.

Deuchler, Martina. 1992. *The Confucian Transformation of Korea: A Study of Society and Ideology.* Cambridge, MA: Council on East Asian Studies, Harvard University.

Dick, Kirby, dir. 2015. *The Hunting Ground.* Chain Camera Pictures.

Donner, Henrike. 2008. *Domestic Goddesses: Maternity, Globalization and Middle-Class Identity in Contemporary India*. Burlington, VT: Ashgate.

Dworkin, Andrea. 1974. *Woman Hating*. New York: Dutton.

Eagle, Morris. 2003. "Clinical Implications of Attachment Theory." *Psychological Inquiry* 23 (1): 27–53.

Eber, Christine, and "Antonia." 2011. *The Journey of a Tzotzil Maya Woman of Chiapas, Mexico*. Austin: University of Texas Press.

Edwards, Derek. 1999. "Emotion Discourse." *Culture and Psychology* 5 (3): 271–91.

Erickson, Amanda. 2018. "In 2018, #MeToo—and Its Backlash—Went Global." *Washington Post*, December 14.

Erikson, Erik Homburger. 1950. *Childhood and Society*. New York: Norton.

———. 1968. *Identity*. New York: Norton.

Evans, Harriet. 2002. "Past, Perfect or Imperfect: Changing Images of the Ideal Wife." In *Chinese Femininities/Chinese Masculinities*, edited by Susan Brownell and Jeffrey N. Wasserstrom, 335–60. Berkeley: University of California Press.

Ewing, Katherine. 1990. "The Illusion of Wholeness: Culture, Self, and the Experience of Inconsistency." *Ethos* 18 (3): 251–78.

———. 1991. "Can Psychoanalytic Theories Explain the Pakistani Woman? Intrapsychic Autonomy and Interpersonal Engagement in the Extended Family." *Ethos* 19 (2): 131–60.

Fairbairn, W. R. D. (1952) 1981. *Psychoanalytic Studies of the Personality*. London: Routledge and Kegan Paul.

Fincher, Leta Hong. 2014. *Leftover Women: The Resurgence of Gender Inequality in China*. London: Zed.

Fisher, Bonnie S., Francis T. Cullen, and Michael G. Turner. 2000. *The Sexual Victimization of College Women: Research Report*. Washington, DC: National Institute of Justice and Bureau of Justice Statistics.

Fiske, Susan T., Amy J. C. Cuddy, and Peter Glick. 2007. "Universal Dimensions of Social Cognition: Warmth and Competence." *Trends in Cognitive Sciences* 11 (2): 77–83.

Flood, Merielle. 1994. "Changing Patterns of Interdependence: The Effects of Increasing Monetization on Gender Relations in Zinacantán, Mexico." *Research in Economic Anthropology* 15: 145–73.

Folbre, Nancy, and Heidi Hartmann. 1989. "The Persistence of Patriarchal Capitalism." *Rethinking Marxism* 2 (4): 90–96.

Follett, Mary P. (1924) 2018. *Creative Experience*. London: Forgotten Books.

Fonagy, Peter. 2001. "The Human Genome and the Representational World: The Role of Early Mother-Infant Interaction in Creating an Interpersonal Interpretive Mechanism." *Bulletin of the Menninger Clinic* 65 (3): 427–48.

Fong, Vanessa L. 2002. "China's One-Child Policy and the Empowerment of Urban Daughters." *American Anthropologist* 104 (4): 1098–1109.

Fosshage, James L. 2009. "Some Key Features in the Evolution of Self Psychology and Psychoanalysis." *Annals of the New York Academy of Sciences* 1159 (1): 1–18.

Foucault, Michel. (1978) 1990. *The History of Sexuality*. Vol. 1. New York: Vintage.

Frank, Katherine. 2006. "Agency." *Anthropological Theory* 6 (3): 281–302.

Freud, Sigmund. (1894) 2013. *The Neuro-Psychoses of Defence*. London: Read Books.

Gailey, Christine Ward. 1987. "Evolutionary Perspectives on Gender Hierarchy." In *Analyzing Gender: A Handbook of Social Science Research*, edited by Beth Hess and Myra Marx Ferree, 32–67. Palo Alto, CA: Sage.

Gallagher, Sally K. 2007. "Agency, Resources, and Identity: Lower-Income Women's Experiences in Damascus." *Gender and Society* 21 (2): 227–49.

Gallagher, Sally K., and Christian Smith. 1999. "Symbolic Traditionalism and Pragmatic Egalitarianism: Contemporary Evangelicals, Families, and Gender." *Gender and Society* 13 (2): 211–33.

Galván, Adriana. 2014. "Insights about Adolescent Behavior, Plasticity, and Policy from Neuroscience Research." *Neuron* 83: 262–65.

Gee, Kevin A. 2014. "Achieving Gender Equality in Learning Outcomes: Evidence from a Non-Formal Education Program in Bangladesh." *International Journal of Educational Development* 40: 207-16. doi:10.1016/j.ijedudev.2014.09.001.

Giddens, Anthony. 1984. *The Constitution of Society: Outline of the Theory of Structuration*. Berkeley: University of California Press.

Gilligan, Carol. 1982. *In a Different Voice: Psychological Theory and Women's Development*. Cambridge, MA: Harvard University Press.

———. 2011. *Joining the Resistance*. Malden, MA: Polity.

Glick, Peter, and Susan T. Fiske. 2001. "An Ambivalent Alliance: Hostile and Benevolent Sexism as Complementary Justifications for Gender Inequality." *American Psychologist* 56 (2): 109–18.

———. 2011. "Ambivalent Sexism Revisited." *Psychology of Women Quarterly* 35 (3): 530–35.

Gold, Ann Grodzins. 2006. "Love's Cup, Love's Thorn, Love's End: The Language of Prem in Ghatiyali." In *Love in South Asia: A Cultural History*, edited by Francesca Orsini, 303–30. Cambridge: Cambridge University Press.

Goldberg, Arnold. 1998. "Self Psychology since Kohut." *Psychoanalytic Quarterly* 67: 240–55.

Goody, Jack. 1973. "Bridewealth and Dowry in Africa and Eurasia." In *Bridewealth and Dowry*, edited by Jack Goody and S. J. Tambiah, 1–58. Cambridge: Cambridge University Press.

———. 1976. *Production and Reproduction: A Comparative Study of the Domestic Domain*. Cambridge: Cambridge University Press.

Gordon, April A. 1996. *Transforming Capitalism and Patriarchy: Gender and Development in Africa*. Boulder, CO: Lynne Rienner.

Gordon, Linda, and Allen Hunter. 1998. "Not All Male Dominance Is Patriarchal." *Radical History Review* 71: 71–83.

Gottfried, Heidi. 1998. "Beyond Patriarchy? Theorising Gender and Class." *Sociology* 32 (3): 451–68.

Gramsci, Antonio. 1971. *Selections from the Prison Notebooks of Antonio Gramsci*, edited and translated by Quintin Hoare and Geoffrey Nowell-Smith. London: International.

———. 1992. *Prison Notebooks*. New York: Columbia University.

Greenfield, Patricia M. 2004. *Weaving Generations Together: Evolving Creativity in the Maya of Chiapas*. Santa Fe, NM: SAR Press.

———. 2009. "Linking Social Change and Developmental Change: Shifting Pathways of Human Development." *Developmental Psychology* 45 (2): 401–8.

Greenhalgh, Susan. 2010. *Cultivating Global Citizens: Population in the Rise of China*. Cambridge, MA: Harvard University Press.

Greenhalgh, Susan, and Edwin A. Winckler. 2005. *Governing China's Population: From Leninist to Neoliberal Biopolitics*. Stanford, CA: Stanford University Press.

Griffith, R. Marie. 1997. *God's Daughters: Evangelical Women and the Power of Submission*. Berkeley: University of California Press.

Guin'ee, Nerine. 2014. "Empowering Women through Education: Experiences from Dalit Women in Nepal." *International Journal of Educational Development* 39: 183–90.

Guterres, António. 2017. "Remarks on International Day for the Elimination of Violence against Women." *United Nations Secretary-General*, November 22. https://www.un.org/sg/en/content/sg/speeches/2017-11-22/elimination-violence-against-women-remarks.

Gutmann, Matthew C. 1997. "Trafficking in Men: The Anthropology of Masculinity." *Annual Review of Anthropology* 26 (1): 385–409.

———. 2006. *The Meanings of Macho: Being a Man in Mexico City*. Vol. 3. Berkeley: University of California Press.

Güvenç, Gülden. 2014. "Construction of Wife and Mother Identities in Women's Talk of Intrafamily Violence in Saraycık-Turkey." *International Perspectives in Psychology: Research, Practice, Consultation* 3 (2): 76–92.

Handrahan, Lori. 2004. "Hunting for Women: Bride-Kidnapping in Kyrgyzstan." *International Feminist Journal of Politics* 6 (2): 207–33.

Harding, Kate. 2015. *Asking for It: The Alarming Rise of Rape Culture—And What We Can Do about It*. Boston: Da Capo.

Hart, Keith. 2014. "Jack Goody: The Anthropology of Unequal Society." *Reviews in Anthropology* 43 (3): 199–220.

Harter, Susan. 2012. *The Construction of Self: A Developmental Perspective*. 2nd ed. New York: Guilford.

———. 2015. *The Construction of Self: Developmental and Sociocultural Foundations*. New York: Guilford.

Hartmann, Heidi I. 1981. "The Family as the Locus of Gender, Class, and Political Struggle: The Example of Housework." *Signs: Journal of Women in Culture and Society* 6 (3): 366–94.

Hatem, Mervat. 1987. "Class and Patriarchy as Competing Paradigms for the Study of Middle Eastern Women." *Comparative Studies in Society and History* 29 (4): 811–18.

Hays, Sharon. 1996. *The Cultural Contradictions of Motherhood*. New Haven, CT: Yale University Press.

He, Jianhua. 2008. "Assessment Report of Gender Equality and Women's Development in [the] Family." In *Green Book of Women: Annual Report on Gender Equality and Women's Development in China, 2006-2007*, edited by Lin Tan, Yongping Jiang, and Xiuhua Jiang, 439–53. Beijing: Social Sciences Academic Press.

Hellman, Judith Adler. 2008. *The World of Mexican Migrants*. New York: New Press.

Henneberger, Melinda. 2012. "Reported Sexual Assault at Notre Dame Campus Leaves More Questions than Answers." *National Catholic Reporter*, March 26. http://ncronline.org/news/accountability/reported-sexual-assault-notre-dame-campus-leaves-more-questions-answers.

Henriques, Julian, Wendy Holloway, Cathy Urwin, Couze Venn, and Valerie Walkerdine. 1984. *Changing the Subject: Psychology, Social Regulation, and Subjectivity*. New York: Routledge.

Hertz-Lazarowitz, Rachel, and Tamar Shapira. 2005. "Muslim Women's Life Stories: Building Leadership." *Anthropology and Education Quarterly* 36 (2): 165–81.

Herz, Barbara, and Gene B. Sperling. 2004. *What Works in Girls' Education: Evidence and Policies from the Developing World*. Washington, DC: Council on Foreign Relations Press.

Hinton, Alexander Laban. 1996. "Agents of Death: Explaining the Cambodian Genocide in Terms of Psychosocial Dissonance." *American Anthropologist* 98 (4): 818–31.

Hirsch, Jennifer S. 2003. *A Courtship after Marriage: Sexuality and Love in Mexican Transnational Families*. Berkeley: University of California Press.

Hirsch, Jennifer S., and Holly Wardlow, eds. 2006. *Modern Loves: The Anthropology of Romantic Courtship and Companionate Marriage*. New York: Macmillan.

Hochschild, Arlie. (1983) 2003. *The Managed Heart: Commercialization of Human Feeling*. Berkeley: University of California Press.

Hochschild, Arlie Russell, and Anne Machury. 1989. *The Second Shift*. New York: Avon.

Hollan, Douglas C., and C. Jason Throop. 2008. "Whatever Happened to Empathy? Introduction." *Ethos* 36 (4): 385–401.

Holland, Dana G., and Mohammad Hussein Yousofi. 2014. "The *Only* Solution: Education, Youth, and Social Change in Afghanistan." *Anthropology and Education Quarterly* 45 (3): 241–59.

Horizon China. 2012. "My 2012 Wedding and House." *Home-Buying Survey of Beijing, Shanghai, Guangzhou and Shenzhen for Phoenix Online* [in Chinese]. http://house.ifeng.com/hezuo/special/hunfang.

Horowitz, Katharine R. 2012. "Social Contexts of Young Moms in the Lake Patzcuaro Basin: Adolescent Motherhood, Gender and the Challenge of Social Pressure." PhD diss., University of Pittsburgh.

Hosking, Dian Marie, and Bettine Pluut. 2010. "(Re)constructing Reflexivity: A Relational Constructionist Approach." *Qualitative Report* 15 (1): 59–75.

Hrdy, Sarah Blaffer. 1999. *Mother Nature: A History of Mothers, Infants, and Natural Selection*. New York: Pantheon.

———. 2009. *Mothers and Others: The Evolutionary Origins of Mutual Understanding*. Cambridge, MA: Harvard University Press.

Huberman, Jenny. 2012. *Ambivalent Encounters: Childhood, Tourism, and Social Change in Banaras, India*. New Brunswick, NJ: Rutgers University Press.

Hudson, Valerie M., and Andrea Den Boer. 2004. *Bare Branches: The Security Implications of Asia's Surplus Male Population*. Cambridge, MA: MIT Press.

Hunnicutt, Gwen. 2009. "Varieties of Patriarchy and Violence against Women: Resurrecting 'Patriarchy' as a Theoretical Tool." *Violence against Women* 15 (5): 553–73.

Hunt, Elle. 2016. "'20 Minutes of Action': Father Defends Stanford Student Son Convicted of Sexual Assault." *Guardian*, June 5. https://www.theguardian.com/us-news/2016/jun/06/father-stanford-university-student-brock-turner-sexual-assault-statement.

Inden, Ronald B., and Ralph B. Nicholas. 1977. *Kinship in Bengali Culture.* Chicago: University of Chicago Press.

Inglehart, Ronald, and Pippa Norris. 2003. *Rising Tide: Gender Equality and Cultural Change around the World.* Cambridge: Cambridge University Press.

Inhorn, Marcia C. 1996. *Infertility and Patriarchy: The Cultural Politics of Gender and Family Life in Egypt.* Philadelphia: University of Pennsylvania Press.

Jacobson, Shari. 2006. "Modernity, Conservative Religious Movements, and the Female Subject: Newly Ultraorthodox Sephardi Women in Buenos Aires." *American Anthropologist* 108 (2): 336–46.

Jahangir, A., and H. Jilani. 2003. *The Hudood Ordinances: A Divine Sanction?* Lahore, Pakistan: Sang-e-Meel.

Jeffrey, Craig, Patricia Jeffery, and Roger Jeffery. 2008. *Degrees without Freedom? Education, Masculinities, and Unemployment in North India.* Stanford, CA: Stanford University Press.

Johnson, Carol. 1996. "Does Capitalism Really Need Patriarchy? Some Old Issues Reconsidered." *Women's Studies International Forum* 19 (3): 193–202.

Joseph, Suad. 1993a. "Connectivity and Patriarchy among Urban Working-Class Arab Families in Lebanon." *Ethos* 21 (4): 452–84.

———. 1993b. "Gender and Relationality among Arab Families in Lebanon." *Feminist Studies* 19 (3): 465–86.

———. 1994. "Brother/Sister Relationships: Connectivity, Love and Power in the Reproduction of Patriarchy in Lebanon." *American Ethnologist* 21 (1): 50–73.

———. 1996. "Patriarchy and Development in the Arab World." *Gender and Development* 4 (2): 14–19.

———. 1999. "Introduction: Theories of Gender, Self and Identity in Arab Families." In *Intimate Selving: Gender, Self, and Identity in Arab Families,* edited by Suad Joseph, 1–20. Syracuse, NY: Syracuse University Press.

———. 2005. "Learning Desire: Relational Pedagogies and the Desiring Female Subject in Lebanon." *Journal of Middle East Women's Studies* 1 (1): 79–109.

———. 2012. "Thinking Intentionally: Arab Women's Subjectivity and Its Discontents." *Journal of Middle East Women's Studies* 8 (2): 1–25.

Jost, John, and Mahzarin Banaji. 1994. "The Role of Stereotyping in System-Justification and the Production of False Consciousness." *British Journal of Social Psychology* 33 (1): 1–27.

Jost, John T., Mahzarin R. Banaji, and Brian A. Mosek. 2004. "A Decade of System Justification Theory: Accumulated Evidence of Conscious and Unconscious Bolstering of the Status Quo." *Political Psychology* 25 (6): 881–919.

Kabeer, Naila. 1999. "Resources, Agency, Achievements: Reflections on the Measurement of Women's Empowerment." *Development and Change* 30 (3): 435–64.

Kağıtçıbaşı, Çiğdem, and Bilge Ataca. 2005. "Value of Children and Family Change: A Three-Decade Portrait from Turkey." *Applied Psychology* 54 (3): 317–37.

Kandiyoti, Deniz. 1984. "Rural Transformation in Turkey and Its Implications for Women's Status." In *Women on the Move: Contemporary Changes in Family and Society*, edited by Deniz Kandiyoti, Barbara Tryfan, and Tomilayu Adeyokunnu, 17–30. Paris: UNESCO.

———. 1987. "Emancipated but Unliberated? Reflections on the Turkish Case." *Feminist Studies* 13 (2): 317–38.

———. 1988. "Bargaining with Patriarchy." *Gender and Society* 2 (3): 274–90.

———. 1994. "The Paradoxes of Masculinity." In *Dislocating Masculinity: Comparative Ethnographies*, edited by Andrea Cornwall and Nancy Lindisfarne, 196–212. London: Routledge.

———. 1998. "Gender, Power and Contestation: Rethinking 'Bargaining with Patriarchy.'" In *Feminist Visions of Development: Gender, Analysis and Policy*, edited by Cecil Jackson and Ruth Pearson, 135–54. London: Routledge.

———. 2005. "The Politics of Gender and Reconstruction in Afghanistan." Occasional Paper 4. Geneva UNRISD.

Kashtan, Mikki. 2017. "Why Patriarchy Is Not about Men." *Fearless Heart*, August 5. http://thefearlessheart.org/why-patriarchy-is-not-about-men.

Kassie, Emily. 2015. "Male Victims of Campus Sexual Assault Speak Out." *Huffington Post*, January 27. http://www.huffingtonpost.com/2015/01/27/male-victims-sexual-assault_n_6535730.html.

Katz, Daniel. 1968. "Consistency for What? The Functional Approach." In *Theories of Cognitive Consistency: A Sourcebook*, edited by Robert P. Abelson, Elliot Aronson, William J. McGuire, Theodore M. Newcomb, Milton J. Rosenberg, and Percy H. Tannenbaum, 179–91. Chicago: Rand McNally.

Keller, Heidi. 2007. *Cultures of Infancy*. Mahwah, NJ: Erlbaum.

Keller, Heidi, Rekubdus Yovsi, Joern Borke, Joscha Kärtner, Henning Jensen, and Zaira Papaligoura. 2004. "Developmental Consequences of Early Parenting Experiences: Self-Recognition and Self-Regulation in Three Cultural Communities." *Child Development* 75 (6): 1745–60.

Kendall, Laurel, ed. 2002. *Under Construction: The Gendering of Modernity, Class, and Consumption in the Republic of Korea*. Honolulu: University of Hawai'i Press.

Khurshid, Ayesha. 2015. "Islamic Traditions of Modernity: Gender, Class, and Islam in a Transnational Women's Education Project." *Gender and Society* 29 (1): 98–121.

Kim, Ai Ra. 1996. *Women Struggling for a New Life: On the Role of Religion in the Cultural Passage from Korea to America.* Albany: State University of New York Press.

Kim, Dongno. 1990. "The Transformation of Familism in Modern Korean Society: From Cooperation to Competition." *International Sociology* 5 (4): 409–25.

Kim, Janna L., C. Lynn Sorsoli, Katherine Collins, Bonnie A. Zylbergold, Deborah Schooler, and Deborah L. Tolman. 2007. "From Sex to Sexuality: Exposing the Heterosexual Script on Primetime Network Television." *Journal of Sex Research* 44 (2): 145–57.

Kingfisher, Catherine E. 2016. "Studying Gender and Neoliberalism Transnationally: Implications for Theory and Action." In *Mapping Feminist Anthropology in the Twenty-First Century*, edited by Ellen Lewin and Leni M. Silverstein, 256–75. New Brunswick, NJ: Rutgers University Press.

Kingkade, Tyler. 2013. "Notre Dame Responses to Lizzy Seeberg Suicide Contrasts with Manti Te'o Girlfriend Hoax." *Huffington Post*, January 17. http://www.huffingtonpost.com/2013/01/17notre-dame-lizzy-seeberg-suicide_n_2499256.html.

Klein, Melanie. 1949. "Some Notes on the Psychoanalytic Composition of Introjected Objects." *International Journal of Psychoanalysis* 22: 8–17.

Kleinbach, Russell. 2003. "Frequency of Non-Consensual Bride Kidnapping in the Kyrgyz Republic." *International Journal of Central Asian Studies* 8 (1): 108–28.

Kleinbach, Russell, Mehrigiul Ablezova, and Medina Aitieva. 2005. "Kidnapping for Marriage (*ala kachuu*) in a Kyrgyz Village." *Central Asian Survey* 24 (2): 191–202.

Kleinbach, Russell, and Lilly Salimjanova. 2007. "*Kyz ala kachuu* and *adat*: Non-Consensual Bride Kidnapping and Tradition in Kyrgyzstan." *Central Asian Survey* 26 (2): 217–33.

Kohut, Heinz. 1971. *The Analysis of Self: A Systematic Approach to the Psychoanalytic Personality Disorders.* New York: International Universities Press.

———. 1984. *How Does Analysis Cure?* Chicago: University of Chicago Press.

Kondo, Dorinne K. 1990. *Crafting Selves: Power, Gender, and Discourses of Identity in a Japanese Workplace.* Chicago: University of Chicago Press.

Koss, Mary P., Christine A. Gidycz, and Nadine Wisniewski. 1987. "The Scope of Rape: Incidence and Prevalence of Sexual Aggression and Victimization in a National Sample of Higher Education Students." *Journal of Consulting and Clinical Psychology* 55 (2): 162–70.

Krakauer, Jon. 2015. *Missoula: Rape and the Justice System in a College Town.* New York: Doubleday.

Krebs, Christopher P., Christine H. Lindquist, Tara D. Warner, Bonnie S. Fisher, and Sandra L. Martin. 2007. *The Campus Sexual Assault (CSA) Study: Final*

Report. Washington, DC: National Institute of Justice, US Department of Justice.

Kusserow, Adrie. 2004. *American Individualisms: Child Rearing and Social Class in Three Neighborhoods*. New York: Palgrave Macmillan.

Kwiatkowski, Lynn. 2016. "Feminist Anthropology: Approaching Domestic Violence in Northern Viet Nam." In *Mapping Feminist Anthropology in the Twenty-First Century*, edited by Ellen Lewin and Leni M. Silverstein, 234–55. New Brunswick, NJ: Rutgers University Press.

Lamb, Sarah. 2000. *White Saris and Sweet Mangoes: Aging, Gender, and Body in North India*. Berkeley: University of California Press.

Lee, Sunghoe. 2013. "Gender, Power and Emotion: Towards Holistic Understanding of Mature Women Students in South Korea." *Gender and Education* 25 (2): 170–88.

Lerner, Gerda. 1986. *The Creation of Patriarchy*. Vol. 1. New York: Oxford University Press.

Lessem, Peter. 2005. *Self Psychology: An Introduction*. Lanham, MD: Rowman and Littlefield.

Li, Chunling, and Shi Li. 2008. "Market Competition or Gender Discrimination: The Trend of Gender Income Inequality and Its Explanations." *Shehuixue yanjiu* [Sociological Research] 2: 1–14.

Lichtenberg, Joseph D. 1989. *Psychoanalysis and Motivation*. Hillsdale, NJ: Analytic Press.

Lom, Petr, dir. 2004. *Bride Kidnapping in Kyrgyzstan*. First Run/Icarus Films.

Loomba, Ania. 2015. *Colonialism/Postcolonialism*. 3rd ed. London: Routledge.

Lutz, Catherine, and Geoffrey M. White. 1986. "The Anthropology of Emotions." *Annual Review of Anthropology* 15: 405–36.

Mack, Sandra. 2015. "Constructing Post-Soviet Identities: An Analysis of the Representation of Bride Kidnapping in Kyrgyz Cinema." In *Gender in Modern Central Asia*, edited by Thomas Kruessman, 51–69. Zurich: Lit Verlag.

MacKinnon, Catharine A. 1989. *Toward a Feminist Theory of the State*. Cambridge, MA: Harvard University Press.

Mahmood, Saba. 2001. "Feminist Theory, Embodiment, and the Docile Agent: Some Reflections on the Egyptian Islamic Revival." *Cultural Anthropology* 16 (2): 202–36.

———. 2005. *Politics of Piety: The Islamic Revival and the Feminist Subject*. Princeton, NJ: Princeton University Press.

Malhotra, Anju, and Sidney Ruth Schuler. 2005. "Women's Empowerment as a Variable in International Development." In *Measuring Empowerment:*

Cross-Disciplinary Perspectives, edited by Deepa Narayan-Parker, 71–88. Washington, DC: World Bank Publications.

Mallon, Florencia E. 1987. "Patriarchy in the Transition to Capitalism: Central Peru, 1830–1950." *Feminist Studies* 13 (2): 379–407.

Man, Joyce Yanyun, Siqi Zheng, and Rongrong Ren. 2011. "Housing Policy and Housing Markets: Trends, Patterns and Affordability." In *China's Housing Reform and Outcomes*, edited by Joyce Yanyun Man, 3–18. Cambridge: Lincoln Institute of Land Policy.

Manago, Adriana M. 2012. "The New Emerging Adult in Chiapas, Mexico: Perceptions of Traditional Values, Gender Roles and Value Change among First Generation Maya University Students." *Journal of Adolescent Research* 27 (6): 663–713.

———. 2014. "Connecting Societal Change to Value Differences across Generations: Adolescents, Mothers, and Grandmothers in a Maya Community in Southern Mexico." *Journal of Cross-Cultural Psychology* 45 (6): 868–87.

Manago, Adriana M., and Patricia M. Greenfield. 2011. "The Construction of Independent Values among Maya Women at the Forefront of Social Change: Four Case Studies." *Ethos* 39 (1): 1–29.

Mann, Michael. 1986. "A Crisis in Stratification Theory? Persons, Household/Family/Lineage, Gender, Classes and Nations." In *Gender and Stratification*, edited by Rosemary Crompton and Michael Mann, 40–56. Cambridge: Cambridge University Press.

Marcos, Sylvia. 2005. "The Borders Within: The Indigenous Women's Movement and Feminism in Mexico." In *Dialogue and Difference: Feminisms Challenge Globalization*, edited by Marguerite R. Waller and Sylvia Marcos, 81–112. New York: Palgrave Macmillan.

Markus, Hazel Rose, and Shinobu Kitayama. 1991. "Culture and the Self: Implications for Cognition, Emotion, and Motivation." *Psychological Review* 98 (2): 224–53.

Marriott, McKim. 1976. "Hindu Transactions: Diversity without Dualism." In *Transaction and Meaning: Directions in the Anthropology of Exchange and Symbolic Behavior*, edited by B. Kapferer, 109–42. Philadelphia: ISHI.

———. 1989. "Constructing an Indian Ethnosociology." *Contributions to Indian Sociology* 23 (1): 1–40.

Marrow, Jocelyn. 2013. "Feminine Power or Feminine Weakness? North Indian Girls' Struggles with Aspirations, Agency, and Psychosomatic Illness." *American Ethnologist* 40 (2): 347–61.

Mathews, Holly F. 1985. "'We Are Mayordomo': A Reinterpretation of Women's Roles in the Mexican Cargo System." *American Ethnologist* 12 (2): 285–301.

———. 1992. "The Directive Force of Morality Tales in a Mexican Community." In *Human Motives and Cultural Models*, edited by Claudia Strauss and Roy G. D'Andrade, 127–62. Cambridge: Cambridge University Press.

———. 2005. "Uncovering Cultural Models of Gender from Accounts of Folktales." In *Finding Culture in Talk: A Collection of Methods*, edited by Naomi Quinn, 105–56. New York: Palgrave Macmillan.

McGinty, Anna Mansson. 2006. *Becoming Muslim: Western Women's Conversions to Islam*. New York: Macmillan.

McHugh, Ernestine. 2004. "Moral Choices and Global Desires: Feminine Identity in a Transnational Realm." *Ethos* 32 (4): 575–97.

Meade, Teresa, and Pamela Haag. 1998. "Persistent Patriarchy: Ghost or Reality?" *Radical History Review* 71: 91–95.

Menon, Usha. 2002a. "Morality and Context: A Study of Hindu Understandings." In *Handbook of Developmental Psychology*, edited by Jaan Valsiner and Kevin J. Connolly, 431–49. London: Sage.

———. 2002b. "Making Śakti: Controlling (Natural) Impurity for Female (Cultural) Power." *Ethos* 30 (1–2): 140–57.

———. 2013. *Women, Wellbeing, and the Ethics of Domesticity in an Odia Hindu Temple Town*. New Delhi: Springer India.

Menon, Usha, and Richard A. Shweder. 1994. "Kali's Tongue: Cultural Psychology and the Power of 'Shame' in Orissa, India." In *Emotion and Culture: Empirical Studies of Mutual Influence*, edited by Hazel Markus and Shinobu Kitayama, 241–82. Washington, DC: American Psychological Association.

Mernissi, Fatima. (1975) 1987. *Beyond the Veil*. Bloomington: Indiana University Press.

———. 1991. *Women and Islam: A Historical and Theological Enquiry*. Oxford: Basil Blackwell.

———. 1994. *Dreams of Trespass: Tales of a Harem Girlhood*. New York: Basic.

Merry, Sally Engle. 2006. *Human Rights and Gender Violence: Translating International Law into Local Justice*. Chicago: University of Chicago Press.

Metcalf, Barbara D. 1994. "Remaking Ourselves: Islamic Self-Fashioning in a Global Movement of Spiritual Renewal." In *Accounting for Fundamentalisms*, edited by Martin E. Marty and R. Scott Appleby, 706–25. Chicago: University of Chicago Press.

Mies, Maria. 2007. "Patriarchy and Accumulation on a World Scale—Revisited." *International Journal of Economics* 1 (3–4): 268–75.

———. 2014. *Patriarchy and Accumulation on a World Scale: Women in the International Division of Labor*. 2nd ed. London: Zed.

Miller, Jean Baker. 2012. *Toward a New Psychology of Women*. Boston: Beacon.

Miller, Joan G., Namrata Goyal, and Matthew Wice. 2015. "Ethical Considerations in Research on Human Development and Culture." In *The Oxford Handbook of Human Development and Culture: An Interdisciplinary Perspective*, edited by Lene A. Jensen, 14–27. Oxford: Oxford University Press.

Miller, Pavla. 2017. *Patriarchy*. London: Routledge.

Miller, Roy A. 1974. "Are Familists Amoral? A Test of Banfield's Amoral Familism Hypothesis in a South Italian Village." *American Ethnologist* 1 (3): 515–35.

Minault, Gail. 1998. *Secluded Scholars: Women's Education and Muslim Social Reform in Colonial India*. Delhi: Oxford University Press.

Mines, Mattison. 1994. *Public Faces, Private Lives: Community and Individuality in South India*. Berkeley: University of California Press.

Ministry of Education of the People's Republic of China. 2007. "In 2006, Our Country's Language and Writing Had a 'New Face'" [in Chinese]. Beijing: Ministry of Education of the People's Republic of China. http://en.moe.gov.cn/publicfiles/business/htmlfiles/moe/moe_1551/200708/25472.html.

Moghadam, Valentine M. 1992. "Patriarchy and the Politics of Gender in Modernising Societies: Iran, Pakistan and Afghanistan." *International Sociology* 7 (1): 35–53.

———. 2004. "Patriarchy in Transition: Women and the Changing Family in the Middle East." *Journal of Comparative Family Studies* 35 (2): 137–62.

Monkman, Karen. 2011. "Framing Gender, Education and Empowerment Research." *Research in Comparative and International Education* 6 (1): 1–3.

Moon, Seungsook. 2005. *Militarized Modernity and Gendered Citizenship in South Korea*. Durham, NC: Duke University Press.

Morrison, Andrew P. 2009. "On Ideals and Idealism." *Annals of the New York Academy of Sciences* 1159: 75–85.

Mukhopadhyay, Carol Chapnick, and Susan Seymour. 1994. "Introduction and Theoretical Overview." In *Women, Education, and Family Structure in India*, edited by Carol Chapnick Mukhopadhyay and Susan Seymour, 1–33. Boulder, CO: Westview.

Murdock, George. 1981. *Atlas of World Cultures*. Pittsburgh, PA: University of Pittsburgh Press.

Najmabadi, Afsaneh. 1998. "Crafting an Educated Housewife in Iran." In *Remaking Women: Feminism and Modernity in the Middle East*, edited by Lila Abu-Lughod, 91–125. Princeton, NJ: Princeton University Press.

Napolitano, Valentina. 2002. *Migration, Mujercitas, and Medicine Men: Living in Urban Mexico*. Berkeley: University of California Press.

Newcomb, Theodore M. 1953. "Social Psychology and Group Processes." *Annual Review of Psychology* 4 (1): 183–214.

Ong, Aihwa. 1987. *Spirits of Resistance and Capitalist Discipline: Factory Women in Malaysia*. Albany: State University of New York Press.

———. 2006. *Neoliberalism as Exception: Mutations in Citizenship and Sovereignty*. Durham, NC: Duke University Press.

Orsini, Francesca, ed. 2006. *Love in South Asia: A Cultural History*. Cambridge: Cambridge University Press.

Ortner, Sherry B. 1984. "Theory in Anthropology since the Sixties." *Comparative Studies in Society and History* 26 (1): 126–66.

———. 1997. "Making Gender: Toward a Feminist, Minority, Postcolonial, Subaltern, etc., Theory of Practice." In *Making Gender: The Politics and Erotics of Culture*, edited by Sherry B. Ortner, 1–20. Boston: Beacon.

———. 2005. "Subjectivity and Cultural Critique." *Anthropological Theory* 5 (1): 31–52.

———. 2014. "Too Soon for Post-Feminism: The Ongoing Life of Patriarchy in Neoliberal America." *History and Anthropology* 25 (4): 530–49.

Otto, Hiltrud, and Heidi Keller, eds. 2014. *Different Faces of Attachment: Cultural Variations on a Universal Human Need*. Cambridge: Cambridge University Press.

Özbay, Ferhunde. 1990. "The Development of Studies on Women in Turkey." In *Women, Family, and Social Change in Turkey*, edited by Ferhunde Özbay, 1–12. Bangkok: UNESCO.

Panksepp, Jaak. 2004. *Affective Neuroscience: The Foundations of Human and Animal Emotions*. New York: Oxford University Press.

Papanek, Hanna. 1979. "Family Status Production: The 'Work' and 'Non-Work' of Women." *Signs* 4 (4): 775–81.

Park, B. C. Ben. 2013. "Cultural Ambivalence and Suicide Rates in South Korea." In. *Suicide and Culture: Understanding the Context*, edited by Erminia Colucci and David Lester, 237–62. Cambridge: Hogfrefe.

Pateman, Carole. 1988. *The Sexual Contract*. Stanford, CA: Stanford University Press.

Patil, Vrushali. 2013. "From Patriarchy to Intersection: A Transnational Feminist Assessment of How Far We've Really Come." *Signs* 38 (4): 847–67.

Paul, Robert. 2015. *Mixed Messages: Culture and Genetic Inheritance in the Constitution of Human Societies*. Chicago: University of Chicago Press.

Pauli, Julia. 2008. "A House of One's Own: Gender, Migration, and Residence in Rural Mexico." *American Ethnologist* 35 (1): 171–87.

Pollert, Anna. 1996. "Gender and Class Revisited; or, The Poverty of 'Patriarchy.'" *Sociology* 30 (4): 639–59.

Potter, Jonathan, and Margaret Wetherell. 1987. *Discourse and Social Psychology: Beyond Attitudes and Behavior*. London: Sage.

Predelli, Line Nyhagen. 2004. "Interpreting Gender in Islam: A Case Study of Immigrant Muslim Women in Oslo, Norway." *Gender and Society* 18 (4): 473–93.

Quinn, Naomi. 1992. "The Motivational Force of Self-Understanding: Evidence from Wives' Inner Conflicts." In *Human Motives and Cultural Models*, edited by Claudia Strauss and Roy G. D'Andrade, 90–126. Cambridge: Cambridge University Press.

———. 1996. "Culture and Contradiction: The Case of Americans Reasoning about Marriage." *Ethos* 24 (3): 391–425.

———. 2005a. "How to Reconstruct Schemas People Share, from What They Say." In *Finding Culture in Talk: A Collection of Methods*, edited by Naomi Quinn, 35–81. New York: Palgrave Macmillan.

———. 2005b. "Universals of Child Rearing." *Anthropological Theory* 5 (4): 475–514.

———. 2006. "The Self." *Anthropological Theory* 6 (3): 362–84.

Quinn, Naomi, and Jeanette Mageo, eds. 2013. *Attachment Reconsidered: Cultural Perspectives on a Western Theory*. New York: Palgrave Macmillan.

Quinn, Naomi, and Holly F. Mathews. 2016. "Emotional Arousal in the Making of Cultural Selves." *Anthropological Theory* 16 (4): 359–89.

Radke, Helena R. M., Matthew J. Hornsey, Chris G. Sibley, and Fiona Kate Barlow. 2017. "Negotiating the Hierarchy: Social Dominance Orientation among Women Is Associated with the Endorsement of Benevolent Sexism." *Australian Journal of Psychology*, August 7. https://onlinelibrary.wiley.com/doi/pdf/10.1111/ajpy.12176.

Raheja, Gloria Godwin, and Ann Grodzins Gold. 1994. *Listen to the Heron's Words: Reimagining Gender and Kinship in North India*. Berkeley: University of California Press.

Rapp, Rayna. 1977. "Gender and Class: An Archaeology of Knowledge concerning the Origin of the State." *Dialectical Anthropology* 2 (1): 309–16.

Repnikova, Maria, and Weile Zhou. 2018. "#MeToo Movement in China: Powerful yet Fragile." *Al Jazeera*, October 22. https://www.aljazeera.com/indepth/opinion/metoo-movement-china-powerful-fragile-181022082126244.html.

Rich, Adrienne. 1980. "Compulsory Heterosexuality and Lesbian Existence." *Signs* 5 (4): 631–60.

Richerson, Peter J., and Robert Boyd. 1998. "The Evolution of Human Ultrasociality." In *Indoctrinability, Ideology, and Warfare: Evolutionary Perspectives*, edited by Irenäus Eibl-Eibesfeldt and Frank K. Salter, 71–95. New York: Berghahn.

———. 1999. "Complex Societies: The Evolutionary Origins of a Crude Superorganism." *Human Nature* 10 (3): 253–89.

Ridgeway, Cecilia. 2011. *Framed by Gender: How Gender Inequality Persists in the Modern World*. New York: Oxford University Press.

Risman, Barbara L. 1998. *Gender Vertigo: American Families in Transition*. New Haven, CT: Yale University Press.

Robbins, Richard E., dir. 2013. *Girl Rising*. Docurama, Cinedigm Distributor.

Rogers, Carl Ransom. 1989. "The Necessary and Sufficient Conditions of Therapeutic Personality Change (1957)." In *The Carl Rogers Reader*, edited by Howard Kirschenbaum and Valerie L. Henderson, 219–35. Boston: Houghton Mifflin.

Roland, Alan. 1982. "Toward a Psychoanalytic Psychology of Hierarchical Relationships in Hindu India." *Ethos* 10 (3): 232–53.

Rubin, Jeffrey W. 1996. "Defining Resistance: Contested Interpretations of Everyday Acts." *Studies in Law, Politics and Society* 15: 237–60.

Rus, Jan. 2009. "La Nueva Ciudad Maya en el Valle de Jovel: Urbanizacion Rapida, Comunidad y Juventud Maya en San Cristobal de Las Casas." In *Chiapas Despues de la Tormenta: Estudios Sobre Economia, Sociedad y Politica*, edited by M. A. E. Saayedra, 169–219. Mexico City: Colegio de México/COCOPA –Camara de Diputados.

Sacks, Karen. 1982. *Sisters and Wives: The Past and Future of Sexual Equality*. Urbana: University of Illinois Press.

Sanday, Peggy Reeves. 1981. "The Sociocultural Context of Rape: A Cross Cultural Study." *Journal of Social Issues* 37 (4): 5–27.

———. 1996. *A Woman Scorned: Acquaintance Rape on Trial*. New York: Doubleday.

———. 2002. *Women at the Center: Life in a Modern Matriarchy*. Ithaca, NY: Cornell University Press.

Schmidt, Elizabeth. 1991. "Patriarchy, Capitalism, and the Colonial State in Zimbabwe." *Signs* 16 (4): 732–56.

Schultz, T. Paul. 2002. "Why Governments Should Invest More to Educate Girls." *World Development* 30 (2): 207–25.

Scott, James C. 1985. *Weapons of the Weak: Everyday Forms of Peasant Resistance*. New Haven, CT: Yale University Press.

Scott, Joan W. 1988. "Deconstructing Equality-versus-Difference; or, The Uses of Post-Structuralist Theory for Feminism." *Feminist Studies* 14 (1): 32–50.

———. 2007. *The Politics of the Veil*. Princeton, NJ: Princeton University Press.

References

Segura, Denise A., and Jennifer L. Pierce. 1993. "Chicana/o Family Structure and Gender Personality: Chodorow, Familism, and Psychoanalytic Sociology Revisited." *Signs* 19 (1): 62–91.

Seymour, Susan C. 1983. "Household Structure and Status and Expressions of Affect in India." *Ethos* 11 (4): 263–77.

———. 1999. *Women, Family, and Child Care in India: A World in Transition*. New York: Cambridge University Press.

———. 2004a. "Introduction." Special issue, "Contributions to a Feminist Psychological Anthropology." *Ethos* 32 (4): 416–31.

———. 2004b. "Multiple Caretaking of Infants and Young Children: An Area in Critical Need of a Feminist Psychological Anthropology." *Ethos* 32 (4): 538–56.

———. 2006. "Resistance." *Anthropological Theory* 6 (3): 303–21.

———. 2013. "'It Takes a Village to Raise a Child': Attachment Theory and Multiple Child Care in Alor, Indonesia, and in North India." In *Attachment Reconsidered: Cultural Perspectives on a Western Theory*, edited by Naomi Quinn and Jeanette Mageo, 115–39. New York: Palgrave Macmillan.

Shapiro, Rebecca. 2013. "Poppy Harlow, CNN Reporter, 'Outraged' over Steubenville Rape Coverage Criticism: Report." *Huffington Post*, March 20. http://www.huffingtonpost.com/2013/03/20/poppy-harlow-cnn-steubenville-rape-coverage-criticism_n_2914853.html.

Shields, Acacia. 2006. "Reconciled to Violence: State Failure to Stop Domestic Abuse and Abduction of Women in Kyrgyzstan." *Human Rights Watch*, September 26. https://www.hrw.org/report/2006/09/26/reconciled-violence/state-failure-stop-domestic-abuse-and-abduction-women.

Shweder, Richard A. 1991. *Thinking through Cultures: Expeditions in Cultural Psychology*. Cambridge, MA: Harvard University Press.

———. 2003. *Why Do Men Barbecue? Recipes for Cultural Psychology*. Cambridge, MA: Harvard University Press.

———. 2008. "The Cultural Psychology of Suffering: The Many Meanings of Health in Orissa, India (and Elsewhere)." *Ethos* 36 (1): 60–77.

Silverblatt, Irene. 1988. "Women in States." *Annual Reviews in Anthropology* 17: 427–60.

Sircar, Ashok, and Diana Fletschner. 2014. "The Right to Inherit Isn't Working for Indian Women, Says U.N. Study." *Wall Street Journal*, March 2. http://blogs.wsj.com/indiarealtime/2014/03/02/the-right-to-inherit-isnt-working-for-indian-women-says-u-n-study.

Sirman, Nükhet. 2000. "Writing the Usual Love Story: The Fashioning of Conjugal and National Subjects in Turkey." In *Gender, Agency, and Change*, edited by Victoria Ana Goddard, 250–72. London: Routledge.

Solnit, Rebecca. 2016. *Hope in the Dark: Untold Histories, Wild Possibilities*. Chicago: Haymarket.

Spiro, Melford. 1993. "Is the Western Conception of the Self 'Peculiar' within the Context of World Cultures?" *Ethos* 21 (2): 107–53.

Sroufe, L. Alan. 2005. "Attachment and Development: A Prospective, Longitudinal Study from Birth to Adulthood." *Attachment and Human Development* 7 (4): 349–67.

Stacey, Judith. 1983. *Patriarchy and Socialist Revolution in China*. Berkeley: University of California Press.

———. 1998. "What Comes after Patriarchy? Comparative Reflections on Gender and Power in a 'Post-Patriarchal' Age." *Radical History Review* 71: 63–70.

Stephen, Lynn. 1991. *Zapotec Women*. Austin: University of Texas Press.

———. 2007. *Transborder Lives: Indigenous Oaxacans in Mexico, California, and Oregon*. Durham, NC: Duke University Press.

Stephens, William N. 1963. *The Family in Cross-Cultural Perspective*. New York: Holt, Rinehart, and Winston.

Sterelny, Kim. 2012. *The Evolved Apprentice*. Cambridge, MA: MIT Press.

Stern, Steve J. 1997. *The Secret History of Gender: Women, Men, and Power in Late Colonial Mexico*. Chapel Hill: University of North Carolina Press.

———. 1998. "What Comes after Patriarchy? Reflections from Mexico." *Radical History Review* 71: 56–62.

Strauss, Claudia. 1990. "Who Gets Ahead? Cognitive Responses to Heteroglossia in American Political Culture." *American Ethnologist* 17 (2): 312–28.

———. 2005. "Analyzing Discourse for Cultural Complexity." In *Finding Culture in Talk: A Collection of Methods*, edited by Naomi Quinn, 203–42. New York: Palgrave Macmillan.

———. 2012. *Making Sense of Public Opinion: American Discourses about Immigration and Social Programs*. Cambridge: Cambridge University Press.

———. 2017. "'It Feels So Alien' or the Same Old S—." Unpublished manuscript, Department of Anthropology, Pitzer College, Claremont, CA.

Strauss, Claudia, and Naomi Quinn. 1997. *A Cognitive Theory of Cultural Meaning*. Cambridge: Cambridge University Press.

Stromquist, Nelly P., and Gustavo E. Fischman. 2009. "Introduction: From Denouncing Gender Inequities to Undoing Gender in Education: Practices and Programmes toward Change in the Social Relations of Gender." *International Review of Education/Internationale Zeitschrift für Erziehungswissenschaft/ Revue Internationale l'Éducation* 55 (5): 463–82.

Subrahmanian, Ramya. 2005. "Gender Equality in Education: Definitions and Measurements." *International Journal of Educational Development* 25 (4): 395–407. doi:10.1016/j.ijedudev.2005.04.003.

Sultana, Abeda. 2012. "Patriarchy and Women's Subordination: A Theoretical Analysis." *Arts Faculty Journal* 4: 1–18.

Supreme People's Court of the People's Republic of China. 2011. "Interpretation [Three] regarding [the] Marriage Law of [the] People's Republic of China." *Court*, August 9 [in Chinese]. http://www.court.gov.cn/qwfb/sfjs/201108/t20110815_159794.htm.

Szoltysek Mikołaj, Sebastian Klüsener, Radosław Poniat, and Siegfried Gruber. 2017. "The Patriarchy Index: A New Measure of Gender and Generational Inequalities in the Past." *Cross-Cultural Research* 51 (3): 228–62.

Tajfel, Henri. 1982. "Social Psychology of Intergroup Relations." *Annual Review of Psychology* 33 (1): 1–39.

Tekeli, Şirin. 1990. "The Meaning and Limits of Feminist Ideology in Turkey." In *Women, Family, and Social Change in Turkey*, edited by Ferhunde Özbay, 139–59. Bangkok: UNESCO.

Tembon, Mercy, and Lucia Fort, eds. 2008. *Girls' Education in the 21st Century: Gender Equality, Empowerment, and Economic Growth*. Washington, DC: International Bank for Reconstruction and Development, World Bank.

Throop, C. Jason. 2008. "On the Problem of Empathy: The Case of Yap, Federated States of Micronesia." *Ethos* 36 (4): 402–26.

Tinsman, Heidi. 1998. "Reviving Patriarchy." *Radical History Review* 71: 182–295.

Tirado, Francisco, and Ana Gálvez. 2008. "Positioning Theory and Discourse Analysis: Some Tools for Social Interaction Analysis." *Historical Social Research* 33 (1): 224–51.

Togashi, Koichi, and Amanda Kottler. 2012. "The Many Faces of Twinship: From the Psychology of the Self to the Psychology of Being Human." *International Journal of Psychoanalytic Self Psychology* 7 (3): 331–51.

Tomasello, Michael. 2014. *A Natural History of Human Thinking*. Cambridge, MA: Harvard University Press.

Tönnies, Ferdinand. (1887) 1957. *Community and Society*. Edited and translated by C. P. Loomis. East Lansing: Michigan State University Press.

Toprak, Binnaz. 1990. "Emancipated but Unliberated Women in Turkey: The Impact of Islam." In *Women, Family and Social Change in Turkey*, edited by Ferhunde Özbay, 39–49. Bangkok: UNESCO.

Trawick, Margaret. 1992. *Notes on Love in a Tamil Family*. Berkeley: University of California Press.

Triandis, Harry C. 1995. *Individualism and Collectivism*. Boulder, CO: Westview.

Trommsdorff, Gisela. 2012. "Development of 'Agentic' Regulation in Cultural Context: The Role of Self and World Views." *Child Development Perspectives* 6: 19–26.

Unterhalter, Elaine. 2007. *Gender, Schooling, and Global Social Justice*. London: Routledge.

Valdés, Guadalupe. 1996. *Con Respeto: Bridging the Distances between Culturally Diverse Families and Schools*. New York: Teachers College Press.

Vandermassen, Griet. 2005. *Who's Afraid of Charles Darwin? Debating Feminism and Evolutionary Theory*. Lanham, MD: Rowman and Littlefield.

Vogt, Evon Z. 1969. *Zinacantán: A Maya Community in the Highlands of Chiapas*. Cambridge, MA: Belknap.

Vygotsky, Lev S. 1978. *Mind in Society: The Psychology of Higher Mental Functions*. Cambridge, MA: Harvard University Press.

Wadley, Susan S. 2002. "One Straw from a Broom Cannot Sweep: The Ideology and Practice of the Joint Family in Rural North India." In *Everyday Life in South Asia*, edited by Diane P. Mines and Sarah Lamb, 11–22. Bloomington: Indiana University Press.

Walby, Sylvia. 1990. *Theorizing Patriarchy*. Oxford: Blackwell.

Wallace, Anthony F. C. 1956. "Revitalization Movements." *American Anthropologist* 58 (2): 264–81.

Wang Feng, Yong Cai, and Baochang Gu. 2013. "Population, Policy and Politics: How Will History Judge China's One-Child Policy?" Supplement, *Population and Development Review* 38 (S1): 115–29.

Weedon, Chris. 1987. *Feminist Practice and Poststructural Theory*. Oxford: Blackwell.

Weiner-Levy, Naomi. 2006. "The Flagbearers: Israeli Druze Women Challenge Traditional Gender Roles." *Anthropology and Education Quarterly* 37 (3): 217–35.

Welch, William M. 2014. "California Adopts 'Yes Means Yes' Law." *USA Today*, September 29.

Welter, Barbara. 1966. "The Cult of True Womanhood: 1820–1860." *American Quarterly* 18 (2): 151–74.

Werner, Cynthia. 2004. "Women, Marriage, and the Nation-State: The Rise of Non-Consensual Bride Kidnapping in Post-Soviet Kazakhstan." In *Reconceptualizing Central Asia: States and Societies in Formation*, edited by Pauline Luong Jones, 59–89. Ithaca, NY: Cornell University Press.

———. 2009. "Bride Abduction in Post-Soviet Central Asia: Marking a Shift towards Patriarchy through Local Discourses of Shame and Tradition." *Journal of the Royal Anthropological Institute* 15 (2): 314–31.

Westen, Drew. 2001. "Beyond the Binary Opposition in Psychological Anthropology: Integrating Contemporary Psychoanalysis and Cognitive Science." In *The Psychology of Cultural Experience*, edited by Carmella Moore and Holly F. Mathews, 21–47. Cambridge: Cambridge University Press.

White, Jenny B. (1994) 2004. *Money Makes Us Relatives: Women's Labor in Urban Turkey*. 2nd ed. London: Routledge.

———. 2013. *Muslim Nationalism and the New Turks*. Princeton, NJ: Princeton University Press.

———. 2015. "The Turkish Complex." *American Interest* 10 (4): 15–23.

Wikan, Unni. 2008. *In Honor of Fadime: Murder and Shame*. Chicago: University of Chicago Press.

Wilkerson, Jared A., Niwako Yamawaki, and Samuel D. Downs. 2009. "Effects of Husbands' Migration on Mental Health and Gender Role Ideology of Rural Mexican Women." *Health Care for Women International* 30 (7): 612–26.

Williams, Normal. 1990. *The Mexican American Family: Tradition and Change*. New York: General Hall.

Winerip, Michael. 2014. "Stepping Up to Stop Sexual Assault." *New York Times*, February 7.

Wittig, Michele A. 1985. "Metatheoretical Dilemmas in the Psychology of Gender." *American Psychologist* 40 (7): 800–811.

Wolf, Eric. 1957. "Closed Corporate Peasant Communities in Mesoamerica and Central Java." *Southwestern Journal of Anthropology* 13 (1): 1–18.

———. 1966. *Peasants*. Englewood Cliffs, NJ: Prentice Hall.

Wolf, Margery. 1960. *The House of Lim: A Study of a Chinese Family*. New York: Pearson.

———. 1972. *Women and the Family in Rural Taiwan*. Palo Alto, CA: Stanford University Press.

———. 1974. "Chinese Women: Old Skills in a New Context." In *Woman, Culture, and Society*, edited by Michelle Z. Rosaldo and Louise Lamphere, 157–72. Palo Alto, CA: Stanford University Press.

Wong, Ying, and Jeanne Tsai. 2007. "Cultural Models of Shame and Guilt." In *Self-Conscious Emotions: Theory and Research*, edited by Jessica L. Tracy, Richard W. Robins, and June Price Tangney, 209–23. New York: Guilford.

World Factbook. 2018. "South Korea." https://www.cia.gov/library/publications/the-world-factbook/geos/ks.html.

Worthen, Holly. 2012. "Women and Microcredit: Alternative Readings of Subjectivity, Agency, and Gender Change in Rural Mexico." *Gender, Place and Culture* 19 (3): 364–81.

Xinhua. 2007. "Chinese Communist Central State Council Decision on Fully Strengthening Population and Family Planning Preparations." *Xinhuanet*, January 22 [in Chinese]. http://news.xinhuanet.com/politics/2007-01/22/content_5637713.htm.

———. 2011. "China's 'Leftover Women' Unite This Singles Day." *China Daily*, November 10. http://www.chinadaily.com.cn/xinhua/2011-11-10/content_4331102.html.

Yan, Yunxiang. 2003. *Private Life under Socialism*. Stanford, CA: Stanford University Press.

Zhang, Zhi Ming, Dilip Shahani, and Keith Chan. 2010. *HSBC Bank Research Report*. Hong Kong: HSBC Global Research.

Zhi, Zihua. 2010. "Survey Says Compatriots Choosing Partners Love Stability." *China*, December 16 [in Chinese]. http://www.china.com.cn/news/txt/2010-12/16/content_21552148.htm.

Zinzow, Heidi M., and Martie Thompson. 2011. "Barriers to Reporting Sexual Victimization: Prevalence and Correlates among Undergraduate Women." *Journal of Aggression, Maltreatment, and Trauma* 20 (7): 711–25.

CONTRIBUTORS

KELLY H. CHONG
Department of Sociology, University of Kansas, Lawrence

MIGUEL DA COSTA FRIAS
E-commerce entrepreneur and writer, Montreal, Quebec

LETA HONG FINCHER
Journalist and scholar; PhD, Tsinghua University, Beijing, China

GÜLDEN GÜVENÇ
Department of Psychology, Işik University, Istanbul, Turkey

Participants in the School for Advanced Research Advanced Seminar "The Psychology of Patriarchy," co-chaired by Holly F. Mathews and Adriana M. Manago, April 19–23, 2015. *Standing, from left*: Kelly H. Chong, Leta Hong Fincher, Gülden Güvenç, Cynthia Werner, Adriana M. Manago, Holly F. Mathews, and Jocelyn Marrow. *Seated, from left*: Naomi Quinn, Ayesha Khurshid, and Susan C. Seymour. Courtesy of the School for Advanced Research.

AYESHA KHURSHID
Department of Educational Leadership and Policy Studies, Florida State University, Tallahassee

ADRIANA M. MANAGO
Department of Psychology, University of California, Santa Cruz

JOCELYN MARROW
Westat Corporation, Rockville, Maryland

HOLLY F. MATHEWS
Department of Anthropology, East Carolina University, Greenville, North Carolina

NAOMI QUINN
Department of Cultural Anthropology, Duke University, Durham, North Carolina

SUSAN C. SEYMOUR
Department of Anthropology, Pitzer College, Claremont, California

CYNTHIA WERNER
Department of Anthropology, Texas A&M University, College Station.

INDEX

adolescence, 56–58, 237
affiliative needs, 19–20
Against Our Will: Men, Women and Rape (Brownmiller), 215–16
agency, 16–17, 21, 136, 215, 235; consent and, 190–93; subjectivity and, 175–78, 183–84, 190, 192, 194
agriculture: in Chiapas, Mexico, 92–93; patriarchy and, 34–35, 39–40; plow, 45–46; social hierarchy relating to, 41–42
Alesina, Alberto, 45–46, 47
All China Women's Federation, 201, 204–5
Alonso, Ana Maria, 155n4
ambivalent sexism theory, 27
anger, 135–36, 164–70, 172–74
antifeminist movement, 96–97
apprenticeship, 83, 92–93
"appropriate" female behavior, 54–55, 123
Arab Families Working Group, 22
Aronson, Elliot, 24, 186
arranged marriage: family and, 1, 124–28, 237–38; family honor and, 124–28; in India, 52, 58, 61–68; in Pakistan, 1, 117, 124–28; respect schema and, 139–41
Association to Promote Contemporary Life, 164
Atalay, Zeynep, 1
attachment theory, 17–19, 61–62
autonomy, 21–22, 54, 89, 136, 144

Bandura, Albert, 16
"Bargaining with Patriarchy" (Kandiyoti), 51
Bargh, John, 17
Barlow, Kathleen, 240
behavioral development, 17, 54–55

benevolent paternalism, 90n4
benevolent sexism, 27–28
Bennett, Judith, 8, 29
Berkshire Conference on the History of Women, 11–12
biology, 35–42, 48nn3–4, 49n9
body, 25, 55–56
Boehm, Christopher, 36, 40, 48n3
Boserup, Ester, 44–45
Bourguignon, Erika, 25
Bowman, James, 6–7
Boyd, Robert, 37–38, 40–41, 49n9
brain, 17
Broussard, Julia, 155n6
Brown, Judith, 46
Brownmiller, Susan, 215–16
Burke, Tarana, 243

capital, 12–13, 48n2
capitalism, 8–10, 13–15, 146
Chang, Kyung-Sup, 178–79
Chiapas, Mexico, 91; agriculture in, 92–93; education in, 92–93, 99–101, 105–8; ethnographic vignettes from, 101–7; family in, 97–109; gender in, 92–96, 98–101, 107–9; gender roles, in Zinacantán, 101–7; marriage in, 1, 97–109; patriarchal bargain in, 96–101; sexuality in, 101–9; social hierarchy in, 98–99, 104
Chicana/o familism, 193n2
child caretaking, 45–46, 182; cultural models of, 51–52, 59; deference and, 26–27; emotional arousal in, 24, 56–58; familism and, 26–27; in India, 20; infant-caregiver relations, 17–20, 52–54, 69n4, 86, 140; multiple child-care, 52–54; sleeping habits and, 52, 54, 69n4

273

child development, 182; attachment theory, socialization, and, 17–19; autonomy and, 54; of self, 17–20, 139; socialization and, 52–56, 236, 242

childhood: father absence in, 144–45; in India, 52–60; what girls must learn in, 56–60

children: domestic violence and, 165–69, 172; *dusta pila* (naughty child), 58–59; marriage of, 56–57; naming of, 54; respect schema and, 140–41

China, 30; All China Women's Federation in, 201, 204–5; deference in, 196, 209–10; education in, 2, 197–201, 204–9, 242; gender in, 196–201, 204, 207–10; leftover women in, 204–10; marriage in, 2, 195–200, 204–10; population control in, 28–29, 204, 206; post-socialist patriarchy in, 198–200, 207–9; property rights in, 33, 34–35, 195–203, 206–10; research methods and findings on, 200–204; state in, 11, 28–29, 198–99, 201, 204–5

Chong, Kelly, 16, 25–26, 28

church participation, 175, 187–90

closed corporate communities, 40

coercion, 26–29, 37–38

cognitive consistency, 24–25, 146

cognitive dissonance, 24–26, 153–54, 186

cognitive schemas, 22–24, 93–96, 186

collective protest, 242–44

collectivism, 48n7

colonialism, 9–10, 31, 62, 115

coming-of-age ceremonies, 56–58

communication, 75–77, 171–72, 174

competitive familism, 184–86

compulsory heterosexuality, 108

Confucianism, 178–79, 180, 183, 194n5

consciousness, 2, 15, 183

consent: agency and, 190–93; kidnap marriage and, 223–24, 227–28; sexual assault and, 226, 232

"Contributions to a Feminist Psychological Anthropology" (Seymour), 14

cooperation, 29, 35–40

coping strategies, 167–70

The Creation of Patriarchy (Lerner), 5

Crenshaw, Kimberlé, 4

cultural models, 3; of child caretaking, 51–52, 59; in India, 75–76; of marriage, 61; in Oaxaca, Mexico, 138–41, 153–54

cultural schemas, 23–24; in Oaxaca, Mexico, 136–46; sexuality and, 108–9

culture: autonomy and, 21–22; deference and, 43; identity relating to, 2–3; kidnap, 212, 218–19, 227, 232–33; patriarchy relating to, 5, 32; rape, 211–12, 215–19, 224–25, 232–33, 242–43. *See also* sociocultural change

D'Andrade, Roy, 138–39

daughter-in-law transitions, 60–62

deference: child caretaking and, 26–27; in China, 196, 209–10; culture and, 43; familism and, 6–7, 37, 44–47; in India, 54–55; self-interest and, 21–22; social hierarchy and, 41–42; systems of, 42–43, 49n10

desire, 82–83

DeVos, Betsy, 216–17

divorce, 61, 203–4

domestic violence, 155n4, 165–69, 172

dowry systems, 33–35, 45, 63, 78, 96

Duke University lacrosse case, 225–26

dusta pila (naughty child), 58–59

economic modernization, 176–80, 190–91, 193n1

education, 1, 22, 149–50; in Chiapas, Mexico, 92–93, 99–101, 105–9; in China, 2, 197–201, 204–9, 242; employment and, 117–22, 148, 161, 242; gender and, 92–93, 99–101; gender empowerment and, 114–20, 125, 129; in India, 63, 64, 68; in South Korea, 179, 183–86;

women's rights and, 117–22, 124. *See also* Pakistani education
elders, 73–74, 76–77, 80–86
emancipation, 2, 13, 160, 162, 239
emotions, 183; anger, 135–36, 164–70, 172–74; emotional arousal, 24, 56–58; emotional expectations, in India, 77–79; emotional expression, in India, 76–77; emotional reactions to familial conflicts, in Turkey, 164–73; emotional regulation, in Turkey, 167–70; emotion work, in India, 74–76, 79–83, 89–90, 90n1; feeling rules and, 76; guilt, 19, 183, 185–86; happiness, 61; *lajya*, in India, 58–59; need for love, 80; *samjhaana* and, 72, 74–76, 79–83, 89–90; socialization and, 18–19
employment: division of labor and, 41, 45–46, 97–98, 159–60; education and, 117–22, 148, 161, 242; motherhood and, 12
empowerment discourses, 22–23, 112
equality, 73–76, 97
Erikson, Erik, 17, 18
ethnopsychology, 89–90
evangelicalism, 175, 187–90
evolutionary theory, 35–42, 48nn3–4, 49n9
Ewing, Katherine, 21
extended household, 6, 39–40
external constraints, 26–29

Fairbairn, W. R. D., 19–20
faith-based organizations, 13
false consciousness, 15
familism: Chicana/o, 193n2; child caretaking and, 26–27; competitive, 184–86; deference and, 6–7, 37, 44–47; development of, 6–7; emotional reactions to familial conflicts, in Turkey, 164–73; filial piety and, 44, 181–82, 207–9; systems of, 44–46
family, 241–42; arranged marriage and, 1, 124–28, 237–38; autonomy and, 21–22; in Chiapas, Mexico, 97–109; intrafamily stress, 164–73; reputation of, 6–7, 37, 44, 123–24; sexuality controlled by, 101, 107–9, 123–29; in South Korea, 176–86, 190–93, 194n8; support systems, 94–95. *See also specific topics*
family duty, 44–45, 182–83, 194n8; loyalty and, 124–28; obedience and, 99–109
family honor, 5–6, 26, 44, 52, 60–61, 100, 117, 211; arranged marriage and, 124–28; Pakistani education and, 123–24; sexual assault and, 217, 227
father absence, 144–45
father right, 11–12
feeling rules, 76
female behavior, "appropriate," 54–55, 123
female domesticity, 122, 179
feminism, 238; antifeminist movement and, 96–97; equality and, 97; intersectionality and, 2–3, 4; psychology and, 14–15
feminista, 95–96
feminists, 1, 95–96, 215–16, 238
fertility rates, 179, 193n3
filial piety, 44, 181–82, 207–9
Fiske, Susan, 27
Folbre, Nancy, 9
Follett, Mary, 146–47
FOMMA. *See* Fortaleza de La Mujer Maya
foraging, 38–40
Ford, Christine Blasey, 216, 243
Fortaleza de La Mujer Maya (FOMMA), 94–96
Frank, Katherine, 14
fraternal right, 11–12

Gailey, Christine, 7
gender: in Chiapas, Mexico, 92–96, 98–101, 107–9; in China, 196–201, 204, 207–10; consciousness, 183; education and, 92–93, 99–101; empowerment, 2,

gender (*continued*)
114–20, 125, 129, 136, 238–39; politics, 237; power and, 11–12, 16; schema theory and, 23; segregation, 9, 56; sociocultural change and, 91–96, 98–99, 189–90
gender roles, 4; in India, 53–54, 69n3; sexism and, 27; in Zinacantán, 101–7
Gilligan, Carol, 183
Girl Rising, 111–12, 130–31
Giuliano, Paola, 45–46, 47
Glick, Peter, 27
Goody, Jack, 34, 44–45
Gordon, April, 9
gossip, 37, 105, 151–52
government. *See* state
Greenfield, Patricia, 92
guilt, 19, 183, 185–86
Guterres, António, 4

Haag, Pamela, 12
happiness, 61
Hart, Keith, 13
Harter, Susan, 16, 93–94
Hartmann, Heidi, 9, 179–80
Hays, Sharon, 12
hegemonic masculinity, 236–37
Hill, Anita, 243
Hinduism, 32, 54–57, 59–60, 67–68, 69n5
Hinton, Alexander, 186
Hirsch, Jennifer, 134, 155n2
Hochschild, Arlie, 11–12, 97–98
homeownership. *See* property rights
"honor" killings, 26
Hope in the Dark (Solnit), 244
hostile sexism, 27–28
human proclivities, toward patriarchy, 35–38
hunter-gatherers, 38–42, 48n7, 49n9
Hunting Ground, 221–22, 230

idealization, 20, 71–72, 84–85
identity, 2–3, 26, 79, 93–95, 103, 107, 146, 183, 228–29

IEL. *See* Institute for Education and Literacy
India: arranged marriage in, 52, 58, 61–68; change in, 62–67, 68; child caretaking in, 20; childhood in, 52–60; communication in, 75–77; cultural models in, 75–76; deference in, 54–55; education in, 63, 64, 68; elders in, 73–74, 76–77, 80–86; emotional expectations in, 77–79; emotional expression in, 76–77; emotion work in, 74–76, 79–83, 89–90, 90n1; equality in, 73–76; gender imbalance in, 52, 69n1; gender roles in, 53–54, 69n3; Hinduism in, 54–57, 67–68, 69n5; kinship in, 51–54, 61, 77–83; *lajya* in, 58–59; listening and telling in, 76–77; marriage in, 52, 60–62, 64–67, 70n12, 72–74; menstruation in, 55–58; Mona's answer, 86–89; Mona's distress, 72–74; psychodynamics in, 83–86, 89–90; Sacred Thread ceremony in, 56–57; *samjhaana* in, 72, 74–76, 79–83, 89–90; sex segregation in, 56; sexuality in, 60, 69n8; shame in, 57–59, 67–68; social hierarchy in, 72–86; socialization in, 51–56, 69n11, 71, 242; social norms in, 20; what girls must learn in, 56–60; wife and daughter-in-law transitions in, 60–62
infant-caregiver relations, 17–20, 52–54, 69n4, 86, 140
inheritance, 33, 34–35, 78, 96, 137, 140, 160–61. *See also* property rights
Institute for Education and Literacy (IEL), 113–15, 118–21, 129
integration, 146–51
internalization, 96–97
intersectionality, 2–3, 4
Islam, 115–16, 119, 126–31, 160–62, 191–92

Joseph, Suad, 20, 127
Jost, John, 28

Index

Kali (Hindu goddess), 59–60
Kandiyoti, Deniz, 5–6, 8, 10, 28, 31–33, 48n2, 96–97, 153, 157, 160, 231, 235, 237; "Bargaining with Patriarchy," 51; on patrilineal-patrilocal complex, 33–34
Kavanaugh, Brett, 216, 226
Kazakhstan, 30, 212–13, 217–21, 223, 228, 233
Keller, Heidi, 18
kidnap culture, 212, 218–19, 227, 232–33
kidnap marriage, 26, 212–13; accommodating, 222–23, 230–31; consent and, 223–24, 227–28; patriarchal value system and, 217–18, 229, 231–32; sexual assault and, 219–24, 220t
kidnap myths, 27, 225t, 226–29
Kim, Dongno, 177, 193n1
Kim, Janna, 108
kin membership, 7
kin selection, 36–37
kinship, 36–37, 48n7, 240–41; in India, 51–54, 61, 77–83
Klein, Melanie, 19–20
Know your IX Campaign, 232
Kohut, Heinz, 20, 72, 84–85, 89

lajya (emotion), 58–59
leftover women, 196, 204–10
Lerner, Gerda, 5
listening, 75–77
love, 185; marriage and, 149, 204–5; need for, 58, 80

machista, 95–96
Machury, Anne, 11–12, 97–98
Mahmood, Saba, 15, 192, 235
Mallon, Florencia, 10
Marcos, Sylvia, 97
marriage: in Chiapas, Mexico, 1, 97–109; of children, 56–57; in China, 2, 195–200, 204–10; cultural models of, 61; divorce and, 61, 203–4; dowry systems and, 33–35, 45, 63, 78, 96; happiness and, 61; honor and, 60–61; in India, 52, 60–62, 64–67, 70n12, 72–74; love and, 149, 204–5; in Oaxaca, Mexico, 133–54, 155nn5–6; pressure to marry, 196, 204–10; sexuality and, 44, 139–40; in South Korea, 1–2, 178, 181–86, 188–90, 194n8; trust schema and, 141–43; wife and daughter-in-law transitions, 60–62. *See also* arranged marriage; kidnap marriage
Marriage Law, China, 198–99
Marrow, Jocelyn, 25, 127–28
masculinity, 8, 23, 48n4, 95–96, 236–37
matrilineal societies, 32, 69n8, 240–42
Maya, 1, 241
McHugh, Ernestine, 237
Meade, Teresa, 12
Menon, Usha, 58–59
menstruation, 19, 55–58
men's understanding, of patriarchy, 236
#MeToo Movement, 216–17, 243
Mexico. *See* Chiapas, Mexico; Oaxaca, Mexico
Mies, Sarah, 12, 13
migration, 144–48, 151, 159–60
Miller, Jean Baker, 21
Miller, Palva, 5
Miller, Roy, 177
Minangkabau, 240–41
mirroring, 85–86
miscommunication, 171–72
Moghadam, Valentine, 10–11, 116–17, 127, 176–77
Mona's answer, 86–89
Mona's distress, 72–74
monogamy, 35
morality, 59–60, 178–79
Moral Origins (Boehm), 36
moral virtues, 15
motherhood, 151–52, 241; changes in role of, 7–8; employment and, 12; nursing and, 52, 69n4, 140; parenting and, 18; power and, 180–82; in South Korea,

motherhood (*continued*)
  180–83; in Turkey, 160–61, 165–69, 173.
  See also child caretaking
mother-in-law, 28–29, 33–34, 54, 157;
  relations with, 42–43, 55, 66–67, 80–82,
  144, 182, 184; in South Korea, 182, 184,
  194n6
mother-son relations, 182, 194n4
motivation, 3, 84, 138
multiple childcare, 52–54
Murick, 240

naughty child, 58–59
needs, 58, 80, 82–83
neo-Confucianism, 178–79, 194n5
neoliberalism, 12–14, 175, 176–80
neopatriarchy, 10–11
New Zealand Values and Attitudes
  Survey, 27–28
non-governmental organizations
  (NGOs), 13, 150–52, 164, 238–39
nuclear households, 39, 42, 65, 154,
  177–81, 184
Nunn, 45–46, 47
nursing, 52, 69n4, 140

Oaxaca, Mexico: conflict, dissonance,
  and choice in, 146–53; cultural models
  in, 138–41, 153–54; cultural schemas in,
  136–46; marriage in, 133–54, 155nn5–6;
  patriarchal bargain in, 141; research
  and data sources on, 137–38; sociocultural change in, 143–46, 154; values in,
  141–46; women's responses to patriarchy in, 135–37
object relations theory, 19–20
Ong, Aihwa, 12–13
opinion communities, 26
Oportunidades Program, 93
Ortner, Sherry, 13, 175–76

Pakistan, 21, 238; arranged marriage in, 1,
  117, 124–28; gender empowerment in,
  114–20, 125, 129; Parhi lihki women in,
  100–101, 112–17, 120, 122–24, 129–30;
  patriarchal bargain in, 122, 124–25,
  130; psychodynamics in, 127–28; social
  hierarchy in, 114, 117–18
Pakistani education: arranged marriage
  and, 124–28; contextual background
  on, 115–17; family honor and, 123–24;
  Girl Rising on, 111–12, 130–31; IEL and,
  113–15, 118–21, 129; research methodology on, 113–14; rights and patriarchal
  norms relating to, 117–22; sexuality
  and, 123–24
Panda, Gitali, 65–67
Papanek, Hanna, 185
parenting. *See* child caretaking;
  motherhood
Parhi lihki women, 100–101, 112–17, 120,
  122–24, 129–30
Pateman, Carole, 8–9, 12
Patil, Vrushali, 3–4
patriarchal bargain: in Chiapas, Mexico,
  96–101; collapsing, 24–26; in Oaxaca,
  Mexico, 141; in Pakistan, 122, 124–25,
  130; precapitalist state formation and,
  7–8; renegotiating, 99–101; in Turkey,
  160, 162, 173
patriarchal belt, 5–6, 116–17, 235
patriarchal contracts, 12–14
patriarchal equilibrium, 29
patriarchal family, 64, 129, 175, 178–80
patriarchal norms: Islam and, 115–16,
  119, 126–31, 160–62, 191–92; Pakistani
  education and rights relating to,
  117–22
patriarchal value system, 26–27; kidnap
  marriage and, 217–18, 229, 231–32;
  sexual assault and, 224–32
patriarchy: defining and situating,
  historically, 5–14, 31; evolving forms of,
  10–11, 22–24; extent of, 31–32; human
  proclivities toward, 35–38; men's
  understanding of, 236; origins of, 31,
  34–35; psychological approach to,

14–26, 64; reclaiming concept of, 3–5. *See also specific topics*
patrifocal, 22–23, 47n1, 67–68
patrilineal-patrilocal complex, 5–6, 33–34
patrilocal extended household, 20–22, 32–34, 45, 101–2, 127, 159
patrilocal household, 5–6, 22–23, 116–17
Paul, Robert, 36, 48n4
personality development, 17–18
Peru, 10
Phenomenal Women Action Campaign, 243
plow agriculture, 45–46
politics, 11, 144–45, 237
polygyny, 35
population control, 28–29, 204, 206
post-patriarchy, 11–12
precapitalist state formation, 7–8
Production and Reproduction (Goody), 34
property rights, 33, 34–35, 78, 96, 137, 140, 160–61, 195–203, 206–10
psychoanalytic theory, 71–72, 83–86
psychodynamics, 72; ethnopsychology and, 89–90; in India, 83–86, 89–90; in Pakistan, 127–28; in Turkey, 157–59
psychology, 235–36; brain and, 17; "Contributions to a Feminist Psychological Anthropology" on, 14; emotion work and, 72; feminism and, 14–15; of human agency, 16–17; psychological approach to patriarchy, 14–26, 64; of self, 17–22, 89–90, 186; social norms and, 15–16; socioeconomic class and, 14–15. *See also specific topics*
psychosomatic illness, 25, 146–47

Quinn, Naomi, 54, 57–58, 67–68, 78, 96, 138–39, 147, 186

rape. *See sexual assault*
rebellion, 64–66
reference groups, 26
reflexivity, 162–64, 174
relationality, 239–41
religion: evangelicalism and church participation, 175, 187–90; faith-based organizations, 13; secularism and, 161–62. *See also specific religions*
reputation: of family, 6–7, 37, 44, 123–24; gossip and, 37, 105, 151–52; sexual assault and, 231–32
resistance, 64–66, 70n13, 188–89, 192
respect schema, 138–41, 148–51
Rich, Adrienne, 108
Richerson, Peter, 37–38, 40–41, 49n9
Ridgeway, Cecilia, 197, 207–8
Risman, Barbara, 194n9
ritual ceremonies, 56–57

Sacks, Karen, 7
Sacred Thread ceremony, 56–57
samjhaana (to make one understand, emotion work): components of, 79–83; defining, 72; Indian model of, 74–76, 89–90
samskaaras, 78, 90n6
Sanday, Peggy, 215–16, 240–41
schema theory: cognitive schemas, 22–24, 93–96, 186; cultural schemas, 23–24, 108–9, 136–46; gender and, 23
Schmidt, Elizabeth, 9
secularism, 161–62
self, 2; affiliative needs and, 19–20; child development of, 17–20, 139; cognitive schemas on, 93–96, 186; psychology of, 17–22, 89–90, 186
self-esteem, 19, 21, 165–69, 173
self-interest, 21–22, 36–37
sexism, 27–28
sex ratio imbalance, 52, 69n1, 206
sex segregation, 9, 56
sexual assault, 26–27; accommodation of, 230–32; consent and, 226, 232; family honor and, 217, 227; kidnap culture and, 212, 218–19, 227, 232–33; kidnap marriage and, 219–24, 220t; kidnap

sexual assault (*continued*)
  myths and, 27, 225t, 226–29; patriarchal value system and, 224–32; rape culture and, 211–12, 215–19, 224–25, 232–33, 242–43; rape myths and, 224–27, 225t, 242–43; reporting, 223–24, 226–27, 230–31; reputation and, 231–32
sexuality: in Chiapas, Mexico, 101–9; cultural schemas and, 108–9; family control of, 101, 107–9, 123–29; in India, 60, 69n8; marriage and, 44, 139–40; Pakistani education and, 123–24
Seymour, Susan, 14
shame, 19, 21, 26, 57–59, 67–68
shengnü (leftover women), 196, 204–10
Singh, Jyoti, 243
social hierarchy: agriculture relating to, 41–42; in Chiapas, Mexico, 98–99, 104; deference and, 41–42; in households, 53, 72–79; in India, 72–86; morality and, 178–79; in Pakistan, 114, 117–18; post-hunter-gatherer, 40–42, 49n9
social identity, 26, 146
socialization: attachment theory, child development, and, 17–19; early, 52–56, 236, 242; emotions and, 18–19; in India, 51–56, 69n11, 71, 242
social media, 200, 243
social norms: in India, 20; opinion communities and, 26; power and, 28; psychology and, 15–16; reference groups and, 26
sociocultural change: gender and, 91–96, 98–99, 189–90; in Oaxaca, Mexico, 143–46, 154; in South Korea, 176–80, 187–90
socioeconomic class: class formation, 10; class struggle, 10; psychology and, 14–15; in Turkey, 157–58, 161–62, 173
Solnit, Rebecca, 244
South Korea, 25–26, 30; church participation and evangelicalism in, 175, 187–90; consent and agency in, 190–93; economic modernization in, 176–80, 190–91, 193n1; education in, 179, 183–86; family in, 176–86, 190–93, 194n8; marriage in, 1–2, 178, 181–86, 188–90, 194n8; motherhood in, 180–83; mother-in-law in, 182, 184, 194n6; sociocultural change in, 176–80, 187–90; state, neoliberalism, and, 175, 176–80; subjectivity in, 175–78, 180–86
Stacey, Judith, 11–12
state: in China, 11, 28–29, 198–99, 201, 204–5; neoliberalism and, 12–14, 175, 176–80; precapitalist state formation, 7–8; women and Turkish state, 160–62
status production, 185–86
Stephens, William, 49n10
Sterelny, Kim, 40–41
Stern, Steve, 141
Strauss, Claudia, 26, 94, 146–47, 186
subjectivity, 162–63, 173–74, 175–78, 180–86, 190, 192, 194
submissiveness, 8, 37–38, 135, 171–72, 188–89
Sultana, Abeda, 8
system justification theory, 28–29

task solutions, 21–22
textile production, 92–93, 102
Thomas, Clarence, 243
Title IX, 216–17, 232
Tomasello, Michael, 38–39, 48n3
trade, 146–47
Trommsdorff, Gisela, 235
Trump, Donald, 216–17
trust schema, 141–43, 149
Tsai, Jeanne, 18–19
Turkey, 13, 25, 30; attempted resolution in, 169–72; conceptual definitions, methodological issues, and reflexivity in, 162–64; discussion on, 172–73; emotional reactions to

familial conflicts in, 164–73; emotional regulation and coping strategies in, 167–70; empirical study in, 164; Islam in, 160–62; motherhood in, 160–61, 165–69, 173; patriarchal bargain in, 160, 162, 173; psychodynamics in, 157–59; social context of patriarchal relations in, 159–60; socioeconomic class in, 157–58, 161–62, 173; suggestions for future work in, 174; women and Turkish state, 160–62
twinship, 20, 71–72, 84–85

understanding, 236. *See also samjhaana*

values: in New Zealand Values and Attitudes Survey, 27–28; in Oaxaca, Mexico, 141–46. *See also* patriarchal value system
violence, 4, 14, 222, 243–44; capitalism and, 13; coercion and, 26; condoning, 8; domestic, 155n4, 165–69, 172; "honor" killings, 26; shame and, 26. *See also* sexual assault

Walby, Sylvia, 3, 9
Weedon, Chris, 15
Westen, Drew, 190
"What Comes after Patriarchy? Reflections on Gender and Power in a Post-Patriarchal Age" panel, 11–12
White, Jenny, 161–62
wife, transitioning to, 60–62
Wolf, Eric, 39–40, 42–43, 46–47, 48n6
Wolf, Margery, 33
women. *See specific topics*
women's accommodation, 32–34, 135–37, 191–92, 223–24, 230–32, 235–36
women's rights, 103, 112–15, 125–26; education and, 117–22, 124; property rights and, 33, 34–35, 78, 96, 137, 140, 160–61, 195–203, 206–10
Wong, Ying, 18–19
Worthen, Holly, 152

Zapatista Movement, 93, 98–99, 101
Zinacantán, 91; gender roles in, 101–7; sexuality in, 101–9. *See also* Chiapas, Mexico